One Step
at a Time

One Step at a Time

A Pilgrim's Guide to Spirit-Led Living

Timothy C. Geoffrion

THE
ALBAN
INSTITUTE

Herndon, Virginia
www.alban.org

The Alban Institute
2121 Cooperative Way, Suite 100
Herndon, VA 20170

Scripture quotations, unless otherwise noted, are from the New Revised Standard Version of the Bible, © 1989, Division of Christian Education of the National Council of Churches of Christ in the United States of America, and are used by permission.

Scripture quotations noted NIV are from Holy Bible: New International Version, copyright © 1973, 1978, 1984. Used by permission of Zondervan Bible Publishers.

Cover design by Tobias Becker, Bird Box Design.

Library of Congress Cataloging-in-Publication Data

Geoffrion, Timothy C., 1957–
   One step at a time : a pilgrim's guide to spirit-led living / Timothy C. Geoffrion.
      p. cm.
   Includes bibliographical references (p 235).
   ISBN 978-1-56699-369-2
   1. Spiritual life—Christianity. 2. Geoffrion, Timothy C., 1957–
I. Title.
BV4501.3.G45 2008
263'.0424611—dc22

                                                          2008036043

08   09   10   11   12   VP   5   4   3   2   1

*To my fellow pilgrims and traveling companions on
El Camino de Santiago de Compostela and the three most
important people in my life—Jill, Timothy, and Daniel.*

Contents

Foreword

∽

HAVE YOU THOUGHT of the spiritual life as a journey, a pilgrimage? I have, but only as a general idea. In *One Step at a Time: A Pilgrim's Guide to Spirit-Led Living*, Tim Geoffrion offers readers specific stories about his own pilgrimage, reflections on the journey, and suggestions about our pilgrimage. Tim's book is one I am looking forward to sharing with others. Having taught and practiced spiritual formation for thirty years, I find this a great addition to the theory and practice of helping people to be formed by God.

Tim tells his story of being on pilgrimage in Spain for thirty-seven days. Before he ultimately decided to make the journey, he had not been particularly amenable to the idea. His wife, who writes books about labyrinths, had asked him a couple of times to go. Then suddenly to his surprise, the next time she asked he said yes. It was a good time for him to make such a journey, a time when he was in a major life transition. He had ended his role as the CEO of a nonprofit organization and needed some time to think about what to do next.

The pilgrimage was really a metaphor for the spiritual life, Tim found. It was far more than a way of getting clearer about what to do next. It led him to make profound changes in his life and gave him clarity about significant matters. Perhaps, he began to think, he couldn't solve the next issue in his life without changing his old way of perceiving things.

And Tim changed. I have seen the change as I have listened to and watched him in the two years since he came back from Spain. In this book, he also has reflected on his experience in a way that can help us all, partially because his growth wasn't a matter of enjoying a "quiet time" and then going back to ordinary life. Rather, the journey seemed to be a matter of moving within ordinary life and then praying and listening. Tim shares stories, theology, scripture, and practical exercises to help us do that. He puts four pieces together:

- His experience on his pilgrimage, warts and all. He shares his deepest feelings. His stories are not nice little vignettes of insights received, but are often about wrenching experiences.
- His theological reflections on pilgrimage as metaphor for the spiritual journey. He wrestles with how to understand what is happening. What might the Spirit be doing?
- His understanding of Scripture's viewpoint. He quotes appropriate Bible passages and comments on them and connects the passage with thinking and feelings.
- Suggestions for the reader. His practical suggestions are broad and appropriate for many styles of spirituality. The reader is encouraged to keep a notebook and to read, try the exercises, and write about what happened.

My attention was grabbed by Tim's stories, and the rest of the book flowed from these stories. He rightly reminds us that growth in the spiritual life, like a pilgrimage, is not linear, straight progress without emotional and spiritual ups and downs. His realistic depiction of this "map" of pilgrimage and growth is better than most charts of the spiritual life that I have encountered, much more real and encouraging than the ones I have used in teaching and writing. He found that the process was a spiraling one for him, which I have noticed as well. The spiral hits certain themes again and again, but every time at a different level.

Tim's thinking and attitude toward his work and other people has been deeply reoriented by the work of the Spirit. This also is quite different from guidance I read in many books on the spiritual life. Many of these books just tell personal anecdotes and give a conclusion that supposedly fits all. Or they provide an "objective" or theoretical approach without sharing the experience of the author. Tim connects the reader to real life and feelings, theology, and the Scriptures, and makes suggestions for those who read. His approach is that of a thinking person's guide to the spiritual journey. This is lived theology.

Tim says that the way he was taught to preach and teach was to start with Scripture, think about it, and interpret it according to his tradition and his teachers. His new approach is to pay attention to life, think, listen to the Scriptures, and then follow the Spirit's leading. This is quite radical for many of us but makes a lot of sense as Tim writes. It is far more alive, far more open to the Spirit, far less intellectually abstract than the old way.

Tim's approach goes along with his discovery and belief that God is already in our lives. If we pay attention, God's gifts and invitation grow increasingly clear. Tim shows us how to look at our experience, think about and listen to what God might be doing, and then do what we have heard or been invited to. Ignatius of Loyola, the practical Spanish mystic who founded the Jesuits and who has written the "Spiritual Exercises," would, I believe, agree. Ignatius told his disciples to first pay attention to their experiences daily, which would keep them better attuned to what God was doing than saying their daily office or reading the Bible, because the practice was rooted and grounded in what God was doing in their lives. It is also the pattern in the Twelve Steps of Alcoholics Anonymous, where the maintenance steps of the program start with a daily inventory and are followed by prayer and meditation.

Tim also asks questions and encourages us to do so. There is no easy answer to his sorrow, the hints he encountered that he needed to grow, and what he learned through connecting with his family. But he found part of the secret in noticing the Spirit's work as he let go and let the Spirit guide, as he gave up his agenda and paid attention to the reality others presented to him. He changed his desire to control and be in charge and found freedom.

I remember having seen Tim discover the power of letting go while setting up Faith, Hope, and Love Global Ministries with his wife, after he had learned how to be more fully guided by the Spirit. Instead of having independent ministries, he and his wife now coordinate his teaching with her leadership of labyrinth prayer and have done so in Burma, France, and the Congo.

Tim's book is designed to help people change for the better in their relationships with God, others, their ministries or vocation, and themselves. This book, along with Tim's previous book, *The Spirit-Led Leader*, can be of use to pastors and laity alike. Pastors may find it useful for their own reading and spiritual formation. They may find it very useful as they preach or lead groups. I can see parts of this being used for a new members class or for a Lenten study. I can imagine staff or clergy groups using the book as the focus of a weekly or monthly study.

Church and business leaders urge others to listen to the small voice in our heads and hearts, but they often give little guidance about ways to do this and how to distinguish their wisdom from the Spirit's. We can learn to listen and walk step by step. Tim can help!

JOHN ACKERMAN

Preface

~

IF YOU OPENED THIS BOOK and are reading these words, something is stirring within you. Perhaps you are looking for help, guidance, encouragement, or simply hope. You may desire something for your life and relationship with God, but you may not be sure how to find it. The stirrings you feel are not uncommon. Others like you have felt such restlessness or yearning.

Sometimes what is stirring within us doesn't yet have a name, and we don't know if it pertains to God, a life-stage issue, unresolved childhood experiences, or something else. We may just feel a need or longing, and we are motivated to try to find the missing pieces. Perhaps something inside us is calling out for deeper understanding, more fulfillment, more authenticity, or more joy. Maybe we are suffering from great disappointment or grief. We may be craving greater satisfaction in our life and relationships. Sometimes we are very conscious that something is wrong in our life. Other times we just know that *something* needs to change.

Our awareness of our needs and desires may dawn on us slowly, while at other times it jars us awake or stings us in an instant. Most of us have had those times when we suddenly realize something very surprising, disturbing, or disappointing. Perhaps we don't really like who we are, where we are, who our friends are, where we work, or any number of other major aspects of our life. We are almost shocked at the realization, and we wonder, how in the world did we get here? Or maybe we set out in pursuit of a dream or desire, only to get what we thought we wanted and discover it is not what we want at all. Such experiences can be very disorienting or troubling. Sometimes they are enlightening.

Others of us are seeking deeper meaning and purpose to life, and we want to make a difference somehow. Some of us are searching for love, to be loved and to offer love to others. We may also want a better life in some way—for ourselves personally, our families, our churches, our nation, and the suffering masses throughout the world—but we may not know what to do. We may feel powerless or overwhelmed.

Spiritually, many of us want to know and experience God more powerfully. We may hear a lot about "personal transformation"—buzz words in many circles today—but sometimes when we look at our own feeble attempts to improve ourselves or our circumstances, we wonder who truly changes and how transformation happens. We may also feel frustrated and disappointed that God doesn't seem to be doing more to help, and, even more, we want to know if there is any hope for us.

If you struggle with any of these issues, as I have, I have written this book for you. I have written for those who want a better relationship with God and a more fulfilling life and who are willing to admit their limitations, struggles, disappointments, and longing. I believe spiritual growth is truly possible and that God is already at work drawing you closer to God and transforming you, whether or not you can see or feel it. The love, joy, and peace you are longing for is not reserved for a few special people but is available to you as well, as you learn to better recognize God's activity in your life and how to flow better with the Spirit's leading day by day.

The backdrop for each chapter is my own life-changing pilgrimage experience on the road to Santiago de Compostela, a relatively rare spiritual practice that helped bring me greater clarity and insight for my own spiritual life. On the Camino, walking five hundred miles across northern Spain in the summer of 2006, my marriage, relationships with my sons, perspective on the world, way of going about relating to others, and way of being in the world and relating to God, nature, and others were all profoundly affected. Through that experience, and ever since, I have been learning more about how the Holy Spirit works in the lives of believers and what it means to be filled and led by the Spirit.

Yet, this book is not about me, but about how God works in those who seek God wholeheartedly. I have written to help fellow spiritual pilgrims learn how to become more intentional on their journey and how to reap greater rewards from their efforts to know God and experience God's power in every aspect of their life. I offer my experiences, reflections, and insights into Scripture and practical Christian living as possible catalysts for your own spiritual pilgrimage, your lifelong journey of seeking God, following Christ, and being led by the Holy Spirit. This journey will be marked by a series of transitions and changes; ups and downs; cycles of doubting, drifting, and renewal; new discoveries; and internal and external transformation—all of which can help you to keep growing and to experience more of the full life Christ intends for you.

If you want to learn more about my spiritual life coaching and consulting work, please see www.timgeoffrion.com. The ministries my wife, Jill, and I conduct in Africa, Burma, and France are described at www.fhlglobal.org. Finally, if you are seeking more resources on spiritual growth and leadership, please visit my blog site at www.spirit-ledleader.com. As this book goes to press, I will be preparing a leader's guide for pastors and small group leaders to use with it; the guide will be posted on www.spirit-ledleader.com.

May the Holy Spirit work powerfully to inspire, teach, and encourage you as you read this book as part of your spiritual pilgrimage.

Acknowledgments

~

WRITING *ONE STEP AT A TIME* has been a great gift to me. I feel deeply grateful for the opportunity to spend nearly six weeks on pilgrimage to Santiago de Compostela and almost two years letting the spiritual principles I write about percolate, take shape, and be refined through a process of reflection, experimentation, observation, Scripture study, conversation, and prayer. Many of the insights that have emerged have their roots in the soil of the pilgrimage, journeyed with my traveling companions: my wife, Jill, and two sons, Tim and Dan. I have been blessed by their willingness to share their lives so openly and fully with me and to engage with me as I have been learning how to better live by the Holy Spirit's leading in my own life and in my relationships with them.

For six weeks in the fall following the pilgrimage, the Ecumenical Institute at Bossey, operated by the World Council of Churches and located just outside of Geneva, Switzerland, kindly opened its doors to Jill and me for a portion of my sabbatical. There I had the opportunity to mix with some thirty young leaders from various parts of the world, who were committed to learning about ecumenism and to serving Christ in their home environments. Along with researching and writing in Bossey's library, Jill and I had the opportunity to attend lectures and hold many conversations with faculty and students on how God was at work in their lives, churches, and countries. All of these experiences were very stimulating and informative and contributed in intangible ways to my ability to write a book on Christian spirituality that honors as many traditions as possible.

In January 2007 I had the opportunity to teach a short course at a Burmese seminary and to interview Buddhist monks, former Buddhists, and various Christian leaders involved in interreligious dialogue and peace initiatives in Myanmar and Thailand. My faith and understanding of spirituality and transformation were profoundly affected by these experiences in southeast Asia. For their protection, I cannot name many of the Christians who spent time with me answering my questions, sharing their perspective on faith, serving Christ in an oppressive environment, and modeling faithfulness and devotion. Yet I am deeply grateful for all they taught me from their own perspective and experience. Some former Buddhist monks, in particular, who had converted to Christianity helped me gain a new appreciation for my own faith in a loving, personal God and in Jesus Christ as Savior. (For more on the appreciation I feel for my time with the Buddhist monks and former Buddhists, see "What the Buddhists Taught Me" at my blog site: http://spirit-ledleader .com/?p=24.)

The Buddhist monks we interviewed were generous with their time and kind enough to explain why their faith in Buddha's teachings and in their own efforts to achieve Nirvana one day was so important to them. Thanks especially to Venerable Bensot Sadhana Ratna from Bangladesh and Batt Sophal and Leng from Cambodia, all three Buddhist monks and students at the Mahamakut Buddhist University in Bangkok, and to Professor Pum Parichart Suwanbubbha, chairperson, Comparative Religion Program, Mahidol University, Bangkok, who told us how important it was to her that she engage in dialogue with Christians who have a vibrant, passionate faith in Jesus Christ rather than with those who think interreligious dialogue means minimizing the differences between religions.

Thanks, too, to Chuleepahn, professor of pastoral care at McGilvary Seminary of Payap University in Chiang Mai. Chuleepahn told us of her work with prostitutes and introduced us to an inspiring Buddhist monk who had been honored by the king of Thailand for his extraordinary outreach to women infected with HIV/AIDS.

I also appreciated the thought-provoking conversations I had with John Butt, senior fellow and former director of the Institute of

Religion and Culture at Payap University, and with the current director, Mark Tamthai. I learned more about how believers from different religions can work together and about spirituality in a pluralistic culture. Other individual Buddhists and Christians helped me better understand how various beliefs from different religions often mix together in the mind and practice of individual believers. In *One Step at a Time*, I do not discuss non-Christian spiritualities, but my many conversations with others who are less committed than I to traditional Christianity, or any Christian faith for that matter, or who minister in pluralistic settings have sharpened my understanding and appreciation for what I hold most dear in my own faith.

Three trips to France while writing the book allowed me to pray and pursue a deeper relationship with God in the context of the awe-inspiring and beautiful Chartres Cathedral, built in the early 1200s. I was able to spend hours alone praying there, and I received clarity or confirmation about many of the chief ideas I write about in *One Step at a Time*.

Jill and I also worshiped most evenings in the Chartres Cathedral with the Chemin Neuf (New Way)—a Catholic order with an ecumenical vocation. Our conversations, prayer, and fellowship with several of the Chemin Neuf community members gave me a deeper appreciation for Catholic spirituality and new insights into the unique contributions of both Catholicism and Protestantism. I am especially grateful to the community's leader, Etienne Veto, PhD in philosophy, who is currently working on a second doctorate (in theology). He has a great ability to explain Catholic theology lucidly, and his insights have deepened my appreciation for the sacred fellowship that exists among the three persons of the Trinity. Etienne also gave me helpful feedback on a couple different sections of the book, for which I am grateful.

In the actual refining of the book, I am indebted to the honest and extensive comments made by John Ackerman, my spiritual director, who carefully read an early version of *One Step at a Time*. John's many suggestions for the book along with his steady support and guidance on a monthly basis have informed and encouraged me greatly in my own relationship with God and have helped me in my writing on spirituality.

I also appreciate Don Reierson, Mike Hoisington, Lynn Christianson, and my son, Tim Geoffrion, whose reading and comments have helped make this a better book. A number of friends and family members were helpful as well at critical times in the writing process by periodically indulging my questions, raising questions or insights of their own, and engaging me in conversation on spirituality and transformation. In particular, Mark Thompson, Dave Stark, and, of course, my wife, Jill, have stimulated my thinking in many ways over the years, helping me to grow spiritually, to serve Christ more effectively, and to refine many of the ideas presented in this book. I am also grateful for the patience and support of Jill as I worked long hours, especially during the eight-week home stretch, and was often distant and preoccupied when I wasn't formally working.

Above all, in the writing of the final manuscript, I am especially grateful for my Alban editor, Beth Gaede, who worked with me step by step, word by word. She repeatedly raised questions that helped me think through and express my ideas better. As I sought to go beyond intellectual concepts to write from my heart and to engage the hearts of others, Beth continually provided honest feedback and helpful suggestions to open my eyes to whatever I was having trouble seeing or accepting on my own.

I am also deeply grateful to all of my students over the years who continue to teach me much by their questions, insights, and example. In a similar way, I have learned a great deal from my spiritual life coaching clients, a number of my sons' friends at Williams College and Yale University, and a host of other individuals who must remain unnamed due to confidentiality. These individuals have deepened my understanding of how God works to draw people to God. From them I have also gained greater insight into powerful spiritual questions and issues with which intelligent, motivated individuals grapple.

Introduction

~

WEDNESDAY, JULY 12, 2006. DAY 19. LEDIGOS, SPAIN. I find myself staring a lot . . . at dilapidated buildings . . . at crucifixes . . . at sunsets. I'm trying to hear better the questions my soul is asking . . . and to listen for some answers.

S PIRITUAL PILGRIMAGE is a lifelong journey of ask-ing questions and seeking answers, of learning how to see more clearly and to listen more carefully, of changing and being changed, and, ultimately, of pursuing God and learning how to better walk with God each step along the way. No matter where we start in our faith and relationship with God, the journey for Christians is marked by seeking to know, love, and serve God bet-ter; to follow Jesus Christ more fully; and to be filled and led by the Holy Spirit as a way of life.

However, spiritual pilgrims also know what it is like to struggle, to fail, to get off track, to be discouraged, to doubt, and to be frus-trated and disappointed with God. True spiritual pilgrims are just like every other fallible human being, except they believe in God and value their relationship with God highly enough to keep pursu-ing God. They want to grow spiritually, and when they lose their way, they grow dissatisfied with their life and look to God for guid-ance and help to get back on track.

This book, then, is not for those who never doubt or who never drift from God. It is written precisely for those people who care deeply about their relationship with God and yet struggle with many different barriers to growth and tend to get stymied in their spiritual

1

journey more easily or more often than they want. It is for those who value the questions of their soul, heart, and mind and who are willing to listen for deep answers—not simplistic, dogmatic answers but ones that resonate with real life and truly lead to loving God and others in practice as well as in theory. It is for those who highly value their faith who want to truly know God and to see the Holy Spirit work within them, in their relationships, and in every other aspect of their lives.

So what is making you care more about your relationship with God at this point in your life? What question, longing, need, desire, conviction, or insight is stirring within you? What is God showing you that you simply cannot ignore any longer?

Why Pilgrimage?

Every year millions of people go on pilgrimage, and the numbers are growing. Many people in the United States seem quite unaware of this phenomenon, but worldwide, annually, millions of people flock to ancient and modern holy sites throughout the world—Christians to Jerusalem, Rome, and Santiago de Compostela, among hundreds of other places; Muslims to Mecca; Hindus to Benares and Mount Kailas; and Buddhists to Kandy. Not everyone walks to get there, but whether they walk, bike, drive, train, or fly, significant numbers of people travel to places they deem to hold special spiritual significance. Some seek hardship as part of the journey; others go as tourists.

The idea of walking hundreds of miles to some medieval religious site might seem bizarre or misguided to many North Americans. What is the point? And if there is a point, do the walkers have their heads screwed on properly? Yet, over the past eleven hundred years, millions of Christians have walked to Santiago de Compostela, while millions of others visit other holy places throughout the world every year. Why do they do it?

Anthropologists have been seriously examining the phenomenon of pilgrimage for the past thirty years or so, ever since the late Victor Turner, former professor at the University of Chicago, put forth his groundbreaking assessment of pilgrimage as "exteriorized mysticism."[1] He found that pilgrims sought to enact rituals that symbolized the movement of their hearts, a transition from one stage or status to another within their community. He described pilgrimage as a liminal—or more properly, *liminoid* (liminal-like, but subtly different from *liminal*)—experience in which pilgrims cross a threshold (*limina* in Latin) as they move from one way of being in the world to another. Pilgrims typically leave behind all structures and identity *en route* to new structures and identities—or at least new ways of being and functioning within one's community. The pilgrimage itself marks the temporary time and mode of existence between the old and the new.

More recently, anthropologists have found that the bulk of pilgrims are not necessarily concerned with transition in their lives as much as with seeking a particular type of community experience and want "to establish direct contact with [their] deity."[2] On one hand, a deep social significance is attached to pilgrimage, especially in the sense of participating in *communitas*—spontaneous, meaningful, egalitarian bonding with others on a common journey. On the other hand, people also have deeply personal, individual reasons for walking, especially spiritual ones, which may or may not involve transition in one's life.

Christian pilgrims have been known to embark upon pilgrimage for many reasons: to fulfill a vow made to God, as penance (punishment for sins committed), to offer thanksgiving, to ask for help or beg for a favor, to seek healing, and to "go to a place where God might just be a bit closer."[3] Catholic pilgrims have also sometimes been motivated to go on pilgrimage in order to receive indulgences, which were granted by the church in place of other penance that believers might be required to do as a consequence of their sin. Eventually, in medieval Catholic tradition, the practice of granting indulgences evolved into declaring complete forgiveness of sins to the pilgrim.

Today those who journey to Santiago de Compostela on pilgrimage can still get a "Compostela," a certificate assuring them of forgiveness for all their sins, providing they have walked at least one hundred kilometers (or sixty miles), attended mass at Santiago de Compostela (the church), and confessed their sins to a priest. While forgiveness of sins and escaping the obligation of penance is still part of the meaning of pilgrimage for many Catholic pilgrims, Protestants and those from other religious and nonreligious perspectives generally walk for different reasons, seeking something they sense they need to see, feel, know, or otherwise experience to go forward.

But frankly, many people need to go on pilgrimage—to make significant shifts in their relationship to God, themselves, and others or to initiate or mark a transition in their life—but simply can't afford the time or handle the physical demands or costs of an extended trip. Many others value a deeper spiritual life and want to be intentional about continuing to grow and change in keeping with how they sense God is leading them in their life, but they lack adequate resources and guides to help them. To address these needs, I have written this book as a guide for both sets of people—those of you who are making shifts in your life but probably can't get away to go on pilgrimage and for you who are devoted to living your whole life in pursuit of a deeper relationship with God.

Spiritual Vitality and Transformation

I was almost halfway into my pilgrimage to Santiago de Compostela before I came to grips with three extremely important spiritual realities. First, the walk was primarily about connecting to God in a profound, extraordinary way for an extended period of time. Second, I felt called to seek a deeper relationship with God—greater knowledge and experience of God—as a way of life. Third, the Holy Spirit was actively at work within me, using the pilgrimage as a tool of transformation in my life, continually calling me back to God and leading me to new realizations, new values, new resolve, and new ways of being and relating to others.

Then, after returning home, I began to sense that God had been preparing me to share with fellow pilgrims the questions, insights, and learning that grew out of pilgrimage. As I continued to reflect on spiritual growth, read the Bible, make changes in my life, listen to others, and engage in conversation with Christians, nonbelievers, Buddhists, Muslims, and other religious people, my desire to write this book kept growing.

While many resources available today present a generic form of spirituality to appeal to as many people as possible, I wanted to offer a nonsectarian Christian view of spirituality and a biblically based understanding of human purpose and fulfillment. I have written this book for you and others who are not satisfied with vague or eclectic spirituality, who want some more definitive answers but still want room to do your own thinking and to relate to God authentically, out of your own experience. This book is for seekers who are open to the Christian faith and for Christians who see themselves as spiritual pilgrims and want to learn how to pursue a deeper relationship with God as a way of life.

Many different individuals and schools of thought, even among Christians, define spirituality in many different ways. In this book, *spirituality* refers to the nature and quality of our relationship to God—both how we know and experience God and how we live out our faith in our relationships and in every other aspect of our life.

According to the teaching of the New Testament, *spiritual vitality* may be defined as a right relationship with God, grounded in God, the Father (Creator and Loving Parent), marked by faith in and devotion to Jesus Christ, and dependent on the active presence of the Holy Spirit working in and through the believer's life. When Jesus Christ said that he came to bring a full life to believers (John 10:10), he meant that he was drawing them into a close, life-giving, loving relationship with God, which is alive, deepening, and fruitfully influencing every other aspect of their life. Spiritually vital Christians develop a faith-based orientation toward life, a godly frame of reference for interpreting their experiences, power for fulfilling their purpose, and meaning for human existence.

Key to spiritual vitality, then, is the Holy Spirit, without whom our faith would be simply intellectual, self-generated, or guided by other spirits. Without the Holy Spirit, our moral convictions may grow out of our personal experiences or a reasonable assessment of what makes for a good social contract, whereby humans can best live in relationship to one another. Our sense of purpose may be self-generated or given to us by parents, teachers, preachers, or other inspirational or influential figures in our life. We may even be extremely religious, in the sense of appreciating symbolism, ritual, the numinous, intuition, synchronicity, or other dimensions of organized religion or *dis*organized spirituality. However, only when we are dynamically engaged with the Holy Spirit does our spirituality truly become Christian, with God as the primary driving force in our relationship with God. That is, the key to truly loving God, ourselves, and others; the key to faith in Christ as one's Savior and Lord; and the key to fulfilling our purpose in life is God's presence and working in us through the Holy Spirit.

The late Robert Webber, author and seminary professor of ministry, defined spirituality simply as "a lived theology."[4] In contrast to alternatives that have emerged in the history of Christianity, he taught that spirituality is neither experientially based nor dependent on our ability to adhere to a certain set of rules. Rather, Christian spirituality is grounded in God and in what God has done on behalf of humanity through Christ and the Holy Spirit as it applies to each individual. The spiritual life means embracing this theology by faith and by living into the new life that comes through God's grace.

In a complementary way, Sandra Schneiders, a pioneer in the academic study of spirituality, captures well the interplay of belief, relationship to God, and relationship to the rest of humanity when she defines spirituality as one's "lived experience" of faith.[5] Spirituality, then, is not just belief, on one extreme, or a collection of religious experiences, on the other. It is grounded in God's activity on our behalf, our response of faith, and our experience of seeking to live out the faith in myriad ways, affecting every dimension of our life.

Spiritual transformation begins by gratefully embracing the God who embraces us in love and by following the Holy Spirit's prompting and leading to order our minds and life in ways that fit with God's will. Ultimately, the Holy Spirit enables us to fulfill God's purposes for us—to know, love, and serve God and to love others as ourselves. Thus, we are given the opportunity to grow spiritually both because God loves us *and* because our spiritual growth serves God's greater purposes of blessing the world through us.

Thus, in urging you to pursue God as your highest priority in life, I am not promoting the self-gratifying type of spirituality that is sometimes promoted. Spiritual vitality and transformation are not about us, but about God and what God wants to do in us and through us. While we will benefit immensely from knowing and experiencing God more powerfully in our lives, God calls us to live for God and to benefit as a byproduct.

How This Book Works:
A Holistic Model for Spiritual Growth

This book is not an academic study of either theology or spirituality. It is neither a philosophical or theological treatise on God nor is it an abstract exposition of spiritual principles. Rather, it is a Christian-based, experience-oriented, reflection-filled, biblically informed, practical discussion of spiritual growth and Spirit-led living.

I assume that we are more likely to keep growing as spiritual pilgrims if we learn to pay better attention to what is happening in our life, think more deeply about our experiences, let Scripture and others inform our thinking, make new choices, and set out to live differently. I also assume a holistic model for spiritual growth that links a closer relationship to God with growth in every aspect of our life, including our heart, mind, emotions, relationships, and behavior.

Each chapter begins with my own experience, usually an excerpt from my pilgrimage journal (edited to fill in gaps or make it more readable). Then, in the second part, I reflect on my experience and invite you to reflect thoughtfully on your own. As we see better what is real in our life and let questions surface and propel us on our spiritual pilgrimage, especially in light of what Scripture teaches, our growth will emerge more naturally and will likely be more sustainable.

The third part of each chapter leads you explicitly to Scripture for the journey. The Bible is the most sacred source of spiritual wisdom in the Christian tradition, providing a unique collection of stories and teaching on God's activity in human history and guidance for spiritual pilgrims. In it, we find the testimony of authentic experience with God from fellow pilgrims, prophets, and spiritual teachers, whom the church in all its forms has identified as reliable and trustworthy witnesses without equal.

Fourth, each chapter offers practical suggestions for next steps that you as a pilgrim can take to keep growing spiritually. While much transformation happens mysteriously in our life due to unseen internal processes, we can also experience significant change as a result of becoming more intentional in our spiritual life—especially when the steps we take are in sync with how we perceive the Spirit to be prompting us. Some suggestions correspond to my own experience, others grow out of time-tested spiritual practices and disciplines honored and followed by many. All are in sync with Scripture, although only those that jibe with how the Spirit is leading you will be helpful.

Finally, each chapter concludes with several questions for further personal reflection and discussion with others. I strongly recommend that you keep a journal while reading and praying through this book. As we take time to write out our thoughts, feelings, intentions, and prayers, we gain greater clarity of mind and heart. When we communicate to God in writing, as composing a letter to a friend or a poem expressing our heart, we are likely to feel closer to God and to experience greater confidence and spiritual strength.

I also recommend that you form a small group or find an accountability partner to discuss spiritual issues that arise from each chapter. Talking with others who share our love for God and commitment to growth can help us gain clarity about the Spirit's leading and provide support as we start taking new steps to follow. Listening to the stories and thoughts of others can inspire, challenge, and encourage us as the Spirit speaks to us through them. Intentionally walking with fellow pilgrims also helps us to see, hear, and feel that we are not alone on our journey.

Traditionally, to grow in our relationship with God, Christians have been taught to start with Scripture, then move to thinking (as informed by theological frameworks constructed by theologians), seek community among those who think similarly, and then, at the end of the process, interpret our experience in light of our beliefs or what the preacher tells us. Good reasons exist for these guidelines, but too often in practice, individual believers don't do enough thinking for themselves or don't value their unique experiences highly enough. The result can be cookie-cutter Christians, shallow followers, or a stunted relationship with God.

The emphasis on experience in this book in no way is intended to undermine the typical Protestant insistence on the primacy of Scripture as a guide for theological understanding or the Catholic respect for tradition. Rather, I am attempting to encourage you believers to think for yourself better and to integrate your experience and religious beliefs more fully, without neglecting Scripture or tradition.

For many years, especially in the 1950s and '60s in the United States, when most people were members of churches, one might easily have found someone who could recite the creeds but not necessarily explain what they mean or how God related to their own personal life. Today, on the other hand, an increasing number of people are comfortable talking about spirituality as an experience with God but don't know what the Bible teaches, how to put their experience in a theological framework, or how their thinking fits in (or doesn't) with the millennia-old Judeo-Christian tradition. Generally, it seems difficult to find believers who, in a balanced and in-depth way, truly value Scripture *and* thoughtful reflection *and* experience *and* intentionality *and* community.

If your spirituality is mostly intellectual, you may need help to get out of your head in order to know God more experientially and to better integrate your faith and every other aspect of your life. If your spiritual experience is mostly intuitive and feelings based, you may need help to ground your beliefs more in Scripture and thoughtful reflection. If you tend to go it alone with a personal spirituality, you may not yet experience the depth and richness that can come from greater communication with others. If you tend to believe or do whatever someone else tells you, without thinking for yourself, you may need help to own your faith for yourself and seek a spiritual life marked by personal experience with God and leading by the Holy Spirit. In short, a holistic model offers help for any of us who tend to be skewed in one dimension or another of human spiritual experience to fill out our spirituality and to deepen in a more balanced way.

The Pilgrim Trail

As a guide to help you and other motivated spiritual pilgrims draw closer to God and experience real transformation in your lives, this book offers a series of steps you can take on your own or with others. Specifically, the chapters will focus on the following:

- Intentionally taking the next step in your spiritual journey (chapter 1)
- Embracing the journey for what it is—full of challenges and opportunities (chapter 2)
- Facing reality better in every aspect of your life (chapter 3)
- Seeking inner change (chapter 4)
- Pursuing God as Father, Son, and Holy Spirit (interlude)
- Knowing God better (chapter 5)
- Following Jesus wholeheartedly (chapter 6)
- Living by the leading of the Holy Spirit (chapter 7)
- Crossing bridges to your best self (chapter 8)
- Staying the course . . . one step at a time (postlude)

Spiritual pilgrims travel a difficult path at times. We have to learn to face reality—truth about ourselves and others that we may not want to see. We discover that to grow closer to God and others and to experience more fulfillment in life, often we need to change. Our growth often depends on making our relationship with God a higher priority and letting go of attachments to the things we value in order to create more space for God in our life and more freedom to follow the Spirit's leading.

However, spiritual growth is not something to be achieved but something to be experienced. It is not a goal so much as it is the fruit of a process of transformation that slowly influences, reorients, and eventually propels us by the leading of the Holy Spirit in every dimension of our life. Though we often don't like to face reality, change, make God a higher priority, or let go of our prized or deep-seated attachments, once we can admit just this one basic truth—our reluctance to change in ways that align with our highest spiritual values—we have begun our journey. Then, as we take steps to act on the truth God reveals to us, our pilgrimage begins in earnest.

CHAPTER 1

Taking the Next Step

~

FOR A LONG TIME I COULD NOT *have really told you why I decided to go on pilgrimage—to walk nearly five hundred miles across northern Spain. At one time I was never going to waste my time and energy doing any such thing! Then all of a sudden, one day, I completely changed my mind. Going on pilgrimage was exactly what I wanted to do, and I couldn't wait to get started.*

It was actually my wife's idea at first. We were in Chartres, France, in the late 1990s. She saw some fit looking, middle-aged people striding by, dressed in athletic shirts, shorts, and walking shoes. "I'd like to do that some day," she blurted out, quite randomly.

"Do what?" I knew she didn't mean just going for a walk, and braced myself for whatever "out there" idea she was going to spring on me.

"There's a pilgrimage route that runs right through Chartres," she explained. "Those people are probably pilgrims. See the scallop shells embedded in the ground? They mark a pathway that goes all the way to Santiago de Compostela."

"To where?" I was puzzled. I had neither heard of the place, nor had I ever noticed the blue and yellow shells.

"It's in Spain. It's the most popular Christian pilgrimage destination in the world, after Jerusalem and Rome. Every year tens of thousands of people, coming from many different directions, walk hundreds of miles to reach the place where James the apostle's bones are believed to be buried. Santiago is Saint James in Spanish."

I was only partly listening. I like being out in nature and quite enjoy hiking, but at the moment, the thought of walking anywhere other than to the town square to get a pain au chocolat

11

and café *(chocolate pastry and coffee) seemed excessive. The picture I conjured up of pilgrimage was walking for miles on end, alongside a long, flat, boring road, with cars sailing past us, spewing exhaust, and making irritating noise. Why would anyone ever want to do that?* "Well," *I said, trying to let her down as gently as possible,* "I'm afraid that has no appeal for me whatsoever."

Nevertheless, about a half a dozen years after first hearing about El Camino ("The Way," *the Spanish name for the pilgrimage route), I was a pilgrim. On June 24, 2006, after declaring some years earlier that I had no interest in walking for days on end, let alone across Spain in the hottest time of the summer, I voluntarily embarked upon a five-and-a-half-week adventure with my wife and two sons, ages eighteen and twenty. We were anxious, excited, and wary as we began, but there was no doubt in my mind. Going on pilgrimage was exactly what I wanted to do.*

Reflecting on the Journey

Think about the times in your life when you suddenly were open to something new and different. What changed your mind or heart? What was it that finally set you free to move forward? What did it feel like to take that first step in a new direction or that next significant step on an already established path?

Maybe you did an about face, changing your mind to do something for God, yourself, or others that you didn't think you would ever do—like joining a study group, volunteering, going to therapy, practicing a new spiritual discipline, or crossing some other threshold that, up to that point, had been too formidable to cross. Perhaps for years you had resisted change or felt defeated when you tried to move forward, and yet, all of a sudden, something shifted, and you took the next, significant step in your life. You ventured forward, maybe boldly, maybe with much trepidation. Perhaps you were excited, perhaps you were ambivalent, but you did it. Now, today, your life is different because you made a decision to finally listen to the inner prompting, and you took action.

Sometimes the most significant actions in our lives relate to major decisions—like choosing a major in college, starting or quitting a job, getting married, leaving a marriage, moving, changing churches, or having children. You turn a corner and find yourself headed in a new direction, associating with new people or doing different things. Maybe you knew what you were doing or maybe you had no idea what you were getting into, but you made your move, and your life was different.

Then there are the more subtle, but still significant, internal changes we make. We may adopt a new attitude, experience a change of heart, choose to act with more integrity, become more empathetic and compassionate. We may feel more open to God, desire to act more faithfully, place a higher value on our health or on caring for our environment. Something shifts and we suddenly see things differently. Our intentions change or become more powerful and we want to take steps to bring our life in better alignment with our values, desires, or vision.

Often, we can give very good reasons why we are making a certain decision or choosing to act in a new or more intentioned way. Other times, such as when I decided to go on pilgrimage, shifts take place in our lives, and we don't really know why or how the changes came about. We may even surprise ourselves or act in a way that seems totally out of character. Or, if we can explain our new actions, we may not know why now and not ten years earlier or ten years later. Whatever the reasons, we feel different, are making different choices, and others around us may even be noticing how much we have changed.

I may never know all the forces that had been at work in my life for perhaps decades preparing me to say yes to the Camino. Was it unresolved grief over my mother's tragic suffering with Alzheimer's disease? Was I still looking for answers to the skin disease that threatened to end my life early, which was diagnosed the day after my first son was born? Maybe it was my increasing dissatisfaction with pat theological answers that put God in a box, a rigid paradigm that had led to disillusionment, frustration, and disappointments in my life and pastoral ministry? Was it my equally unsatisfying experience trying to think my way to God through graduate school or my limited ability to be the husband and father I wanted to be? All these factors, and others, had propelled me on my spiritual journey over the years, but what was driving me this time?

There is no question that my dissatisfaction with life and my spiritual questions have been continual prods, but I was drawn to pilgrimage by much more positive forces. More times than I can count I have experienced love and encouragement from God in the midst of unanswered questions and painful circumstances. These experiences have made me think that a more serious effort to seek God would lead to more insight and a deeper connection to God. My history of setting aside a week a year for spiritual reflection and prayer no doubt laid the groundwork for a five-week pilgrimage. Ever since my trip to Taizé, France, in 1998, I have come to love my annual spiritual retreats. I have become increasingly open and eager for more of what I might learn and experience by seeking God intentionally.

On the Camino, though motivations varied, most everyone, like me, was intent on getting something significant from the experience. Most were Europeans, and the majority was Spanish, but many came from as far north as the Czech Republic, Estonia, Germany, Norway, and Russia. We even met a handful of Americans and Australians, who traveled thousands of miles just to make the journey.

Some were trying to make a new start, some were seeking clarity in their minds and hearts, others were looking for divine guidance, some wanted to get away from their normal environment to be out in nature, others were interested in walking in the steps of millions of other Christians, and still others were simply open to being surprised by God in some way. Many walked for nonspiritual reasons, too. School groups and bike clubs took to the trail for fun. Some were seeking an adventure. Others liked getting out of the house in the summer to enjoy the beauty and peace of the Camino. For some it was a cultural experience or a multigenerational family tradition.

In my case, once I decided to go on pilgrimage, I realized that, most of all, I wanted to seek guidance from God. I also wanted to be changed, but I didn't know exactly how. I had enjoyed leading a nonprofit ministry and offering spiritual leadership to staff for more than ten years, but I had been feeling a strong yearning to devote more time to studying, writing, and teaching. Walking on pilgrimage seemed like a perfect opportunity to focus intensely on seeking God's wisdom and guidance for the next phase of my life. I also hoped the experience would be a catalyst to personal growth in some way.

Crossing Bridges

Throughout the pilgrimage, the image of crossing a huge bridge kept popping into my head. I had left behind the land from which I came and I was going to a new place. I was in neither the old nor the new world. I was moving and being moved along a path that would take me to a place that I could not yet envision. I was crossing over a chasm that separated one way of thinking and being in the world to another, though I could not know what the new way was going to be like.

Parts of me were greatly resisting. Even though I often felt dissatisfied with my life at home, it was familiar, and I had surrounded myself with many comforts to distract me from my periodic feelings of angst. I was also afraid of what might be on the other side of the bridge. What might God ask of me, if I trusted enough to keep walking on an unfamiliar path?

Yet, at the same time, I felt a push and a pull. My restlessness and desire for something more or different was almost compelling me to move forward. At the same time, some force, which I assumed was the Holy Spirit, was opening my heart and mind to new possibilities and drawing me to them. My life wasn't being instantaneously changed. Rather, I was experiencing a slow process of transformation, which included periodically running back in the direction I had come from, before turning again to resume the journey.

Since returning home, I have come to understand, with the help of anthropologists, that I was going through a period of profound transition in my life, an extended liminal experience, which included changing jobs and entering the empty nest phase.[1] Some of what I experienced on pilgrimage is unique to transitional phases and not characteristic of what we might think of as "normal" life. However, life is a series of large and small changes, too. We may not be continually changing jobs or significant relationships, but we all move from stage to stage in life and must negotiate many transitions. In addition, biblical writers call believers to continually seek greater maturity and spiritual transformation until we finally become like Christ—something that we fallible human pilgrims can at best pursue as an ongoing goal all of our lives.

Thus, I have come to realize that what I was doing on the Camino is a rare and intense form of what can be a way of life—intentionally and regularly pursuing a deeper relationship with God and ever deepening personal transformation. Most Christians will never be able to walk to Santiago de Compostela or any other significant holy site. Yet, could not everyone, even if they never leave their hometown, still live their life as spiritual pilgrims? Could we not learn to continually stay open to movement, as God leads us onto new or different paths, and across bridge after bridge, throughout our lifetime?

In practice, we may never be able to fully understand why we make the changes we do or why we finally become ready to take another significant step in our spiritual life. We may not know all of what is driving us or how God might be at work transforming us at any given juncture. We may not know how we got on any given bridge, let alone what lies on the other side.

What seems most important in our spiritual journey is simply heeding the call to take the next step forward . . . and then the one after that . . . and the one after that . . . in perpetual pursuit of a deeper relationship with God. As we seek to know and experience God more fully and to let ourselves be changed and grow, we may know only that we need to set our face forward and move—that it is time to take the next step.

Scripture for the Journey

In the Judeo-Christian tradition, biblical writers portray spiritual vitality in various ways, all of which come down to knowing and loving God, trusting in the love and grace of God, and seeking to serve God's purposes with our life (Deut. 6:4–5; Mic. 6:8; Eph. 2:8–10).

In the New Testament, spiritual vitality is rooted in Yahweh, the God of the Hebrew Scriptures; is intimately linked to Jesus Christ; and depends on the Holy Spirit, who grounds us in our present relationship with God and keeps us moving forward on our spiritual journey.

When we, as spiritual pilgrims, look to Scripture for guidance, we find a complementary balance between resting and moving, relying on God and taking action, enjoying the blessings of God and perpetually seeking more and all of what God intends for us. Jesus invited believers to find rest in him and to follow him (Matt. 11:28–30). The Holy Spirit has been given to us so that we can continue to grow in our relationship with God and to be transformed in our being and doing in the world (Gal. 5:22–23; 2 Pet. 1:3–10). Ultimately, when this life's journey is finished, our final destination is to enter into the full presence of God, completely conformed to the image of Christ (Rom. 8:29).

The balance between rest and movement can also be found in the writings of the apostle Paul, whose understanding of salvation is often described by scholars as "now and not yet." On one hand, followers in Christ can experience grace, forgiveness, reassurance of eternal life, power, love, and the other fruit of the Holy Spirit in this life, now (Rom. 3:23–26; 6:23; 8:1–10; Gal. 5:22–23). However, at the same time we are still plagued by desires, thinking, and behavior that are contrary to God's will and undermine our relationship with God, even when we want to do good (Rom. 7:21–23). Ultimately, Paul teaches, we must wait for the next life to be completely transformed with Christlike qualities, when we receive an immortal body (Rom. 8:11, 29; 1 Cor. 15:50–54; Phil. 3:20–21).

Thus, while we already experience great blessings through our faith and the Holy Spirit, much more still lies ahead—more growth, more freedom from sin, more knowledge and understanding of God, more experience with the love of Christ, and more ability to act justly and show mercy. A dynamic relationship with the Holy Spirit promises to change us from the inside out and transform our relationships with God and others, helping us become more and more like Christ.

Spiritual pilgrimage, then, is that quest for the "more." It begins "now" and continues until we reach what is "not yet." The pilgrim simultaneously rests in a present relationship with God and sets out in pursuit of God. Clearly, it is not as if God is out there somewhere hiding or in an obscure, distant land and needs to be found. God is within us as well as beyond us. Pilgrims seek more of the God who is already journeying with them.

For those ready to take the next step in their spiritual journey, biblical writers teach us that a good place to start is by opening our heart and mind to God as fully as possible, and by responding accordingly to whatever God may reveal. For example, as we allow ourselves to see our Creator more fully, we are likely to bend our knees in awe and gratitude to the Source of our life. As we are moved by the love of God, we may feel drawn to reach out to Love and to seek to be more filled with love ourselves. As we realize how much our spiritual vitality is affected by sin, we will acknowledge its presence, seek forgiveness from God, and turn away from it (repent). When we read in the New Testament that God has designated Jesus Christ to be the Savior of the world and leader for Christians, believers will respond with trust, allegiance, and devotion. As we come to perceive the work of the Holy Spirit (Christ's Spirit) to empower, transform, and guide us from day to day, we may feel motivated to better listen to and keep in step with the Spirit.

Spiritual pilgrimage is about an inner journey of transformation that shows its fruit in our external world. As pilgrims, we pursue a deeper, more unified relationship with God, who is the Creator of the universe, the Savior of humanity, and the Holy Spirit. God precedes us, journeys with us, is the destination ahead of us, and simultaneously is both infinitely beyond us and present within us. On occasion we may have the opportunity to traverse an external, holy pathway (a pilgrimage route) for a fixed period of time. However, the more important inner journey, which spiritual pilgrims perpetually make over the course of their lifetime, is one of ever deepening personal and spiritual transformation.

So we read in the Psalms, "Blessed are those whose strength is in you [God], who have set their hearts on pilgrimage. . . . They go from strength to strength, till each appears before God in Zion" (Ps. 84:5, 7 NIV). For the ancient Hebrews, Zion referred both to the actual city of Jerusalem and the symbolic setting for the fulfillment of all God's promises to Israel. The psalmist here portrays life as an ongoing journey, in which God is both the ultimate destination and the Presence who provides pilgrims with the strength needed to keep moving forward. Consequently, we who trust in God's promises and know God in a deep, existential way are simultaneously at home with God, perpetually in pursuit of God, and dependent on God the whole way.

Jesus himself shows us how important it is to seek out God by modeling what we now call spiritual disciplines—practices such as solitude, prayer, Sabbath worship, serving the needy, fellowship, witness, and using spiritual gifts, among others still observed today.[2] His extended times alone with God the Father seemed to be especially important to him, ahead of and in the midst of his uniquely demanding ministry.[3]

In the book of Hebrews, the writer sums up the value of pursuing God actively by simply saying, "And without faith it is impossible to please God, because anyone who comes to him must believe that he exists and that he rewards those who earnestly seek him" (11:6 NIV). Elsewhere, the writer says, "Let us then approach the throne of grace with confidence, so that we may receive mercy and find grace to help us in our time of need" (4:16 NIV). God is receptive to us and wants to help us in the ways we most need on the journey.

When the apostle Paul urged believers to actively seek a deeper connection with Christ as a way of life, he didn't draw on the concept of spiritual pilgrimage. Instead, in the case of the Philippians, he used a citizenship metaphor to help them understand that their real home and destination was "heaven"—not an otherworldly place of escape but a different dimension of reality that has bearing on this life as well as the next. Paul wrote: "Our citizenship is in heaven. And we eagerly await a Savior from there, the Lord Jesus Christ, who, by the power that enables him to bring everything under his control, will transform our lowly bodies so that they will be like his glorious body" (Phil. 3:20–21 NIV).

These verses help us by reminding us that there is a bigger reality that is relevant to us. We have a Savior, the Lord Jesus Christ, and the kingdom of God that stand in contrast to the Roman emperor of Paul's day and any earthly political or social system. Paul is saying that Christ brings salvation with lasting transformation for those who trust in him. He also serves as the rightful leader of our lives who can guide us into the life we were meant to live, offering true hope for our deepest longings and eternal needs. Remembering that we are citizens of heaven reminds us to value our relationship with God, to look to Christ for hope, and to see ourselves first and foremost as people of faith in Christ's service. To mix the citizenship and pilgrimage metaphors, all of life for a Christian can be seen as a long journey in which we are simultaneously at home in relationship to God through faith in Christ and continually heading toward our ultimate home.[4]

Next Steps

What is stirring within you? Do you feel a yearning to know and experience God more fully? Do you sense a prompting to make a change in your life or to seek transformation, even if you don't know where the process may lead? The step you are considering may seem out of character for you or even weird to your friends or family, but perhaps a part of you wants something more or different, and you are ready to do something about it.

If this describes you, what action do you need to take in order to flow with the impulses arising within you? Whether you are considering a full-blown pilgrimage of some sort or are simply moving forward to adopt a new spiritual discipline or cultivate your spiritual life in some way, many of the same principles apply. Here are some recommendations based on my experience for the first (or next) steps on your spiritual pilgrimage.

Just Say Yes!

You may be concerned about what forces are prompting you and whether to trust your impulses. Wisdom does indeed suggest that one safeguards important decisions to some extent. By trying to be as self-aware and thoughtful as possible, you can make better choices about how to meet your needs and how to respond to your inner stirrings in healthful ways. You can also pray and seek godly counsel to help you discern what might be from God and what kind of action is likely to be most fruitful. The Bible is also an invaluable resource to help you know the actions that fit with spiritual maturity and to make it harder for you to deceive yourself with selfish or harmful impulses.

Yet, sometimes, you just need to let go and get going. The truth is, pilgrims don't always need to know why they finally say yes to a new idea or inclination to seek God and make changes in their life. There are probably multiple influences at work within you, and God's hand is often unseen. Sometimes when you feel the stirrings, the best thing is to simply say yes and then let God shape your heart and mind and guide your steps as you go forward.

Set a Direction

Sometimes our inner stirrings are vague longings or ideas, and other times we know exactly what we need. You don't always need to have figured out the best way to go forward in order to get started on your journey, but having some direction is quite helpful.

When I started on pilgrimage, I had only a very general sense of what the specific journey might be about, but I had a direction. I knew I wanted to seek God in a more intentional way and to experience some kind of spiritual transformation, and I had chosen a specific spiritual discipline to help me. Spiritual pilgrimage is not about wandering aimlessly, but about seeking something and Someone of great value to us in the best ways we can over time.

Make a Plan

Positive thinking without a plan is a prescription for paralysis. Positive thinking with a plan puts you on a path to possibilities. (Do you like the alliteration?) First, make a firm decision to do something that you are not currently doing to pursue God in a fresh way, whether as a one-time, special endeavor or as a new way of living your life. Then, once you have committed yourself to action, figure out what it will take to make your plan a reality.

To set out in pursuit of God in a more intentional way, you can utilize any number of readily available spiritual exercises or tools, such as fasting, solitude, extended silence, a spiritual retreat, a mission trip, Bible studies, journal writing, daily devotions, walking meditatively, labyrinth walking, and other such practices. Pick something that is a stretch for you that will engage you for an extended period of time, both on a daily basis and for as many days as possible. The more frequently and the longer you practice a spiritual discipline, the more it will become a part of your life, and often the greater its effect.

If you don't know what to do next, start praying for wisdom and seek the counsel of a pastor or some other spiritually mature individual. While you are searching, make visual reminders of your goals in order to prompt you to pray or make the call you think might be helpful in your process. Set aside times to explore specific opportunities. Tell someone else about your intention.

Once you have an idea of what you want to do, then you are ready to create a plan of action and think through what it will take to make it a reality. Where, when, how will you find the time, money, support needed to carry through on your idea? Ask others to pray with you to help make your vision a reality.

It is also important that you don't just try to tack on some spiritual practice and otherwise leave your normal life intact. Something will have to give. Your plan needs to consider what will not be done if you take time for a new spiritual practice, so that you won't add stress to your life by trying to do too much or neglect something important by not allotting enough time to another priority. For example, if you decide to take a thirty-minute prayer walk when you get home from working out each morning, but that is when you normally connect with your spouse, call your parents, or get ready for upcoming meetings, then find another way to adequately attend to these other values.

The general goal of seeking God can be vague, but the plan for your next steps should be very specific. Where are you going? When? With whom? What will you do there or on the way? How do you need to structure the time to best facilitate your connecting with God? If you will be doing your spiritual practice with others, such as on a retreat or pilgrimage, what parameters do you need to set on your interaction with them while you are there in order to stay focused?

Get Away

Most spiritual practices can be done right at home, but if you get the chance to get away to do something special that would enhance your spiritual life, do it. One of the great things about actually leaving home, limiting our belongings to what could fit in a backpack, and traveling to a designated pilgrimage route in northern Spain was that it was easy to realize we were doing something different and special. You may have to work harder to create the same space and perception if you don't walk the Camino, but it is worth the effort.

The more you can quietly focus your mind on God, let go of the preoccupations that normally clutter your heart and mind, and gently listen with a minimal number of distractions (home life is often full of them), the better the chance that you will actually be able to hear God's voice or sense God's moving within you. Rather than settling for "drive-by" praying, create a ritual of separating yourself from your normal routine to connect with God. For example, start with just two minutes (a full 120 seconds) and work your way up to twenty uninterrupted minutes a day for thirty days when you are fully engaged with God. In these times, focus on journaling, reading Scripture, or prayer. Even better would be to get away for at least overnight to a spiritual retreat center, campground, monastery, or some other special place. Have it in your mind when you go that you are going on a minipilgrimage—not a vacation, but a time to seek God with special focus and intention. Get caught up on sleep, relax, breathe deeply, go for a walk, and gently turn your attention to God.

Some day you may even want to walk an established pilgrimage route. If you are not able to take a big trek any time soon, you could do a segment of a known pilgrimage route with the time you do have available. In Spain, we met a number of pilgrims who would walk for a week or however much time they had one year, then come back another year to do the next portion.

Get a Guide

We had a very helpful guidebook with maps, details on towns, where to get food and water, where to find a bed, and some inspirational thoughts to ponder. When you are creating your own pilgrimage or devoting yourself to a new spiritual practice, I recommend consulting with a pastor, spiritual director, or retreat center first. Find someone who can help you envision what you hope to get out of the practice, who can give you tips along the way, and who will be available to help you debrief it afterwards. On an ongoing basis, my spiritual director is an important guide, among others, for my life as a pilgrim. We meet about once a month, and he helps me by listening for how God is at work in my life and by helping me learn to notice better for myself.

Ask Others to Join You

Consider asking companions to join you in the journey. There are pros and cons to going on pilgrimage with others, be it a walk around the block, a Bible study, a spiritual retreat, or something more extensive. At best, others can support you, share the experience with you, help you work out what you are learning along the way and afterwards, and provide community to bring out the social dimension of God's activity and your personal transformation. At worst, they can be a distraction or stumbling block. If you succumb to their influence, you may allow yourself to be preoccupied with conversation, stuck in old ways of thinking and being in the world, or overly focused on your companions' concerns and issues. If, on the other hand, you are able to let your interactions with others serve as testing ground to strengthen you in your new resolve to pursue a deeper relationship with God and personal transformation, then rubbing shoulders with companions could make you stronger. Apart from rare times of solitude in life, we all journey with others. One of life's spiritual tasks is to learn how to do so well.

I was very glad my wife and sons accompanied me on the Camino for all the positive reasons listed above. In addition, I learned more about God and God's love by interacting with them, whether the learning came from working through conflicts or just enjoying each other's company. However, I also learned that I had to make a point of creating solitude for myself each day and to work harder to stay on track with the individual aspects of my pilgrimage.

In normal life, we are usually surrounded by other people and, to be active in a Christian community or church, we have to travel with fellow pilgrims. For most of us, traveling through life alone is neither an option nor is it necessarily desirable. Still, you can be intentional about whom you invite to share in the spiritual dimension of your life. Though you cannot pick who attends your church, you can choose your friends and those with whom you fellowship. You can seek out the company of certain individuals who will enhance your journey, and you can carve out time to be alone, when you need solitude and time to focus your attention just on God.

Make Room for God

Create space and maintain boundaries in your daily life in order to leave room for God. This practice is important in all dimensions of your life. If you are a people pleaser, you will be very vulnerable to the demands, real or imagined, of others. If you are overly task oriented, your endless to-do list will offer little or no space in your minds for quiet, for listening, or for God. Perpetually seeking God as a way of life requires learning to connect with God consciously and regularly in the midst of responsibilities and relationships as well as in the moments of quiet time and retreat.[5]

Pray

Prayer may sound passive, but it is not at all. When you consciously expresses your heart's desire and intentionality, often something will shift within you. Aligning your words with what you sense to be the Spirit's leading reinforces the work God is doing within you and enables you to move forward in sync with God's prompting. Prayer can also allow you to realize your weaknesses and dependency on the Holy Spirit, prompting humility and moving you to seek God's grace and help. When your prayer reaches this level of honesty, openness, humility, and intentionality, you have truly already taken significant steps on your spiritual pilgrimage.

One favorite prayer practice of my spiritual director, John Ackerman, is to put yourself in the place of Bartimaeus. Once when Jesus was walking from Jericho to Jerusalem, Bartimaeus, a blind beggar, was sitting on the side of the road and started calling out to Jesus. No one could quiet him, he was so intent on being heard. Finally, when Jesus did hear him, he told him to come to him, and said, "What do you want me to do for you?" Bartimaeus eagerly and quickly replied, "Let me see again" (Mark 10:51). Jesus then healed him.

Bartimaeus models for us eagerness to seek help from Jesus and willingness to express the desire of his heart. Try imagining that Jesus is asking you what you would like him to do for you. Answer from your heart, and notice what comes out of your mouth with energy. Let that desire turn into a daily prayer for a week, month, or as long as it takes for you to feel heard by Jesus. The Bartimaeus prayer is not a formula to get something from Jesus. Rather, it is a way of identifying what matters most to you and is stirring powerfully deep within you. Praying this way can also remind you that Jesus is eager for you to engage him with that level of authenticity. It is the beginning of a process of self-discovery and a dialogue with Christ, not the end.

Get Support

I recommend starting the next phase of your pilgrimage with an accountability partner, someone with whom you will meet or talk regularly to help you stay on track with whatever steps you have set for your journey. Each of us must walk our own individual pilgrimage, but we do not and ought not to try to walk alone. Others are pursuing God all around you, and seeking out their support will strengthen you, help you sort out what you are experiencing, and help you avoid the discouragement or distractions that waylay many pilgrims, as Jesus's parable of the sower warns.

What other help and support do you imagine you will need that is not covered by the suggestions already given? Whatever you think you need, ask others for help. The right kind of accountability and support will greatly increase your chances of following through on your plan and enhancing your spiritual journey.

For Further Reflection

Friday, April 28, 2006. Deephaven, Minnesota. (Journal entry, written two months before leaving on pilgrimage.) I suspect the main reason I need to go on pilgrimage is to separate myself from my normal world almost entirely. I will set down every commitment and habit and attachment. When I get home, I will be in a much better position to know what I want to pick up again. I pray that I will be better positioned to move with greater determination and force. Ah ha. I'm seeking my own transformation—to move powerfully out of the inertia that holds me prisoner in my current lifestyle more into the life that will bring greater satisfaction and meaning.

Use the journal excerpt above and the following questions to guide your journal writing. Discuss your thoughts, feelings, and intentions with some fellow pilgrims from your spiritual community.

- What is stirring within me to which I need or want to say yes?
- What spiritual practice has recently been suggested to me or has popped into my head that seems like the right thing for me to do next on my spiritual journey?
- What specifically am I going to do? What is my next step? When will I take it? Whom will I tell?
- What support will I need to take the next step in my spiritual life? Who will be my accountability partner(s)? How will I get and ask for the help I need?
- What other thoughts were prompted by this chapter on taking the next step on my spiritual journey that I want to think more about or act on?

CHAPTER 2

Embracing the Journey

~

FRIDAY, JUNE 24, 2006. DAY 1. RONCESVALLES, SPAIN. Early this morning, around seven, we stood at the edge of the little village of St. Jean Pied-de-Port, France. I was so excited to be starting the Camino. I was awake half the night writing in my journal and trying to calm my nerves.

A couple of grassy paths led in different directions. We squinted to read the fog-shrouded signs in the early morning light. We finally found one that pointed us to Roncesvalles, our first stop en route to Santiago de Compostela, Spain. Another sign announced that our destination was only eight hundred kilometers (five hundred miles) away!

Over the next seven hours and fifteen minutes, we walked thirty-one kilometers (nineteen miles), ultimately climbing to 1,400 meters (4,600 feet) as we went up and down the French Pyrenees through fog and much rain. We didn't get a ray of sun the whole day, but near the summit, the view finally expanded to reveal verdant, rolling hills. Absolutely beautiful. I took off my pack and spun around to look in every direction. I felt so free and full. I momentarily forgot the conditions and stress of the climb, and started singing and jumping around. We made it to the top . . . and it was only the beginning of our adventure.

We crawled into an old shepherds' shelter, a five-by-nine-foot, five-foot-high cubbyhole made of rocks with a wooden door and flat metal roof. The four of us wedged ourselves in the small space, cramped by boulders and debris left by previous visitors. It felt great to finally be able to sit down out of the pouring rain and eat the sandwiches we had packed. At this point, we didn't feel the need to talk much—partly because the physical exertion had been so exhausting and partly because the stimulation of a new adventure was plenty. I drank in the silence, while my heart and mind became filled with hopes and dreams for what this pilgrimage might mean for me.

When the rain tapered off, we decided to tackle the remaining distance. The last 3.6 kilometers (2 miles) were downhill, over gravel, through woods, in the steady dripping rain. I was getting so tired and sore toward the end that the fun began to dissipate. The walk was actually a bit dangerous, and we couldn't arrive at our destination soon enough.

Finally Roncesvalles appeared through the sparse forest. We would spend the night in the small Spanish village where Charlemagne had been defeated in 778. Now the town is mostly a key link on the Camino with a dormitory where 120 pilgrims pack in, sleeping on bunk beds in one large room. Dozens of others squeeze in, rolling out their sleeping bags wherever they can find a spot on the floor. Nearby a small church symbolizes a deeper meaning of the pilgrimage. There, each night, a priest offers mass and a pilgrim blessing for those who seek God's help for the journey.

Now I'm waiting for someone to arrive to check us in. I'm soaked and exhausted, but still thrilled. I can't believe we're really doing this!

Reflecting on the Journey

Finally underway, I felt very ready to begin a new chapter in my life. I was eager to experience something that would help me break out of the emotional and psychological eddy that kept me swirling in the same waters. I had glimpses of where I wanted to go in my vocation, marriage, and friendships, but I didn't know how to get there. I wanted to learn how to flow better with God's Spirit in my life, yet I couldn't seem to move out of my way of thinking and being in the world. I felt frustrated and unsatisfied but unable to get downstream to whatever might be waiting for me there. Now, with the first steps of the journey, I felt hopeful that there would be real movement in my life.

At the summit of the Pyrenees, I was singing, "On a clear day, you can see forever . . ." Actually, I could not see very far down the mountain at the moment, but my mind was spinning and my heart was beating faster, imagining new possibilities for my future. I didn't really know what I was seeing yet, but I knew it was going to be different. I could see hope.

The other song I kept singing over and over again was, "We Are the Champions." I only knew a few lines of the rock band Queen's immensely popular hit, but it felt great to belt them out. By taking these first steps, by actually getting out of my home environment to take this pilgrimage, I felt like a champion. I was overcoming a huge, limiting force in my life. I had faced the inertia in my work life, the fears about letting go of the known and pursuing my vision of creating a global ministry, and my doubts and apprehensions about hiking five hundred miles—and I was finally moving forward. On top of the mountain, I felt on top of the world. Soon, I began changing the lyrics while keeping the tune. My singing turned into a prayer:

> God, you have brought me to this place.
> I feel so happy—at last.
> Please give me wisdom.
> Please give me insight.
> Show me the best way.
> Show me a better way . . . to live.

Looking back, I see that the first day of the pilgrimage was a time for high expectations and for feeling the joy of moving forward with my life. It was a time for celebration and a time for creating happy memories in anticipation of the difficult journey ahead. Remembering the joy and the visceral experience of Day 1 helped me later on when I felt so exhausted or wanted to go home early. That first day provided a stake in the ground, a hope to hold on to, so that I would not forget why I came on pilgrimage in the first place and how much this journey meant to me.

Of course, I had no idea at the time what was really going to happen and what I was going to experience. I knew it would be hard, but I didn't know what I would face and when. I wondered how I would respond to the challenges when they came and how they would affect me.

Soon I would begin to find out.

Unexpected Graces

We got our pilgrim passports stamped by a plain-looking volunteer in a sparsely furnished room, with tables crammed together in a U shape, uninspiring paint on old walls, and incandescent lights emitting no warmth. We dragged ourselves to the dormitory and managed to find four bunk beds together in a sea of 120 beds in one large room. Not exactly the Hilton—or any other living arrangement I have ever been in—but any dry, clean place with beds looked good at the moment. We wanted to collapse at 4:00 p.m., but we had to do something with our soaked clothes and wet backpacks. We also wanted to attend the pilgrim service in the chapel and get dinner before crashing for the night.

My mood started deteriorating when I discovered that all of my prescription pills had fallen out of their container, partly dissolving inside my pack. There was white goo everywhere, on everything, with no washing machines, soap, or towels at hand. After staring in dismay at the mess for several minutes with no idea what to do, a fellow pilgrim intervened. He was kind enough to show me a few tricks for cleaning out the pack with a undershirt, and then washing the soiled garments separately.

The stranger's kindness was my first glimpse of the unexpected graces and camaraderie that sprung up spontaneously throughout the pilgrimage. The moment was powerful and transformative. When I thanked him, I wasn't just being polite. I truly felt grateful—something I was not used to feeling very often. I liked the feeling. I liked it a lot. Experiencing simple, unsolicited generosity from a fellow pilgrim made me want to do the same for somebody else.

However, the mess and loss of my pills sobered me up pretty fast. I was feeling more and more exhausted and was still looking at soaking wet clothes. I eventually found a small dryer in the basement that we could use—a rare luxury, we were to discover. Usually, if we had rain-soaked clothes that did not dry overnight, we had to attach the wettest items to the outside of the packs with safety pins. There was always the hope that the sun would shine the next day and dry the clothes in the open air. This night the dryer was a real gift.

When I finally made it to the pilgrim service, I was happy just to be sitting down and happy to be in a place of worship. Most of my energy was gone. I didn't understand the priest's Spanish, but the rhythm of his voice helped me relax, think, and pray. An internal dialogue began in my head with an imaginary counselee.

A faceless person has just come to me for help. His voice was full of despair. He only said four words to me: "I am so lost."

Without thinking, I heard myself respond immediately, "But you are not lost to God."

I was stunned by my words. Where did they come from? Who's lost, and how did I know he was not lost to God?

I suddenly realized I was counseling myself. Here I was a Protestant minister in a Catholic service, led by a priest speaking a language I could not understand, embarking upon a traditionally Catholic spiritual event, in a completely foreign culture. What was I doing here?

Yet, at the same time, I felt more at home here than I usually do in my own English-speaking church, within my own denomination, in my American culture, or with pretty much any other aspect of the world I left behind.

Actually, I felt I belonged nowhere, except with my family and out on the road, in prayer, and in the world as a caring, giving person. Yet I often feel so alone. . . .

I feel lost. But to God, I am found.

Tears fell to the cement floor.

The service came to an end. I gladly received the priest's blessing—offered in words I could not translate. In that moment, the man in the long white robe speaking and making familiar gestures was giving something important to us pilgrims en route to Santiago de Compostela. For me, as he made the sign of the cross in the air, he was saying, "Go in faith, because God is going with you."

Day 2—The Letdown

We got up before dawn the next day to head for Larrasoana, eighteen miles away. However, all the excitement of Day 1 was gone. The moment we walked out of the dormitory, the rain began in what promised to be an all day immersion—an endless combination of drizzle, drip, splash. Soon, mud caked my only pair of shoes, water soaked my socks. I was starting out already extremely sore and tired from yesterday's hike. I could tell this was going to be a long day. The intriguing adventure now seemed like an obligation and dreaded chore. How was I ever going to get through it?

Jill thought she could help me by being cheery. However, her happiness only made me more irritable, and I snapped at her. Our prepilgrimage fantasy of long, idyllic walks together on the Camino, encouraging one another spiritually while bonding at ever deeper levels, was quickly being replaced with a rerun of all too common patterns. First a misunderstanding occurs, someone gets hurt, and soon we have devolved into quarrelling or moody silence. Fortunately, my younger son, Dan, saved the day with a witty interjection. "Oh, don't worry, Mom. Dad is just being Eeyore."

When I heard what he had said to his mother, I was hurt. "What? That's not fair," I wanted to say. Then, before my defensive reaction left my lips, I was amused. I suppose I did sound quite a bit like Winnie-the-Pooh's gloomy, the-glass-is-half-empty donkey friend. To listen to me, you would have thought the rain symbolized a curse on the pilgrimage and the mud on my shoes meant the trip was ruined already on Day 2.

I suppose part of my sourness came from anger, fueled by frustration and fear. I had just turned my right ankle twice and the left one once within the first mile. I felt angry, not so much because of the throbbing pain, but because I was afraid that I done damage to myself that was only going to intensify. I chose to imagine the worst, and I immediately started drawing dark, neurotic conclusions from my experience. I must be screwing up. I am to blame for my condition. My body is not going to cooperate with me, and my hopes and dreams are going to be undermined.

My thoughts weren't rational. They were driven by anxiety, and my negativity was threatening to take everyone down with me. Happily, Dan's Eeyore appellation snapped me out of my self-absorbed funk.

Released from the power of the anxious mood, I started to think and pray about what was going on. I realized that my lack of physical balance, which caused my ankle to twist, mirrored the spiritual and emotional imbalance in my life. I also saw that in such situations, I have choices. I can spend time churning over possible causes of my grumpiness and physical distress, start blaming myself or others, and worry about what might happen as a result. *Or* I can focus on the present and view my experience as an opportunity for growth or action. Given the present state of affairs and the options available to me, what can I do *now*?

Scripture for the Journey

The Bible contains many stories of men and women of faith who were called to embark upon a holy journey or who were given a special assignment that called for pursuing a God-inspired vision. Often, they encountered many difficulties, temptations, and sometimes great pain and suffering en route. How they handled these experiences was as important as obeying God's call to go in the first place.

Take Abram (whose name was later changed to Abraham), for example. Yahweh sent him on a great journey: "Go from your country and your kindred and your father's house to the land that I will show you" (Gen. 12:1). God was promising him great blessings—land, a great name, and numberless offspring. God also intended to bless the many nations of the world through him (Gen. 12:2–3, 7; 15:5). Though Abraham's calling and covenant with God was extraordinary, we can learn many things from his exemplary response of faith and faithfulness that can help us on our own spiritual journeys.

First, Abram had to believe in God's promises, get up, and move. Then, his pilgrimage didn't end with the completion of his physical trip from Haran to Canaan. Far from it. In fact, the narrative doesn't tell us much at all about his cross-country migration. Instead, some fourteen chapters of Genesis relay story after story of Abram's journey of faith and faithfulness *after* he reached the promised land.

He had to fight several great battles and rescue his nephew Lot from his captors. He was tested in various and sometimes extreme ways. He became fabulously rich, and had to navigate intense conflict within his family—some brought on by his own doing and some caused by others. Through all the ups and downs, Abram is held up as a man who trusted in God and did not give up his faith in the midst of trials and difficulties.

At the same time, God is held up as the ultimate reward for the one who journeys in faith. Once when Abram tithed the bounty from a military victory by giving 10 percent to Melchizedek, the high priest, he refused to take anything for himself because of a pledge he had made to God. Afterwards "the word of the LORD [Yahweh] came to Abram in a vision: 'Do not be afraid, Abram. I am your shield, your very great reward'" (Gen. 15:1 NIV). Later, Abram was rewarded for his faith and faithfulness with God's complete acceptance and approval. We read, "Abram believed the LORD [Yahweh], and [Yahweh] credited it to him as righteousness" (Gen. 15:6 NIV).

Many other role models for spiritual pilgrimage are found throughout Scripture as well. Moses's calling to deliver the Israelites from Egypt was unique, yet he still models for us a response of trust and obedience throughout the immensely challenging and difficult journey. David is well-known for such serious moral failings as adultery and murder during his rule as king of Israel. Nevertheless, he was also called a man after God's own heart. Why? Because he did "everything" the Lord wanted him to do. (See 1 Sam. 13:14; Acts 13:22 NIV.) In this case, "everything" cannot possibly mean perfection, and his wrongdoing certainly did not please God. Rather, David was a man after God's own heart because, in spite of his stumbling, he was a man who loved God and who kept getting up and returning to his calling to lead Israel faithfully for forty years. He faced numerous threats, setbacks, challenges, and betrayals, but he kept looking to the Lord for forgiveness, guidance, and help in order to fulfill God's purposes for his life.

In the New Testament, Jesus stands out as one who lived his whole life serving God's purposes. His experiences show us to expect many difficulties on our own journey, and his example teaches us how to handle them. When Paul teaches the Philippians how they are to live out their own calling within community, he tells them to have the same unselfish attitude within them that Christ had (Phil. 2:5). Then he illustrates this attitude by drawing on a passage widely regarded as taken from an early Christian hymn (Phil. 2:5–11).

To Paul, Jesus modeled sacrificial, obedient service to God and humanity, which, in his case, culminated in his crucifixion. Yet the true conclusion to his earthly sojourn was his exaltation following his resurrection: "Therefore God exalted him to the highest place and gave him the name that is above every name, that at the name of Jesus every knee should bow, in heaven and on earth and under the earth, and every tongue confess that Jesus Christ is Lord, to the glory of God the Father" (Phil. 2:9–11 NIV). Few of us will be asked to die for our faith, and none of us will ever receive the title of Lord, but Paul was teaching followers of Jesus to expect to journey through valleys of sacrificial service and suffering and to reach the mountain top of resurrection and reward from God. The spiritual journey includes many hardships, but God is faithful to those who walk by faith and seek to serve God's purposes with their life.

Similarly, the author to the Hebrews holds up Jesus as a model of faith and faithfulness throughout one's life. He explicitly urges believers to emulate Jesus: "Let us run with perseverance the race that is set before us, looking to Jesus the pioneer and perfecter of our faith, who for the sake of the joy that was set before him endured the cross, disregarding its shame, and has taken his seat at the right hand of the throne of God. Consider him who endured such hostility against himself from sinners, so that you may not grow weary or lose heart" (Heb. 12:1b–3).

Finally, the apostle Paul stands out as another powerful biblical figure whose journey was marked by great faith, passion, surprising turns, flexibility, and determination, as is true for all faithful pilgrims. For years he zealously lived a righteous life as a religious Jewish leader and persecutor of what he thought was a false sect, comprised of the followers of Jesus (Phil. 3:4–6). Then his dramatic experience with Christ on the road to Damascus radically reoriented his faith and mission. Paul now expressed devotion to God by preaching the gospel of Jesus Christ as an evangelist and church planter, even in the face of great opposition (Acts 9:1–22).

The depth of his reliance on God's leading and confidence in God's working in his life is seen throughout his missionary journeys. For example, in the middle of evangelization efforts in Asia Minor, he received a vision of a man from Macedonia pleading with him to cross the sea to come to him. Paul concluded this was a message from God, got on a boat, and eagerly set out for Greece at once (Acts 16:9–11). However, soon after arriving in the Macedonian city of Philippi, he and his fellow evangelist, Silas, were arrested, beaten, and thrown in jail. Yet they were not defeated by their misfortune. Rather, the story continues with their praying and singing hymns to God in the middle of the night, while chained to a wall.

When an earthquake loosened all of the bindings, they chose not to escape. They believed they were securely in God's hands and serving Christ by remaining in the prison, and their witness led to the salvation of the jailer and the baptism of his whole family. The next morning Paul and Silas were released and completely exonerated by the city officials (Acts 16:25–40).

Paul's attitude of faith helps us in our own journeys by giving us an example of what it looks like to be wholly committed to God and to serving Christ's purposes. In his second letter to the Corinthian church, he makes these priorities and perspective on life explicit, along with his conviction that the spiritually vital life is one in which God is working powerfully in and through believers. He writes:

> For we do not proclaim ourselves; we proclaim Jesus Christ as Lord and ourselves as your slaves for Jesus' sake. For it is the God who said, "Let light shine out of darkness," who has shone in our hearts to give the light of the knowledge of the glory of God in the face of Jesus Christ. But we have this treasure in clay jars, so that it may be made clear that this extraordinary power belongs to God and does not come from us. We are afflicted in every way, but not crushed; perplexed, but not driven to despair; persecuted, but not forsaken; struck down, but not destroyed; always carrying in the body the death of Jesus, so that the life of Jesus may also be made visible in our bodies. For while we live, we are always being given up to death for Jesus' sake, so that the life of Jesus may be made visible in our mortal flesh (2 Cor. 4:5–11).

Though Paul did not use pilgrimage language, he was clearly on a God-led journey of faith that called for faithfulness amid very difficult and sometimes painful circumstances. He chose to frame everything he experienced by how his situation related to God's will and furthering the gospel. As a result, Paul's life and ministry became Christocentric, meaning he focused himself on knowing, following, serving, and reflecting Jesus Christ in every way possible.

At the heart of Paul's ability to remain centered on Christ and to keep working for God's purposes in the midst of his great trials was his trust in God's grace and promise of resurrection. He valued the spiritual over the material, because he saw the former as eternal and the latter as temporary. He explained his perspective and faith to the Corinthians this way:

> We know that the one who raised the Lord Jesus will raise us also with Jesus, and will bring us with you into his presence. Yes, everything is for your sake, so that grace, as it extends to more and more people, may increase thanksgiving, to the glory of God. So we do not lose heart. Even though our outer nature is wasting away, our inner nature is being renewed day by day. For this slight momentary affliction is preparing us for an eternal weight of glory beyond all measure, because we look not at what can be seen but at what cannot be seen; for what can be seen is temporary, but what cannot be seen is eternal (2 Cor. 4:14–18).

Paul considered this life as an opportunity to serve God's purposes in the world and as preparation for eternity. He saw that our experiences of God's grace can produce great thankfulness and a closer relationship with God. Our afflictions and suffering can help us become more like Christ and prepare us for the indescribable and immense glory of the next life. Living for the sake of others spreads God's grace and helps more and more people enter into a grateful, close relationship with God. Defining his path in these terms, Paul fully embraced his journey.

For most of us spiritual pilgrims, we may not have as much clarity and conviction about our purpose as did Abraham, Moses, David, Jesus, Paul, and many other notable biblical figures. Yet, they can still help us on our journeys. They teach us to keep moving forward, seeking God and serving God's purposes. They model looking at difficulties and afflictions through the eyes of faith and staying open to whatever God might want to show us, teach us, or work in us through our experiences. They show us that we can expect many graces and gifts from God, alongside many unanswered questions and frustrations. They teach us to highly value the spiritual dimension of life, to trust in God's promise of resurrection from the dead, and to see this life as preparation for eternity.

Next Steps

While much is outside of your control on pilgrimage, there are many steps you can take to prepare for what lies ahead of you, for handling the challenges constructively as you encounter them, and for making the most of your opportunities. Here are some suggestions.

Embrace the Journey

What a difference it makes when I start off a new initiative with a positive attitude and spiritually prepared to make the most of the opportunity. When we arrived in St. Jean Pied-de-Port the day before our pilgrimage was scheduled to begin, I was pretty excited. But excitement alone is not enough to keep one focused and on track throughout the journey.

From a Christian perspective, spiritual pilgrimage takes you on a lifelong journey of seeking to know, love, and serve God; to follow and become more like Christ; and to experience the Holy Spirit working in you and through you. Along the way, you will face a whole range of experiences and emotions, some of which may be extremely difficult for you to handle. Often, though, you may not know what to think or how to go forward. You may feel stuck in the journey, disillusioned, bitter, or otherwise bound up by life's experiences so far.

If this condition at all describes you, perhaps the next step for you is to accept that the path of faith and faithfulness will be hard and perplexing at times and that the only way forward is to trust God and not lose sight of what the journey is all about. Spiritual pilgrimage is not about you, but about God and what God wants to do in you and through you. Embracing the journey means entering into it wholeheartedly, maintaining a perspective of faith, looking for God's presence and activity in your experiences, listening for the Spirit's leading, and persevering faithfully.

Prepare Adequately

Think about what you need to do to prepare adequately. Too many times in my life I have arrived at a meeting, a worship service, a ministry setting, or some other special event unprepared mentally, emotionally, physically, or spiritually. The results are predictable. I am not at my best, I try to fake enthusiasm or faith, I run out of energy, I fail to offer the leadership needed, or I simply cannot handle the conflict or other emotional demands of the situation.

Before starting a new journey, taking on a new mission, or practicing a new spiritual discipline, think about what it will take to make your efforts worthwhile and successful—however you define success. For each person, the preparation checklist will be somewhat different. The important thing is that you think through what it will take for you to be ready and able to take your next steps fruitfully.

For example, to walk five hundred miles, physical preparation seemed to be one of the most important things my family and I needed to do. Jill and I walked one to two hours, four or five days a week for several months prior to leaving for the Camino. We were building up our endurance and making sure our shoes were right. Physical fitness isn't just for pilgrimages, though. Sometimes the best thing you can do to enhance your spiritual life is to get in better physical shape, eat more healthfully, minimize mood altering food and drink, and get enough sleep.

Identify Goals

Think about what you want to get out of your experience. In our case, we held a few family meetings before we left to come up with goals for the trip and to identify the various contributions each member could make. Our goals ranged from experiencing the joy of simplicity to improving our Spanish skills to learning to let go of needing to feel in control. Some of us wanted to gain a stronger body, others were interested in exploring Roman art and architecture. Jill and I wanted to help our sons learn to step into their adult selves and to take more leadership in our family. A couple of us wanted to gain a greater vision of our identity and where we were going with our lives.

Each new spiritual practice has the potential of bringing something different into your life. By setting specific goals, you gain insight into what is important to you at a given time in your life or stage in your spiritual growth. While God may have very different intentions in mind, you can't start with God's unique perspective. You have to start with your own desires and goals, informed by Scripture and prayer, and move forward accordingly. Then spiritual wisdom calls for remaining open to let the Holy Spirit shape your heart and mind along the way to become in better sync with God's will.

Get the Right Gear

Packing well and having the right gear is essential, both literally and metaphorically. For five and a half weeks of walking, we had to get our packs down to about fifteen to seventeen pounds. We needed to get shoes that were light but sturdy enough to carry us five hundred miles. We needed to anticipate what kind of weather we would encounter and how we would care for our personal needs while living in such limited facilities.

In everyday life, the right spiritual gear includes items like a readable translation of the Bible and tools for quiet times with God, such as a journal, prayer book, hymns, study guides, devotionals, or whatever resources will support and enhance your experience. Think through what items would be helpful for you, get them, and put them in a place where they are readily available to you to use when it is time to practice your spiritual discipline.

Consider Your Contributions to Community

Think about what contributions you and others have to make to your pilgrim community. When our family talked about the contributions each of us had to make, our individual gifts and personalities emerged even further. I was designated Travel Agent, Reframer (of difficult situations), Route Planner, Family Spiritual Life Coach, Grammar Professor, Injector of Witty Remarks, and Biblical Consultant. Jill was Researcher, Medical Attendant, Naturalist, Roman Art Lecturer, Packing List Coordinator, Pray-er, Local Clairvoyant, Holder of Everyone's Interests. One son was Spanish Expert, Señor Charming, Map Expert, Family Mediator, Holder of Everyone's Interests. My other son was the Physical Coach—Stretch Meister, Reframer, Photographer, Holder of Everyone's Interests, and B.S. Detector.

When you walk alone, you have to rely on yourself, the Holy Spirit, and the kindness of strangers. Yet, since much of life is lived within community, drawing on the strengths of others and offering your own contributions to the group can make your pilgrimage much more vibrant. Unfortunately, you can waste much energy either thinking that you have nothing to contribute or being envious of others who seem to have much more to offer than you have. An alternative approach is to assume that God has made you uniquely— with unique contributions to make in any given context.

Standing tall by believing and declaring that you have something to contribute to others does not necessarily come from vanity or haughtiness. When done with humility and Spirit-inspired confidence, such stepping up is living by faith, and offering your strengths and gifts to others is faithfulness. Likewise, looking to others to contribute to you does not necessarily come from weakness or selfishness; it is humbly recognizing your limitations and gratefully accepting the gifts God has given you through others. We rely on others to strengthen us and enhance our ability to serve Christ; thus, drawing on others' strengths and contributions is another aspect of faithfulness, because doing so helps each of us fulfill our purpose better.

Create Helpful Rituals

One of the characteristics that separates human beings from the rest of creation is our ability to utilize meaningful symbols and rituals to strengthen and encourage ourselves. On pilgrimage, we created a family prayer that we said each morning in the dark before heading out for the day. Each member of our family contributed to its creation, and reciting it helped us keep God and our highest values in mind. It also bound us together with a common intention.

> We thank you, Christ.
> We ask for a good day, fun day, and safe day.
> May we know and express your wisdom and kindness.
> May your love flow to us and through us.
> Thy will be done. Amen.

Creating rituals and setting daily intentions (who you want to be, what you want to do, and how you want to do it) work similarly to setting goals. They provide ways to clarify and reinforce what is most important to us on pilgrimage and in every other aspect of our life as well.

Find a Good Place to Focus on Your Spiritual Life

When walking across Spain, the journey itself provided "a good place" for me to seek God and spiritual growth. In everyday life, though, we may need to work harder to create sacred space in which we can focus on God. I am referring to both physical location and the environment in that special place.

For example, whether on a real or virtual pilgrimage, silence is golden. Temporarily turn off electronic and other devices that intrude upon your ability to focus and be at peace, in order to leave the maximum room to listen to your own thoughts and to the Holy Spirit. Solitude is also helpful in freeing you from impulses to interact with others, to try to please them, or to otherwise divert your attention from God to them. Beautiful spots are inspirational for many of us and can help us lift the eyes of our hearts to God. Holy places—such as churches, chapels, sanctuaries, or any other place designated for worship—usually provide symbols to remind people of God and their heart's desire for a closer relationship with God.

Over the years, we have increasingly tried to make our home and yard a sacred space for ourselves and others. Sure, we have to live normal life there, too, but we have we tried to create an atmosphere of spiritual vitality to reinforce our faith and other spiritual practices. We have placed symbols of faith everywhere on our walls and furnishings, we have painted our rooms with warm colors that produce a feeling of welcome and peace, we invite ministers and ministries to use our home as a retreat center, and we have tried to add visual beauty in whatever ways we can.

Solemnize the New Journey in Some Special Way

Marking an important next step in your spiritual life can be as simple as telling a friend that you have a new spiritual goal or practice, or as complex as creating a dedication service with pastors and a formal program. Whenever I sense God prompting me to step out in a new way—perhaps to join a small group, to attend midweek services, to start journaling, to do a special Bible study, to take a day or two (or week) to go on a spiritual retreat, to make being kind or thoughtful a higher priority, or any other such intention or action—sharing what I am doing with others can be very encouraging and helpful. I don't make a show of what I feel inclined to do, and I don't make wild promises that I can't keep, but I often tell my wife or other close friends how I feel God is working in my life. Telling a select few how I am seeking to take another step in my spiritual journey makes the intention more real and helps me follow through better. Receiving their support strengthens my resolve and my ability to persevere.

The weekend before we caught our flight to Spain, we scheduled a dedication service. We invited about thirty people who could witness our intention, pray with us, and offer moral support as we prepared to leave on pilgrimage. My sons were also baptized as part of the service. We dressed up in our pilgrim gear, shared our family prayer, and asked for prayer for us while we were gone. The day was inspirational for all of us and set the tone for the walk. As the pilgrimage took on a life of its own, our remembering the service helped us remember why we were walking.

Be Mindful of Fellow Pilgrims

In addition to contributing to one another along the way, having in mind the particular personalities, needs, and interests of fellow group members from the very beginning is helpful. My natural tendency on a new adventure is to become completely self-absorbed in my excitement and anticipation. Inevitably, this kind of self-centeredness affects my relationships and the social dynamic. When I consciously pay attention to who is journeying with me and discipline myself to look out for the well-being of others, everything seems to go more smoothly. I avoid creating a host of ill feelings, including hurt and resentment, because I have been charging ahead oblivious to the group. Plus, I avoid the emptiness that often develops after indulging myself to the neglect or exclusion of others.

Expect the Unexpected

Whenever God sends you on a journey, you can usually count on many twists and turns, unexpected developments and detours before you reach your final destination. You will know that your path will surprise you at times, but you won't know what the surprises will be until you encounter them. Sometimes everything will seem right and better than you could ever imagine. Other times, you won't be able to imagine how things could get worse. (But be warned: they almost always can!) You may think you are headed in one direction, only to have the path veer in another. Sometimes an unexpected problem forces you to change course, and sometimes a different way suddenly or slowly emerges as the best way.

This reality calls for openness and flexibility. When you start the journey of seeking God or following Christ more fully, you simply cannot know all of what you need to experience to keep growing or what you will face as you try to live by faith and be faithful. You may need to make adjustments as you face your limitations, or you may sense a call to make changes in your attitudes or behavior. Openness and flexibility are responses of faith because they express a willingness to trust God as you are being led along an unknown path of personal development and spiritual transformation.

Expect Emotional Roller Coasters

No matter how thrilling your spiritual pilgrimage or how grand your calling may seem at the onset, if you are like many people, living life as a spiritual pilgrim is going to feel like an emotional roller coaster. Both highs and lows are the norm. When you set out on a new journey, experiencing a thrill mixed with nervous anticipation is not unusual. In only a matter of time, though, you will most likely also experience moments of confusion, discouragement, exhaustion, frustration, pain, anger, despair, or any number of other difficult or draining emotions. Then, as God works in your life, utilizing your gifts or efforts to contribute to the world, your emotions can suddenly swing upward again as you see God bring good out of loss or suffering. You may feel great joy, satisfaction, meaning, inexplicable peace, or other encouraging feelings that uplift you and may even take you back to the mountaintop. And up and down you may go throughout the journey.

Be Prepared to Persevere

Unexpected difficulties, the emotional roller coaster, and having to face your own weaknesses and false expectations all call for perseverance. Not uncommon is for spiritual pilgrims to discover that the journey is harder than they thought or to let the challenges overwhelm or distract them. The main mistakes our family could have made on the pilgrimage would have been to try to go too far in one day, to seek comfort by getting sidetracked, to turn on one another, to curse the journey (or God), or to give up altogether.

To continue the journey successfully, we had to learn how to pace ourselves and make the journey work for the long haul. Sometimes we needed to slow down; lick our wounds; take a rest; or take some time to think, write, and pray before tackling the next segment of the journey. We had to learn to be honest about what we were experiencing and to talk through conflicts, even if it felt like we were going backwards relationally. We had to remind ourselves not to get distracted by our pain or any of the other troubles or annoyances and that we were on pilgrimage for a reason. Even if we had to make adjustments or compromises along the way to survive or cope with the challenges, we never wanted to lose sight of our ultimate destination.

One more thing. Discovering the right direction to walk is not the same as reaching the final destination. Entering into spiritual disciplines and reordering one's life according to biblical teaching can be hard work at times, and extremely stretching—as the pursuit of any worthy goal usually is. Be prepared to persevere. "Never give up, never surrender," a slogan popularized by the sci-fi movie *Galaxy Quest*, was our mantra.

Forgive

Finally, be ready to forgive yourself and others, and start again. At times you will fail, you will have a bad attitude, you may even quit for a while. None of us is perfect, and the spiritual battles sometimes feel overwhelming. At times you will get confused and lose focus, doubt and start holding back, feel let down by God and lose heart, rebel and become willful, succumb to temptation and hurt yourself or others. This is normal. There are many ways to get tripped up on pilgrimage, get stuck, or get off track. Often, painful consequences follow.

The question is not will you stumble, but what will you do once you discover something is wrong. Here, facing the truth is essential. You need to ask, what is really going on? Confession is critical. Acknowledging when you have allowed something to interfere with your connection with God, your relationships with another person, or your ability to follow Christ is key to breaking the power of whatever has led you astray. Once you have confessed your failure, your next step is to reorient your mind and heart toward God by seeking and receiving forgiveness and asking for the courage and strength to get back on track again. When your confession is done from a position of faith rather than self-condemnation or defeatism, it will be both humbling and restorative. Getting up and starting out again on the right path, by the grace of God, is what separates true spiritual pilgrims from poseurs and tourists.

When pilgrims have done their spiritual work of facing the truth, confessing their sins, receiving forgiveness, and getting back on the right path, they can forget about yesterday and focus on the many new possibilities of today.

For Further Reflection

SUNDAY, JUNE 25, 2006. DAY 2. Joy and ecstasy—exhaustion and pain—frustration and feeling lost—reassurance and blessing—grumpiness and alienation—insight and new beginnings. Twenty-four hours into the pilgrimage, and it seems clear that the Camino is going to bring a roller coaster of different emotions and powerful encounters with God and others. Unexpected experiences of grace are already feeding my soul. However, my own weaknesses, limitations, and rough edges are starting to show up as well. How is all of this going to play out?

Use the reflection above along with the following questions to guide your journal writing. Discuss your thoughts, feelings, and intentions with some fellow pilgrims from your spiritual community.

- Where does my life as a spiritual pilgrim get hard? How I am tempted to get off track or lose focus?
- What would my life and relationship with God look like if I truly embraced the spiritual journey lying before me?
- What have I learned from past experience that might help me handle the ups and downs, the distractions, the failures, or the discouragement that I am experiencing now or expect to experience along the way?
- What do I need to do as soon as possible—attitudinally, in communication with fellow pilgrims, with my schedule, with my finances, in my relationship with God, or in some other way—to get back on track or stay the course better?

- What support do I need from others to walk by faith and stay faithful? Whom and when will I ask for the help I need?
- What other thoughts were prompted by this chapter on embracing the journey that I want to think more about, share with others, or act on?

CHAPTER 3

Facing Reality

~

TUESDAY, JUNE 27, 2006. DAY 4. *Puente La Reina. Beautiful vistas for the first twelve kilometers (seven miles) this morning— valleys, mountains, modern windmills, sculpted fields. I love being out in nature, enjoying sights that I so often miss.*

I'm also starting to see myself and others differently. I keep crossing the path of farmers, carpenters, old women washing their laundry outside, shepherds walking their animals through the village, and other individuals who live in the small towns we're passing through. I don't know what I expected, but I've been surprised by their warmth, helpfulness, and hospitality. Most of our interaction is limited to saying, "Hola!" But there are lots of smiles, little gestures of welcome and encouragement, and occasionally help with directions when we feel insecure or lost. These people seem sincere and genuinely happy. They have something to teach me.

I want to be free enough to live a simple, happy life as the norm. I want to live more frugally—not because I'm cheap or obsessed with money, but because I can be content with what I need. I would like to more consistently place a higher value on generously helping others than in indulging myself. Yet I'm seeing already that living simply doesn't automatically make me happy and that living happily is not a simple matter.

We've been walking for only four days, and I clearly see some aspects of myself that I need to face if I am going to experience more joy and contentment in my life. Our family needs to make some changes, too, if we are going to relate to each other better. Each of us loves each other a great deal, but in some ways, we're stuck. Something needs to shift.

I realize that being together all the time might be accentuating our differences, and the physical stress is certainly bringing out our worst on occasion. At the same time, we are also being forced

51

to face certain realities that we have been able to minimize or avoid at home. Our wonderful little family is truly wonderful, but we also have significant issues that need to be addressed. As far as I can tell, the sooner the better.

Reflecting on the Journey

My idealism and fantasies were being punctured by relational realities. Our family was having to deal with issues of poor communication, misunderstanding, fear of conflict, unresolved pain, clashing personalities, and other stressors that most marriages and families have to face. I didn't like dealing with any of it, but ignoring these realities simply was not an option.

In retrospect, I realize that I might have been able to minimize some of the conflicts better, but I was just plain too tired of pretending any longer. True to my midlife sensibilities, I had grown increasingly unwilling and unable to put up with so much dissatisfaction and dysfunction in myself, my marriage, and my family. It was time to face the truth and to do something about it.

Meanwhile, many other physical, mental, emotional, social, and spiritual realities were also confronting me. I had to face them for my own well-being and for the sanity of others. For example, if I didn't take time to think or seek out intellectual conversation, I would start to get uptight, bored, frustrated, or even agitated. If I didn't get enough time alone, I would get crabby. On the other hand, if I didn't spend enough time touching or simply talking to my wife, I would feel lonely. I discovered that being myself sometimes brought laughter, joy, and camaraderie to our family; at others times, my idiosyncrasies drove them nuts. Spiritually, if I neglected my relationship with God, I soon felt empty.

Pause for a moment to do some self-reflection. How well-grounded in reality do you think you are? That is, how good is your grasp of what is truly going on in the various dimensions of your life—your body, material possessions and physical world, relationships and social network, mental state, emotional health, and spiritual life? If you took a moment right now to identify some aspects of your life that you have been neglecting, denying, or conveniently choosing to ignore, what would they be? Say the first things that come to mind and make a note of them before reading on.

Spending the summer walking across Spain taught me many lessons about the importance of facing the truth about my strengths, weaknesses, resources, opportunities, and calling. My experiences taught me to pay better attention to how I take care of my body, to my physical environment, to my relationships with those around me, and to how I manage my energy, time, and needs. I was forced to come to grips with various fears, attitudes, desires, and habits that were affecting my relationship with God and other important aspects of my life.

We don't have to go on pilgrimage to wake up to truths we have ignored or have simply not had to face, however. Sometimes, what is real comes to us uninvited in normal everyday life. Once "the honeymoon is over," for example, every couple has to face the truth about their individual differences and the difficulties of creating a life together. Unfortunately, too often we refuse to face up to inner or relational conflicts, or to some other situation requiring honest evaluation and change, until we are forced to do so. Sometimes, in fact, we do not deal with reality until we experience a divorce, a setback at work, a personal failure, an addiction, a suicide, a betrayal, or some other unnerving or shocking circumstance. By then, the consequences of our delay may be far worse than they would have been had we faced reality sooner and dealt with issues at hand in a timely manner.

On pilgrimage, the stress of the long walks and the practical demands of daily living were the first catalysts to help me become more grounded in reality. On just a physical level, the twenty-five to thirty thousand steps we took each day, carrying twenty-pound packs over varied terrain, made me very conscious of every muscle of my body and even the ground under my feet. I became much more sensitive to what was real in my body and environment. I quickly learned to pay attention to my physical and emotional limitations, because our survival, let alone enjoyment of our experience, depended on it.

At first I tried to ignore the pain in my feet and the weariness of my legs. I told myself, "Gut it out," "Be a man," "No pain, no gain," and any other pithy aphorism I could think of to deny how bad I was feeling. Sometimes, I tried to shame myself into pressing on: "You're not going to let that family with two little girls walk farther than you, are you?" "You can't let your sons think you're a wimp!" In one way or another, I was trying to motivate myself to keep going.

Yet no matter how tough I told myself to be, at some point each day my body would reach its limits. As much as I tried, I simply couldn't ignore the terrain, the weather, the uninvited person who wanted to walk alongside us, the woman snoring on the bunk above me, or the sweltering heat. If I ignored for too long the pain in my feet or my needs for water, food, shade, rest, encouragement, conversation, friendship, or hope, there were going to be undesired ramifications.

Truly, facing reality mattered. For example, we could not afford to tolerate someone's critical attitude, unkind words, or unrealistic expectation of themselves or others. To do so would have made the trip harder than it needed to be, and much more painful. We did not try to control one another (too often!), but we were committed to being honest with each other, especially when someone's attitudes or behaviors were negatively affecting the whole group.

We also could not afford the luxury of denying the fact that the mountain trail, for example, was more difficult than one or more of us could handle. To miscalculate might mean blisters, injury, exhaustion, heat stroke, emotional meltdown, or collapse. A number of small crosses along the route periodically warned us that even death was a possibility. On the other hand, to budget our time, energy, and physical capabilities well might mean discovering extraordinary views, preserving energy for meaningful encounters with others, or being better able to enjoy any number of other special opportunities.

Paying attention to how others in the group were feeling was important, too. Some days we could barely move our legs as we

trudged along. Other days, at least one of us felt especially ener-
gized and wanted to walk an extra five or six miles. Knowing which
day was which and discerning how well our feelings matched our
physical capabilities mattered greatly to our experience of the day.
Then, to be a well-grounded husband and father, I had to be sure
that I wasn't making decisions for the group based on how I alone
felt. I also needed to see what was true for everyone else. Usually, all
I needed to do in most cases was to pause long enough to look at
the heavy eyes and at the drooping posture of my wife, and I knew
the wisest and most loving decision was to bring the day to an end.

This kind of attentive responsiveness to the needs, desires, and
capabilities of others does not come naturally to many of us, especially
when we want to do something that might be threatened if we were
to face the truth about others. However, to be only concerned about
one's own reality is likely to cause us to neglect or hurt someone we
love or care about. To be truly well-grounded, we need to get past
our own self-oriented way of being in the world and consider what
others are experiencing. We need to care about what life looks like to
our spouse, children, fellow parishioners, co-workers, and neighbors
and to people from other countries, races, or religions.

Squarely facing reality may also mean confronting our grand
ideas and romantic notions about who we are and about marriage,
family, humanity, religion and spirituality, and other important areas
of our life. Yet, facing truth we would prefer not to consider or
acknowledge need not limit us. On the contrary, the more grounded
in reality we are, the better we can pursue the vision and relationships we most value. Why? Because once we stop fooling ourselves
about where we are or what we have accomplished or attained, the
truth may motivate us to start doing something that may improve
our lives or actually help others better. Seeing things for how they
really are—both from our own perspective and that of others—
brings what is needed into sharper focus. That is, the more grounded
in reality we become—physically, mentally, emotionally, relationally,
and spiritually—the more clearly we will be able to see the gap
between what we are experiencing and what we long for. A greater
awareness of the gaps may become a natural catalyst to make needed
changes.

For example, on the Camino, I thought that a family of pilgrims ought to walk together as a family. However, as time went on, for various reasons, everyone seemed unhappy with this enforced policy. I was at a crossroads. I could ignore everyone's complaints and stubbornly stick to my philosophy or I could listen carefully and accept that something wasn't working. Fortunately, I chose the latter.

As often is the case, personal and relational needs proved to be more complex and varied than my idealism allowed for. Sometimes, my wife needed me to walk with her, whether we talked or not. Sometimes one of my sons wanted to talk to me about something private, so the two of us would head out together and carry on lengthy conversations for perhaps the entire day. As we each faced the truth about our occasional needs for solitude, we created opportunities for each one to walk individually for part of the day, depending on each one's interest. Soon, each of us discovered that we very much enjoyed walking for miles in silence, sometimes preferring to journey alone and sometimes simply alongside a family member without talking. By listening to one another and paying attention to what was real, and by being willing to flex, our pilgrimage experience and relationships with one another became much richer and more joyful for everyone.

Becoming well-grounded in reality requires a holistic, multiperspective effort involving physical, mental, emotional, relational, and spiritual dimensions to our life. It also includes truly seeing those around us and grasping our impact on them and theirs on us. Then as we let these various insights, perspectives, and experiences influence the decisions we make and how we will communicate with those we love, we will embark upon a transformation process that will lead to new realities.

Scripture for the Journey

In searching the Bible for what it means to be well-grounded in reality and in God, a word study on *ground* offers us many insights. Naturally, the Bible has many references to the earth, the soil beneath our feet, the place where trees and vegetation are planted, and the surface on which we stand or to which things fall. But beneath the disparate, expected references to ground, we find something far more significant.

First, biblical writers, and presumably those who heard or read their words, held a deep appreciation for human dependence on the earth, along with the Spirit, for life. Second, ground was used as a metaphor in various ways to talk about the quality of one's relationship to God. In both cases, we see that facing the truth about life, seeing what is happening in and around us better, is only the first step in becoming well-grounded in reality. When the Holy Spirit grounds us in spiritual reality, we begin to see every aspect of our life as rooted in God and dependent upon God's working in and through us. We also gain insight into spiritual dynamics at work within us and in our relationships with others.

Ground and Spirit—Sources of Life

In Genesis, we read, "The Lord God formed the man from the dust of the ground and breathed into his nostrils the breath of life, and the man became a living being" (2:7 NIV). The Hebrew word for ground, *'adamah*, is the basis for the name given to the first man: Adam (*'adam*). Thus, in the Hebrew mind, one could not think of the first human being without also considering the source of Adam's being—and by extension, of Eve and every girl and boy created thereafter.

Those of us who work in multistoried office buildings or who spend most of our time in cyberspace or in the world of ideas may miss the significance of what ancient Israel took for granted for millennia: the ground is the material basis for human existence, while the Spirit of God is the instrumental cause that brings physical, spiritual, and eternal life to humankind. That is, humans come from the ground and depend on what comes from the ground to live. The Holy Spirit makes the human spirit come alive within one's body, fills believers in Christ with God's life-giving presence, and recreates life after death. In addition, in social relationships, the ground and Spirit sustain and enliven community. (See Rom. 8:11–14; Titus 3:3–7; 1 Cor. 12.)

The importance of the ground and Spirit for physical, communal-relational, and spiritual life—three overlapping, interdependent dimensions to life—was emphasized in God's covenant with Abraham. The Lord promised to provide a particular land for a particular people (Israel), while at the same time envisioning that through Abraham's descendents, he would become a source of a spiritual blessing for the entire world. The Lord said to Abram: "Leave your country, your people and your father's household and go to the land I will show you. I will make you into a great nation and I will bless you; I will make your name great, and you will be a blessing. I will bless those who bless you, and whoever curses you I will curse; and all peoples on earth will be blessed through you" (Gen. 12:1–3 NIV).

In other words, the promised land would serve as a tangible sign of God's blessing on Abraham and Israel, while also functioning as the setting from which Abraham's descendent(s) would bless the entire world. Two thousand years later, Jesus Christ, a descendent of Abraham, a Jewish teacher and prophet from Nazareth (a village situated within the promised land) fulfilled many of the expectations of the Jewish messiah. (See Luke 4:16–21; Matt. 16:13–20.) After his resurrection, Christian apostles identified him as the one who fulfilled the prophecy in Abraham's covenant on a spiritual level also, by providing forgiveness of sins and eternal life for all those throughout the world who put their faith in him. (See Acts 3:24–26; 4:12.) Through Christ's Spirit (the Holy Spirit), the body of Christ is formed, comprised of small communities of believers (churches), who together make up the full body of Christ, the church. The apostle Paul equated the church with Israel and taught that its ministry includes strengthening believers and shining the light of Christ to the world. (See Eph. 2:11–22; 3:7–11.) God's blessing of the world, then, is rooted in Abraham, focused in Jesus Christ, and extends to the entire world through the church as believers faithfully reflect the light and love of Christ by means of the Holy Spirit within them.

When Christian theologians speak of salvation history, they are often describing one grand story linking ground and Spirit to physical, communal-relational, and eternal life. God created human life from the ground through the Spirit, established a people in a particular land, and set the stage for the birth, life, ministry, death, and resurrection of Jesus, the Savior of the world. God then blessed (redeemed) humanity by providing eternal life through faith in Jesus Christ and rebirth through the Holy Spirit. (See Rom. 4:16–24; Heb. 9:11–28.) Communities of believers are called to serve God's purposes by reflecting the light and love of Christ to others and thus continue God's story until the end of time.

Becoming well-grounded in reality includes seeing more clearly our dependence on ground and Spirit for physical, communal-relational and spiritual life and acting accordingly. We will have our eyes opened to the source of hope for humanity, which is both grounded in real life historical places and events and extends to the unseen and eternal world. We will embrace our purpose to live in relationship with God, face our limitations and failings, recognize our need for a Savior in Christ, seek the Holy Spirit's transforming presence in our lives, reach out more earnestly for the life and hope that only God can provide, and do so within the context of fellow spiritual pilgrims in community.

Ground as Metaphor

The modern phraseology of "being well-grounded" or the instruction to "keep both feet on the ground" or to "stay grounded" in reality is not found in the biblical text. However, among a variety of helpful metaphors to describe a spiritually vital life, such as streams of living water, flying as an eagle, or new birth, numerous ground metaphors and analogies teach important spiritual truths in the Bible. In general, when biblical writers refer to the actual promised land, they are emphasizing Israel's connection to God through the covenant. When references to ground and land are metaphorical, they are usually stressing someone's connection (or lack thereof) to God through faith, obedience, and the Spirit.

In numerous Scripture passages, writers talk about one's relationship to God and God's ways by contrasting level, secure ground to uneven ground; dry ground to flooded river- or seabeds; stable ground to shaking or slippery ground; and rich, fertile ground to hard or weed-infested ground. Our hearts, attitudes, and behavior can all be described as either a type of land or the effect land has on us.

When the psalmist talks of standing on level ground, he is alluding to a metaphorical meaning of the Hebrew word *mishor*, which can mean either "level place" or "uprightness." We read: "My feet stand on level ground [*mishor*]; in the great assembly I will praise the LORD" (Ps. 26:12 NIV); and, "Teach me to do your will, for you are my God; may your good Spirit lead me on level ground [*mishor*]" (Ps. 143:10 NIV). Having a right attitude toward God (praise) and living according to God's ways (uprightness) are analogous to standing or walking on level ground, led by the Spirit, in a way of life that allows us to be sure-footed and secure.

Dry land (*charava* or *yabbasha*) connoted safety and security for Israel, as opposed to the dangerous, flowing waters of the Red Sea or Jordan River. For example, when Moses raised his staff to part the Red Sea, the Israelites could pass through safely on dry land (*yabbasha*; Ex. 14:16, 22). Similarly, when Israel was poised to enter the promised land, the priests first needed to step into the Jordan River at flood stage and risk drowning. However, once they did, the waters receded, and they were able to stand on dry ground (*charava*) with the ark of the covenant (Josh. 3:15–17). The people could now cross safely, and the priests' standing on dry ground symbolized both the faithfulness and provision of God and the safety and security that comes from trusting God. In both cases, dry land not only indicated that it was safe to cross the river but also symbolized that it is always safe to trust in God and God's promises. Thus, as we read such passages, we are being invited to think about the ways God has provided dry land in our life and to consider how we are going to respond God's call.

In other narratives, God shook the ground to create instability and panic when, for example, the goal was to undermine the confidence of Israel's enemies (see 1 Sam. 14:15). The psalmist used the image of slippery ground to describe the unsure footing of the wicked, which would bring them to ruin (Ps. 73:18; compare to 73:2). When someone or something is defeated, humbled, or even destroyed, the person or thing is "cast to the ground" (for example, Ps. 89:44; 143:3; 147:6; Isa. 25:12). Simply put, to be on firm ground is normally a good thing; when God shakes it or our feet are knocked out from under us and we land on it, it is usually a bad thing.

In the New Testament, the particular promise of land for Abraham's descendents is replaced with the promise of a heavenly and eternal home in order to help believers keep in mind what is real about their spiritual identity.[1] Believers belong to another (spiritual) world, heaven, and serve heaven's (God's) purposes and ought not get sidetracked with pursuing political goals of their own, get discouraged in the face of suffering and loss, or lose their faith when they face persecution for their faith. Instead, they are to remember that they are part of a heavenly kingdom with an inheritance that can never perish, spoil, or fade in a loving and joyful relationship with Jesus that cannot be taken away from them (1 Pet. 1:1–9).

In the well-known parable of the sower, Jesus referred to the kingdom of God as a seed planted in ground. Here, the type of ground is very important. Hard ground won't take the seed. Rocky places have little soil, inhibiting the growth of plants or crops. Ground infested with thorns will choke out new vegetation. Only good soil will produce a bountiful harvest (Mark 4:3–8, 13–20).

Similarly, in a parable drawing differently on the image of the ground, Jesus contrasted a house built upon solid ground rather than sand (Matt. 7:24–27). Here the figure of speech has changed because what is being created is a house instead of vegetation. However, the general concept remains the same: the type of ground in one's life is extremely relevant for spiritual vitality and fruitfulness.

All these texts ask in one way or another, what is true about your relationship with God? How well do your relationships with others in community line up with God's values of compassion and justice? Biblical writers assumed that those who heard or read their words would realize the importance of the type and quality of land. Their concern had to do with the personal and communal meaning(s) their audience would draw from the metaphors. Their implied questions include, what kind of ground best describes you? Or, what kind of ground are you standing on? If you had to describe your spiritual life as a type or kind of ground or the kind of ground you are standing on, metaphorically, how would you do it? Are you firm, soft, rocky, hilly, flat, plain, beautiful, barren, fruitful, or some other type of ground? The ground may be level or inclined, dry or wet, stable or shaking, hard, thorny, or good. We may have had little or nothing to do with how the ground got that way. But our current condition is what is real and what each of us must face.

Next Steps

As a spiritual pilgrim, facing what is real is essential for spiritual vitality and growth in every aspect of your everyday life. The more well-grounded in reality you are in every dimension in your life, the more clearly you will see truth about human existence, including your need for others and God. You will better realize who you and others are, the present state of affairs, what can and cannot be done, what the challenges are in fulfilling your calling and purpose, and how God does and can belong in your life. Without such illumination, you will likely believe half-truths, deceptions, or delusions, hindering your relationships, growth, fruitfulness, and everything else important to you.

Becoming a better-grounded person, then, requires continually facing the truth about yourself and your life and usually requires help from the Holy Spirit and others to do so. If you feel clueless about what is real in any of the various dimensions of your life, ask God and trusted others for insight. If you are scared to face reality, then ask God for courage and ask friends for support. If you feel weak, then ask God for strength and get help to develop strategies to go forward with your life. If you feel overwhelmed or don't know where to start, simply start somewhere.

The following are additional suggestions or questions to help you take some practical steps toward becoming better grounded in reality and in God in every dimension of your life. Add your own ideas and practices to the list.

Pray for Eyes to See

In *The Spirit-Led Leader*, I introduced a prayer I created to help me become a better-grounded person. Whenever I pray this prayer, I am asking God to help me see reality more clearly and become better able to flow with the changes the Holy Spirit wants to bring about in my life. It goes like this:

> Lord, please help me to see what I need to see,
> to have the courage to face the truth, and
> strength to act on what you reveal.

Every day, spiritual pilgrims can also ask the Holy Spirit to help them answer some hard, practical questions: What do I need to make a higher priority in my life? What do I most need to do today? What must I set aside in order to better pursue my vision? What must I face up to in myself, in others, or in my environment in order to make this day a success? What do those traveling with me need? What does love look like in concrete behavior?

In contrast to dwelling in the realms of ideas, hopes, dreams, and imagination (my preferred venue), being grounded focuses your attention on what is real in the present moment and what is likely going to be real in the future, depending on the action or inaction you take now. Just as you might take your temperature if you think you might have a fever, stick your head out the window to see how cold it is, or try on a new pair of pants before buying them, so you need to find helpful methods to best ascertain what is going on "in the real world" in which you are trying to live and serve.

Don't Be Afraid of the Truth

You don't need to fear that becoming better grounded will undermine your motivation or ability to create or pursue a reality different from the status quo. Facing the truth about your circumstances may be sobering at times, but it need not stop you from dreaming or working toward a better future. Rather, you should be well-grounded so that you have a more solid launching pad from which you can run, leap, or simply move ahead when the time is right.

Sometimes the truth the Spirit reveals is a beautiful thing. For example, maybe what you most need to see is that God truly loves you and has given you unique qualities to enjoy and share with others. In my spiritual life-coaching work (a unique blend of spiritual direction, life coaching, and personal consulting), I hear many people struggle to truly see their many good qualities, such as their giftedness, abilities, uniqueness, vision, passion, or the depth of their love.[2] When the Spirit is the source of revelation, you may experience unusual power to finally embrace your goodness, beauty, and many strengths and new confidence to pursue your vision and calling in life.

At other times the truth we need to see is hard to face but still important in order to keep growing. For example, maybe you need to face a difficult or painful issue that you have been avoiding. It may have to do with your marriage, kids, job, friendships, health, or financial situation. The truth you most need to face may be about how you are spending your time and energy or how you are dealing (or not dealing) with a conflict. Perhaps you have not come to grips with some aspect of your relationship with God, such as your level of trust, surrender, openness, or obedience. Often, we turn our eyes away out of fear of what we might see or unwillingness to know the truth, lest we feel obliged to act on it.

The most helpful question you can ask yourself when you feel afraid of facing the truth may be, how is life working for me? If you have no longing for God, if your marriage is as good as it possibly could be, if your children love you and your relationship with them is healthy and helpful to them, if your work is flourishing and you are maximizing the use of your gifts, if you are consistently resolving all of your conflicts peacefully and constructively—in other words, if you are living a loving, fruitful, purposeful, harmonious life, with nothing holding you back or interfering with your ability to pursue your dreams and fulfill your purpose in life, then your life is working well as is. If not, you may very well need to see something that you have been avoiding, something you need to change that will help you experience the life God intends for you. The truth is not your enemy but your friend—the means to getting "unstuck" and flowing better with the Holy Spirit's leading.

Slow Down and Pay Better Attention

From a practical perspective, better grounding yourself in reality often requires slowing down, paying more attention to details, and seeing clearly what is going on. If you tend to be impulsive or let your feelings drive you too quickly, you may need to learn to shut your mouth, listen longer, and ask more thoughtful questions. If you tend to be in your head, you may need to learn how to feel your feelings and trust their contribution. You may also need to learn to articulate what is going on inside your heart and mind—perhaps more patiently and kindly, for the sake of building bridges to others. Of course, at times acting, and doing so quickly, is the best thing to do. But the person who regularly takes the time to be well-grounded mentally, emotionally, physically, and spiritually often will be in the best position to make rapid decisions and take quick action when needed.

Know the Condition of Your Physical Body

How have you kept in shape? How have you let yourself get out of shape? One of my wife's lessons from the pilgrimage was that she, as a forty-eight-year-old woman, was simply not as physically strong and capable as our teenaged sons. It was no fun for her when her fantasy bubble burst, but facing the truth about her physical capabilities was essential for her to know how to pace herself and to make wise choices each day.

When is the last time you had a physical exam? Is it time for another? What physical factors do you need to consider when making long-range plans for yourself—and others? I am not suggesting that you stop dreaming or stretching yourself beyond your current limits, even if others try to talk you out of something because they think you are being unrealistic. Rather, I am reminding you that as you seek to pursue your dreams and fulfill your purpose, remember that your body is usually needed to get you there. So face the truth about its condition.

Learn to Think More Deeply and Clearly

I sometimes find that I am going so fast that I don't really know what I am thinking or feeling. I am just "doing." Do you know the state of your mind? How well can you articulate your philosophy of life? What do you believe about God, and why do you believe these things?

Being well-grounded mentally includes having a *thought-full* approach to life. You may perceive that your life is working just fine without thinking much about your philosophy of life or the foundation for your beliefs, but the reality is often otherwise. You may say you are comfortable with your way of thinking and being in the world, but do you complain, worry, fight, and churn about many things that are wrong? Does it occur to you that perhaps your way of thinking or looking at your life is askew or could be improved?

Furthermore, many of us hold a jumble of conflicting beliefs and philosophies that confuse others trying to relate to us as well as confusing ourselves. Frequently feeling confused may be a sign that it is time to do some deeper level thinking. If others regularly respond to you with frustration or puzzlement, it may be an indication that your life contains contradictions that are interfering with your relationships. Is it time to make a concerted effort to think more clearly and deeply?

How Well Do You Know, Experience, and Express Your Feelings?

How well do you know what you are feeling, let alone express what you are feeling to others? Some of us thoroughly enjoy a full range of emotions, while others feel choked off from many different emotional experiences. For example, if you ask some people what they are feeling, you may get a blank stare in return or their answers are limited to "happy" or "angry." Sometimes, they simply use nonfeeling adjectives, "good" or "bad," and you are left without any insight whatsoever into what is actually going on in their lives.

Whether you can articulate your emotions or not, you might be overly controlled by them. For some people, everything seems to be a big deal. You may be so influenced by others that you are continually keying off what other people are thinking, saying, or doing, rather than maintaining your own equilibrium and perspective on reality. Or you may be just fine as long as everything goes the way you planned, but you become discombobulated whenever something is out of place or doesn't fit your agenda. We all have emotional responses to life's circumstances, but when we seem to be at the mercy of our feelings, we and others around us often suffer and our ability to consistently be people of love diminishes.

Being well-grounded emotionally includes knowing what you feel, being able to articulate your feeling to others, and experiencing the full range of emotions without being controlled by them. Beneath these feelings and emotional responses to life's circumstances are conscious or subconscious beliefs and thoughts that you have about God, yourself, others, and life in general—very important personal perspectives that you need to know in order to keep growing as an individual and in relation to others.[3] Examining the many benefits and factors involved in exploring what is beneath your feelings is beyond the scope of this chapter. Suffice it to say that one important dimension of becoming better grounded in reality, and of communicating with others, is becoming more fluent in naming and expressing your feelings and learning to explore underlying beliefs and thoughts influencing them.

Establish Solid Connections with Others

How well-connected are you to others? To face reality in someone else's life or in our relationship with them, we often need to make a solid connection with them first and then pay close attention to what we see, hear, feel, or perceive. Your connection with others may grow out of truly hearing an important idea they are expressing, sympathizing with them, physically touching them or being touched by them, or enjoying shared experiences. Often, the connection is made using words while drawing heavily on nonverbal signals, too.

Much research has been done on the importance of nonverbal communication. According to at least one psychological study, only 7 percent of communication depends on the actual words spoken.[4] That means up to 93 percent of communication does not involve words. Thus, if you want to truly see what is real for someone else, you need to learn to read their nonverbal signals—tone of voice, facial expressions, and body language. Then, since none of us will ever be able to do this perfectly, good listeners (observers) will also check out their perceptions with the other person. You ask questions such as, "Your mouth got really tight. Are you upset?" "You turned away from me. Did I say something that alienated you?" "Your voice has gotten really loud. Are you frustrated or angry?" and "You stopped talking. Are you hurt?"

You also need to learn to listen well to the words that are spoken. As most of us know, just hearing sounds coming from someone else's mouth does not constitute listening. Good listening means hearing the actual words uttered and being able to reflect back to the person both what was said and what you think they meant by these words.

Whether you are a friend, co-worker, manager, or leader—let alone pastor, counselor, or some other kind of caregiver—your ability to connect well, communicate both verbally and nonverbally, and listen well to others is absolutely critical for establishing and maintaining meaningful relationships with others. What would your spouse or significant other, children, parents, and co-workers say about how well you listen to them and understand them? What do you think you might gain from paying closer attention to your spouse's face, to the way your children fold their arms, or to your co-worker's body stance when you are talking together? When is the last time you took initiative to make a quality connection with someone—not for the sake of how you might benefit but in order to simply see the truth about them more fully and clearly? You may or may not consider yourself a good listener, but what would others say about how well you listen and notice what is real for them? If you are not sure, ask them.[5]

Face the Truth about Your Spiritual Life

What is true about your relationship with God? What would you like to be true? How do you explain the gap between what is and what you would like the relationship to be? The more honest you are with yourself about the state of your spiritual life, the better prepared you will become to create or receive a new vision for your relationship with God. The following questions may help you assess where you are spiritually:

- What are the deep spiritual longings of my heart?
- What do I want in my relationship with God?

- What do I need?
- How do I think God is at work in my life?
- What would be different if I integrated my faith more fully into every aspect of my life?
- What happens in my mind, heart, and relationship to God when life gets hard or painful?
- How do I think God is calling me to faith or action?

Asking questions such as these will help you face reality in your spiritual life. You will become better grounded in reality as you accept the truth of what you see. To be well-grounded spiritually first requires honestly assessing your relationship with God (facing current reality) and then letting the Holy Spirit deepen your connection to God so that you may live a more spiritually vital life (creating new realities).

One suggestion is to pray with one of these questions for seven straight days, writing down any thoughts and feelings that emerge for that week. The next week, take up another question. Or you could pray one question a day and then keep going through the list, multiple times, until you feel as if you have a good handle on the answers that are true to you. Add your own questions.

Whatever method you choose, make a habit of continually praying all your questions—while you lie in your bed, sit at your desk, do home projects, drive in the car, walk a labyrinth or out in nature, or do something else you like. Over time, clear answers will likely emerge. This is how the Spirit works—often both giving you the pertinent questions for your spiritual pilgrimage and leading you to the answers you most need (though not necessarily want) to hear.

The goal at this stage is not so much to create an ideal vision for your relationship with God but to clearly identify what is currently real in your heart, mind, and behavior related to your spiritual needs and longings. By becoming more cognizant of what is truly going on inside of you, you become more eager and prepared for significant spiritual growth. If, on the other hand, you are fooling yourself about your interest in growth or love for God or if you are closing your eyes and ears to what God is trying to communicate to you, you are going to stay stuck. You won't know what to do that will help you grow at this particular point in your life or what kind of help you most need from others.

For Further Reflection

On the Camino, in so many ways, my pilgrimage experience and my ability to lovingly relate to others was significantly affected by my willingness—or unwillingness—to face truth about myself and my fellow pilgrims. The more I walked, and the more I paid attention, the more I realized a profound truth that continues to affect every aspect of my life: I have to do a better job facing reality in my life—or else.

As a resource in moving forward, reflect on the quotation above and use the following questions to guide your journal writing. Discuss your thoughts, feelings, and intentions with some fellow pilgrims from your spiritual community.

- Am I asking the Holy Spirit to help me see reality better? If so, what am I seeing?
- How is my body working for me? How well am I caring for my body?
- How well have I thought through my faith and the implications of my faith for my life? How am I seeking to develop my mind?
- Can I come up with at least five feelings I have had in the past twenty-four hours? (What are they?) How well can I experience emotions freely without being driven by them? How well can I talk about my feelings to others?
- To whom do I feel well-connected? What do I like about my relationships as they are? What is missing?
- What could I do to see others' faces better when they are speaking, to listen more carefully to their tone, to watch their body language more closely, to hear them out more fully, and simply to pay better attention to what is real for them? What

is going on (or not happening) in my interactions with others that is worth noticing?

- If I am really honest and observant, what do I see as I look at my spiritual beliefs, feelings, actions, and sense of connection to God? What do I like and feel good about? What is missing?
- What help do I need from others in my community of believers? Whom will I ask for what I need? When will I ask for help and support?
- What other thoughts or feelings are stirring within me from this chapter on facing reality better? What specifically do I intend to do differently or more consistently?

CHAPTER 4

Seeking Inner Change

～

THURSDAY, JUNE 29, 2006. DAY 6. TORRES DEL RIO. *Spiritually, I don't know what is happening. We're less than a week into our pilgrimage, and already I sense that most of the work takes place as I walk. I feel so free here! I feel like a sponge, soaking up every bit of the beauty and gift of the Camino. I feel full, yet more hungry and thirsty than ever. What is this journey I'm on? Why do I need to be here so badly?*

MONDAY, JULY 24, 2006. DAY 31. TRIACASTELA. *Just one week to go. Most days so far have been long trudges over rocky paths, up and down hills, or through arid wastelands—though we have seen some beautiful valleys and mountains along the way. The temperature the last few days has hit one hundred degrees. Our feet blister, ache, or swell. Getting up at 5:15 a.m. has gotten old. Today, we are taking a rest day. We're so exhausted.*

Still, the walking has been an incredible, grounding, and illuminating experience. Most of the time, I'm not aware of what is happening internally while I'm walking. Then, all of a sudden, emotion will surge out of me—anger, longing, sadness, frustration, disappointment, regret, relief, hope. More than a few gangly weeds along the Camino are no longer standing, because of a sudden thrashing from my walking stick! Sometimes, these outbursts seem to be the best way to express the feelings raging through me. . . . Then suddenly, clarity and conviction emerge. Often peace has followed.

Good things are happening. We're changing. I'm changing.

Trudging along for fifteen miles a day under the hot sun was having a powerful transformative effect on my life that I only partially understood at the time. Day after day of getting up before dawn, pushing my body through painful miles, well beyond the point where I usually wanted to stop, was changing me in ways I am still sorting out. At times I was so weary or sore that I could not think at all, while at other times I became very introspective. Sometimes I would walk for miles with no conscious thought or discernible sequence of ideas, then all of a sudden, a conclusion or conviction would burst through to the surface of my consciousness. Apparently, I had been thinking all along, but the mental process was subconscious.

Emotionally, pilgrimage was helping bring my inner turmoil as well as desire and joys out in the open. Sometimes, the beauty of the walk, the refreshing nature of time alone outdoors, or the freedom that comes from simplicity would lead to spontaneous song, joy, laughter, and lightness that felt like such great gifts. At other times, I felt near desperation, emptiness, sadness, and loneliness. I was surprised occasionally by the anger that erupted. Superficial, apparent causes—annoying fellow pilgrims, disappointments, hunger, along with other irritations and aggravations—usually explained the surge of emotion. At the same time, deeper level frustrations, hurt, fear, and unfulfilled desires would surface, helping me realize that I needed to deal with some unresolved issues in my life that had little to do with whatever was happening at the moment.

I was doing a lot of reacting to circumstances, rather than consciously developing new ideas or changing my behavior in any thoughtful manner. The walk and my encounters with others were sparking thoughts, feelings, choices, and conversations that often seemed stronger than anything I could will or plan. Many times I saw important issues rise to the surface without immediate resolution or growth. At first it seemed that I needed the toxic thoughts and feelings to consume me, sometimes even to overflow onto those around me, before I could do anything with them. Often, it seemed, I had to feel the pain and distress of what was wrong in my life or memory before I could experience healing, release, and renewal.

Reflecting on the Journey

I realize now that I was in the midst of an extraordinary purification and transformative process while on pilgrimage. The intense, extended, five-hundred-mile journey was exposing various kinds of toxicity in my mind, heart, and relationships. As time went on, I sensed that the Holy Spirit was sifting through it all and leading me to healthier places.

> As you reflect on your life, in what ways have mixed motives, impure thoughts, negative attitudes, or inappropriate behavior hurt you or someone else you love? As you have matured over the years, what have you learned about becoming more pure and experiencing inner change? Take a few minutes right now to list whatever issues and memories come to mind that relate to purity or impurity in your life. How has your spiritual life been affected by these factors?

Mystics sometimes describe the process of purification as "purgation." Being freed from attachments to self, sin, and an over-preoccupation with human living is seen as a prerequisite for deeper, spiritual illumination. This dynamic understanding of spiritual growth certainly has some merits.

When I reflect on why purification would be so important to my spiritual life, I quickly see how toxic so many fears, attitudes, or behaviors of mine have been and are at times. Over the centuries, the church has identified seven specific clusters of vices or "deadly sins," which are often listed as lust, gluttony, greed, sloth, wrath, envy, and pride. Roman Catholics in particular view these sins as so lethal to a person's spiritual life that they put the believer in danger of eternal condemnation.

No comparable list appears anywhere in Scripture in one place, but New Testament writers frequently identify numerous sinful attitudes and behaviors that are contrary to God's will and the Holy Spirit's leading.[1] Paul also indicates that the result of setting one's mind on the "flesh" (one's sinful impulses) is "death." He writes: "For those who live according to the flesh set their minds on the things of the flesh, but those who live according to the Spirit set their minds on the things of the Spirit. To set the mind on the flesh is death, but to set the mind on the Spirit is life and peace. For this reason the mind that is set on the flesh is hostile to God; it does not submit to God's law—indeed it cannot, and those who are in the flesh cannot please God" (Rom. 8:5–8).

In addition to what biblical writers call sin, I have also seen the detrimental effect of other psychic garbage that may accumulate within us. Many of us suffer at times from false guilt over concern to please others, undue influence of parents or authority figures, aversion to conflict, distorted biblical teaching, and other such psychological or spiritual contaminators.

Then there are the life-poisoning effects of fear. The four basic human fears identified by psychologist Robert McGee cover well most of the fears that tend to prevent us from experiencing the fullness of life as Christ envisioned: fears of failure, rejection, blame, and shame.[2] When fear controls us, our ability to love ourselves, let alone God or others, is greatly inhibited. Fear can imprison us in crippling anxiety or compulsive behavior.

Let's face it, between sin, distorted thinking, and fear, along with a multitude of other influences (often the effects on us of someone else's sin or limitations), we are all filled with inner forces that sap our energy, interfere with our relationship with God, and hinder our ability to fulfill our purpose in life. The fruit of these forces runs contrary to the good we are called to pursue and often leads us to hurt ourselves and others, sometimes significantly. The more we are purified from these influences, the better.

The purer our minds, hearts, and souls are, the more we can live the life God intends for us. We will feel lighter, more confident, and peaceful about ourselves. We can trust our judgment more, because we will be less worried that we are secretly trying to serve ourselves at the expense of someone else. We are more likely to be proud of our life, and we certainly don't have to worry about someone finding out what we have done. We will feel healthier and more motivated to contribute in the world out of love and joy. We will feel more eager to express our creative, God-given abilities and personalities. God will be glorified as others can better see the beautiful creation that each of us is, and Christ will be able to shine more purely and brightly through us.

Purity is not just for Puritans. Greater purity would be a great gift to any of us.

Purgation in Practice

Of course, when I set my intention on personal transformation via pilgrimage, I had no idea what I was getting into. I had been reading some mystics and, naively, I had romanticized purgation. Committing myself to Christ and promising to pick up my cross to follow sounded so great when I was on my knees in prayer *before* heading out. However, once I actually got on the Camino, my enthusiasm quickly started to wane. My kids got sick of hearing me talk about the imagined glories of purgation. I was actually scaring them—and, frankly, I had only the vaguest idea what I was talking about.

I assumed I needed my mind and heart to be cleansed, but I didn't know in what ways, how to do it, or even how to let it happen. I was in for many surprises. Enduring physical hardships and having to confront painful truth about myself as I went along was much harder than I imagined. Such rude awakenings are not uncommon whenever we move from the resolution stage to implementation in our spiritual life.

As we might expect, purgation strips us of those thoughts, attitudes, and behaviors that interfere with our relationship with God and ability to live out our purpose. However, what can surprise us is how ingrained and self-defeating our way of living is. We may know we are dissatisfied with our life or relationship with God, but we are so caught up in our usual way of thinking and acting that we are sometimes clueless about how we are undermining our own spiritual vitality and growth.

At other times, we may know very well what is wrong within us, but we feel as if we can't change or simply don't want to let go of something holding us back. When we become aware of what is going on, our next step is to take whatever action is within our power to take, even if it is simply to ask God to show us where to go from here. We can ask God to purify us, and we can seek to purify ourselves.

Letting Go

On the Camino, just before the city of Ponferrada, most pilgrims participate in a longstanding custom that helps them let go of whatever is holding them back. With still more than 125 miles to go to reach Santiago, they come upon a huge cross, the *Crucero*, anchored in a pile of rocks. Traditionally, pilgrims deposit a small stone at the foot of the cross, an action that symbolizes putting something behind them before continuing on with their pilgrimage. I suppose we could say the ritual gives pilgrims an opportunity to name the purging that needs to happen, and that has already begun, in their life. The act helps them set aside whatever has been weighing them down or holding them back. Laying the rock at the foot of the cross also becomes a prayer, both an act of surrender to the will of Christ and a request for forgiveness and help to move forward.

When I reached the Crucero, I knew I wanted to lay down my ideas about what it meant for me to be a minister and how I would define success. I had been feeling so much internal pressure to identify concrete evidence that my work is valued and esteemed by myself and others. I was no longer pastoring congregations or leading a nonprofit organization. Now that I was on sabbatical, without knowing what my next ministry was going to be, I couldn't point to facts or figures anymore (such as attendance numbers, lives changed, size of budget, scope of programs, and the like). I wanted to feel proud of my work and have others look at me and say, "Wow, what a successful person. He must be something special."

Such thinking, though, was killing my soul. Over the years, my bouts with self-absorption and losing my grounding in the love and grace of God have periodically taken me off track or undermined my spiritual vitality. My preoccupation with my image, my accomplishments, the praise of others, and quantifiable signs of success was once again contaminating my psyche and stealing my joy and heart for the journey. I needed to be purged of these things and set free to focus more clearly on my relationship with God and my own sense of calling. Pride in work well-done is fine, and feeling a sense of accomplishment is normal and healthy, but when our focus shifts from God and our calling to ourselves in such insecure or self-absorbed ways, something is out of whack.

Whatever "success" God has in mind for me is God's business. My role is to seek God and serve Christ as faithfully as I know how, in light of my own sense of calling. Specifically, in my case, I needed to come to see the world as my parish, even though I may not be preaching or teaching a single person in any pew on most Sunday mornings and no one is putting any money in the (nonexistent) offering plate. I needed to let go of calculating and striving so hard, so that I could be freer to set my mind and heart on growing spiritually and responding to opportunities for teaching and encouraging others.

Now, as a result of the purging and transforming experience I had on the pilgrimage, I am taking a different tack in my ministry. I am still planning and preparing, but trusting the Holy Spirit more to lead me to those I am to teach and serve. I am focusing more on cultivating my relationship with God, the gifts and abilities God has given me, and *who* I am as well as *what* I do. I am seeking to focus on what I can best offer to others, based on my knowledge, skills, experience, resources, and opportunities, and to trust God for the fruit.

Whatever the specific need for transformation, purgation can help us see that many of our impulses grow out of fear, anxiety, selfishness, ego, or wanting to control our circumstances or others. Reflecting on this reality also can help us see these forces for what they often are—sad, pathetic, self-defeating, spiritually inhibiting enemies of our soul that seriously limit our ability to love and to know love. The more we let go of these inclinations and behaviors, and the more we focus on growing in and expressing our love for God and others, the more we will experience the life we truly desire and that God desires for us. Our lives will be more joyful and full, and our work and witness will become more powerful and effective. The Spirit will take care of producing fruit from our efforts, in God's timing and in God's way.

Scripture for the Journey

Purification and inner change are challenging spiritual issues and two of the most important. They are important because lack of personal purity interferes significantly with our relationship with God, and inner change is key to becoming more like Christ and to reflecting the love and goodness of God. They are challenging because true inner change is often frustratingly elusive, and many of us feel defeated, not knowing how to be free from guilt or from the power of sinful desires.

When we look to Scripture for help, we find that Jesus and others taught extensively about purification and inner change. Biblical writers refer to spiritual phenomena that are, in the end, mysterious and beyond our ability to fully grasp, yet the heart of the New Testament message is fairly clear and agreed upon by most scholars: God purifies sinners by grace through faith, in order to bring salvation to believers, and that ongoing cleansing and renewal of our hearts, minds, and behavior is part of a Spirit-led sanctification process.[3]

Jesus's Teaching on Purity

Jesus is known for his teaching on love, and rightly so. What is less well-recognized is that he was also concerned with the many internal and societal forces that inhibit our ability to love God, ourselves, and others, chief of which is an impure heart. He taught that impurity of all kinds leads to behavior that is opposed to God's will for human life.

On a number of occasions, Jesus clashed with the religious leaders of his day, who seemed to value their own personal agendas and rituals more than having a right heart toward God and caring for others in loving ways. Once, for example, he vividly exposed the hypocrisy of the Pharisees, who were upset that Jesus's disciples weren't participating in cleansing (hand washing) rituals before eating. Jesus responded by attacking the Pharisees' focus on outward rituals rather than on a clean heart, objecting to any religious teaching that valued impotent, symbolic gestures over true inner transformation (Mark 7:1–23).

Jesus's audience did not need an explanation about why being defiled (made impure) alienated them from God. The holiness tradition and sacrificial system of Judaism would have made that clear to all the Jews living in Palestine. Rather, Jesus explains to his disciples that they should not be fooled into thinking that they can purify themselves simply by splashing some water on themselves. What they needed to address was the root cause of their impurity, the evil that comes from the heart and is expressed in all sorts of impure thoughts, which often lead to corresponding actions:

> Then he called the crowd again and said to them, "Listen to me, all of you, and understand: there is nothing outside a person that by going in can defile, but the things that come out are what defile. . . . It is from within, from the human heart, that evil intentions come: fornication, theft, murder, adultery, avarice, wickedness, deceit, licentiousness [extreme decadence], envy, slander, pride, folly. All these evil things come from within, and they defile a person" (Mark 7:14–15, 20–23).

As well as warning against the evils of impurity, Jesus extolled the virtue of a pure heart. While preaching the Sermon on the Mount, Jesus expressed the greatest benefit of purity in very simple terms when he said, "Blessed are the pure in heart, for they will see God" (Matt. 5:8). In context, he is stating an existential reality: there is a link between the absence of inner corruption and contamination and one's ability to perceive God's nature and presence. Jesus is upholding the tremendous value of inner purity while possibly anticipating the vital role of the Holy Spirit in purifying those who seek to know and experience God.

The Purified also Purify Themselves

Throughout the New Testament, no writer questions Jesus's assumption that purity is important to our spirituality and that impurity has negative effects on us, our relationship with God, and our relationships with others. All authors assume this basic spiritual reality and then focus on one or both of two different, yet interrelated, aspects of purity. One type of purification produces forgiveness and fellowship with God and other believers, and the other refers to specific choices we make and how we live in obedience to the teaching of Scripture and the Holy Spirit, as we become more and more like Christ. Consider three verses in 1 John:

"If we walk in the light as he himself is in the light, we have fellowship with one another, and the blood of Jesus his Son cleanses us from all sin" (1 John 1:7).

- Walking in the light, in keeping with a Hebrew understanding of "to walk" (*halak*), refers here to a way of living (behavior) that corresponds to the light (truth) revealed in Christ.
- The blood of Jesus cleansing us from all sin refers to the sacrificial atonement interpretation of Jesus's death, the understanding that believers receive forgiveness from God on the basis of Christ's actions.

"If we confess our sins, he who is faithful and just will forgive us our sins and cleanse us from all unrighteousness" (1 John 1:9).

- Confession is something we do and refers to our need to acknowledge that we are sinners in need of cleansing and forgiveness from God.
- "He who is faithful and just" refers to God, and "cleanse us from all unrighteousness" to what God does. In other words, God does the purifying of us, leading to a right relationship with God.

"And all who have this hope in him purify themselves, just as he is pure" (1 John 3:3).

- The "hope" to which John is referring is the complete transformation of the believer to become like Christ when Christ returns (3:1–2).

- John's reference to those who "purify themselves" indicates that those whom God has cleansed of their sins also have a role to play in their purification: they seek to rid themselves of impurity and to live a pure life. In this life, human transformation is only partial at best, yet the hope of becoming completely like Christ in the next life motivates believers to "purify themselves" now. Though John does not elaborate in detail what he is referring to, the verses that follow indicate that he means that those who have been cleansed from their sin will stop sinning, will do what is right, and, above all, will love others, in keeping with "the truth" (3:4–20).

Likewise, Paul gives Timothy, his disciple, a similar message. Believers, who are already experiencing the grace of God, need to make an effort to cleanse themselves of everything that might hinder their spiritual vitality and ability to serve God: "In a large house there are utensils not only of gold and silver but also of wood and clay, some for special use, some for ordinary. All who cleanse themselves of the things I have mentioned will become special utensils, dedicated and useful to the owner of the house, ready for every good work. Shun youthful passions and pursue righteousness, faith, love, and peace, along with those who call on the Lord from a pure heart" (2 Tim. 2:20–22).

In this passage we see more clearly the true goal of purification. Christians are not called to clean up their lives in order to have a neat but empty house. The real point of being cleansed by God and purifying ourselves is to be filled with the fruit of the Holy Spirit so that we can relate to God and others more purely and vibrantly and serve Christ more effectively.

The Paradox of Seeking Purification

Other New Testament passages give us further insight into the transformation process and into purification in particular. In one form or another, every biblical writer teaches that purification, or purgation, comes about in a paradoxical way. Being changed from the inside out requires letting go of what we know to be contrary to God's will while simultaneously letting go of trying to change ourselves. As one popular adage explains the seemingly contradictory truths, the Christian life requires that we "work as if it all depends on us, and pray as if it all depends on God." We have decisions to make about what we think, say, and do—with very real consequences for the choices we make. Yet, in the end, a true change of heart and mind that leads to a closer relationship with God and greater spiritual vitality is something that the Holy Spirit must do within us.

Not surprising, then, is to find in Scripture multiple examples of individuals praying for themselves or others for real inner change. What mystics describe as a process of purgation, leading to illumination and union with God, biblical writers call and pray for using different language. For example, in the apostle Paul's prayer for the Philippians, his description of spiritual growth is similar to what we might expect from a mystic. He wrote: "And this is my prayer: that your love may abound more and more in knowledge and depth of insight, so that you may be able to discern what is best and may be pure and blameless until the day of Christ, filled with the fruit of righteousness that comes through Jesus Christ—to the glory and praise of God" (Phil. 1:9–11 NIV).

Like seeking purgation, he prays for purity and righteousness. In place of illumination, he prays for depth of insight and greater discernment. In keeping with the idea of union with God, he seeks deepening love for God and others.

Paul prays for others because he knows what the spiritual pilgrim must never forget. As believers, we are called to an ongoing journey of transformation that requires God's ongoing activity and our responsiveness to God. Thus, the psalmist both prayed, "Create in me a pure heart, O God, and renew a steadfast spirit within me" (Ps. 51:10 NIV), and wrote, "How can [young people] keep [their] way pure? By living according to your word" (Ps. 119:9 NIV). Likewise, Paul taught, "Since we have these promises [we are God's children and temple, in whom God lives], dear friends, let us purify ourselves from everything that contaminates body and spirit, perfecting holiness out of reverence for God" (2 Cor. 7:1 NIV).

God loves us even with all of our imperfections and works only with flawed human beings—because that is the only kind there are.

Nevertheless, biblical writers consistently call on believers to make a concerted effort to seek freedom from whatever is hindering their spiritual life, while simultaneously trusting in God's forgiveness and relying on the Holy Spirit to produce the real work of transformation.

Pilgrims' Progress

In a letter ascribed to Peter by the early church, we find Christians described as pilgrims journeying through foreign lands. Peter writes: "Dearly beloved, I beseech you as strangers and pilgrims, abstain from fleshly lusts, which war against the soul" (1 Pet. 2:11 KJV). On pilgrimage, every traveler must also deal with desires that well up within every human being that are at odds with God's will for heavenly pilgrims. These "fleshly lusts" are actually waging war against the pilgrim's soul, Peter says. They are the enemies of our spiritual life. They come from within us, but they are working against us. Christian pilgrims progress as they grow in their ability to say no to sinful desires and yes to the Holy Spirit. (See Titus 2:11–14.)

In 2 Peter, although spiritual pilgrimage is not explicitly mentioned, the author paints a vivid picture of believers who think differently about themselves and their purpose in life because of their faith and God's presence in their life. Peter writes:

> [God's] divine power has given us everything we need for life and godliness through our knowledge of him who called us by his own glory and goodness. Through these he has given us his very great and precious promises, so that through them you may participate in the divine nature and escape the corruption in the world caused by evil desires. For this very reason, make every effort to add to your faith goodness; and to goodness, knowledge; and to knowledge, self-control; and to self-control, perseverance; and to perseverance, godliness; and to godliness, brotherly kindness; and to brotherly kindness, love. For if you possess these qualities in increasing measure, they will keep you from being ineffective and unproductive in your knowledge of our Lord Jesus Christ (2 Pet. 1:3–8 NIV).

Through Christ and the Holy Spirit, pilgrims participate in the divine nature as they journey through life. Not that we are gods, but God is so intimately connected to us that we are able to draw on God's power to avoid the corruption of the world (impurities) and to seek further inner change (godly qualities) and fruitfulness (in service)—in keeping with God's will for our lives.

Next Steps

The purpose of purgation goes well beyond ridding yourself of impurities of heart, mind, and behavior. Biblical writers consistently indicate that the ultimate goal is inner transformation so that you will be able to know, love, and serve God better; to follow Christ more fully; and to become more Spirit-filled and Spirit-led in every aspect of your life. Thus, as you seek spiritual growth, you are called to trust in Christ for forgiveness of your sins, put aside known sin, and be filled with God.

The actual process of being purified differs from person to person, includes significant turning points along with many incremental changes, and may, at times, look like two steps forward, one back. Occasionally, as in the children's game Chutes and Ladders, you may think you have made great progress only to stumble and "slide" back to what seems like a much earlier stage of development.

Often, God purifies us in ways that are unexpected or seemingly quite out of our control. God may choose to give us a Damascus road experience such as Paul had, where we are suddenly confronted with truth that we have not been able to see. In such encounters, we experience "aha" moments when all becomes clear and we feel compelled to think and act in new ways.

God also uses our failures, frustrated plans, natural consequences, and even tragedies to open our eyes to needed changes. Sometimes others help, such as when a friend confronts us or when a rival or a competitor exploits our blindness or stubborn refusal to change—and we are suddenly different as a result. Some of us require an intervention, when family and friends try to prick the bubble of deception that envelopes a loved one. In such situations, a group gathers to confront the individual, who might be suffering from alcoholism, under the influence of a cult, or entrapped by some other addiction or harmful behavior. Sometimes the light comes on and changes become possible only with extensive help from others.

At others times, if we are motivated to seek inner change to become a more pure person, we can take initiative and seek to purify ourselves, to use biblical language. First, let's look at what is not helpful, before talking about some specific attitudes and actions any of us can take that might be helpful in the purification process.

What Is Not Helpful

I am leery of most self-inflicted abuse or deprivations to try to purge oneself. Self-flagellation, or any modern equivalent, is dangerous and likely grows out of unhealthiness and not spiritual wisdom or insight. In the United States, a growing number of anorexic and bulimic individuals are literally killing themselves slowly by depriving themselves or purging themselves of food. In various places in the world throughout history, people have witnessed the great evils of so-called ethnic cleansing, whereby some groups seek to annihilate an entire ethnic group, driving them from their midst or actually killing them. These evils and other such harmful practices have nothing to do with the purgation taught by biblical writers or mystics.

Purgation also doesn't necessarily mean creating a bunch of rules or overly strict community guidelines intended to force members to be holy. This is Paul's point when he writes in Colossians that believers don't become superspiritual by depriving themselves of normal human pleasures. Some spiritual leaders can devise rules or harsh practices that sound like advanced teaching but are actually useless to promoting real inner change. Paul wrote:

> Since you died with Christ to the basic principles of this world, why, as though you still belonged to it, do you submit to its rules: "Do not handle! Do not taste! Do not touch!"? These are all destined to perish with use, because they are based on human commands and teachings. Such regulations indeed have an appearance of wisdom, with their self-imposed worship, their false humility and their harsh treatment of the body, but they

lack any value in restraining sensual indulgence (Col. 2:20–23
NIV).

Purging ourselves also doesn't mean eliminating everything that
is fun in our lives, as if spiritual maturity means walking around with
scrunched-up foreheads and frowns. One can be a serious Christian
and hysterically funny at the same time. One can serve sacrificially
and still admire beauty and appreciate the countless number of little signs of God's creativity and handiwork in the universe. We can
still laugh, play, and love passionately. In fact, the more we are purified from those sin-based impulses that offer deceptive alternatives
to the abundant life Christ envisioned, the freer we are to truly live
creative, joy-filled, and fulfilling lives.

Purgation, then, is not about squeezing all the life out of your
life, as some may think, or trying to change your personality, a transformation beyond your ability to effect. Rather, it is about getting
rid of those thoughts, attitudes, and behaviors—"everything that
hinders and the sin that so easily entangles" (Heb. 12:1 NIV)—that
interfere with your ability to love God, others, and yourself. Purgation makes you lighter and freer so that you can live more fully out
of your authentic, best self by the Holy Spirit's influence and leading. The more you get rid of the garbage and extra weight, the easier it will become to put your full self into the pursuit of God and
God's purposes for your life.

What Is Helpful

If you are motivated to seek inner change, many vehicles are available
to you. No one magic formula exists, but there are some general
principles and proven helpful attitudes and practices you can adopt.

Look honestly at your life. Some people, out of fear of or aversion
to anything that might lead to feeling guilty, will reject the kind of
honest self-appraisal I am recommending here. Some, due to debil-
itating emotional or even spiritual abuse, run far from any talk of sin
or self-examination. Some might recoil because they still have to
recover from being shamed so much as a child that any reminder of

past guilt and shame is hurtful. Others might feel depressed as they face the moral weaknesses of the human race.

However, I am not advocating the kind of harmful practices too many people have suffered from. I have no interest in encouraging you to become so introspective that you become self-absorbed and consumed by your failures and weaknesses. Wallowing in guilt and shame has no benefit, and I certainly have no interest in somehow controlling you or holding you down. Far from it!

Looking honestly at yourself vis-à-vis the biblical vision for human life actually can help you. Such introspection can move us out of denial to face the truth about ourselves as individuals, as a church, or as a society. It is a first step to a better place.

Ask God to break your heart over sin. Some of the most vivid and dramatic experiences of my life involve suddenly seeing the sin in my life for what it is, breaking down, and weeping. I have experienced this degree of remorse only a few times in my life, but when I have, I have felt great cleansing and renewal. I am not "cured" for all time in such moments of purification, but I feel a new freedom, gratitude, joy, and inner strength. Purer choices and behavior often follow.

Those who are used to self-analysis or who are well-versed in the teaching of Scripture might be able to articulate easily what makes sin wrong. However, what is truly needed for most of us is not analysis but contrition. Sometimes, our hearts break naturally when we finally see some awful truth about ourselves. Other times, we need the Holy Spirit to get through to us.

Live by God's love and grace. Facing the truth about impurity in your life is not the end of the story for Christians but a helpful catalyst to appreciating the magnitude of God's love and grace for you, his beloved child. I remember being taught as a teenager that when the devil points out our sin, he does it to crush us. When the Holy Spirit reveals our impurities, God will point us to the foot of the cross. There, as we experience forgiveness and freedom from thinking, attitudes, and behavior that have been mucking up our life, the joy we can feel is pure, powerful, and restorative.

Become more discerning. Learn to distinguish well between the healthy instincts that spring up within us naturally or come from the Holy Spirit, on the one hand, and the unhealthy, destructive impulses also common to human experience, on the other. A Bible, a good friend or two, perhaps an adversary who speaks truth to you, enough moments alone in silence, and prayer should be enough to greatly increase your discernment skills.

Stay open to whatever God may show you. This is far from easy, because most of us resist change, and we are often afraid or reluctant to give up something we have come to depend on. We know that if we are truly open to whatever God may have in mind for us, we may very well have to change something we don't want to change. This is where you need to pray for God to give you courage to face what you don't know, and for grace and strength to let go of sin, distorted thinking, unhelpful attitudes, hurt, or whatever else God might reveal to you that needs to go.

One of my favorite spiritual practices, *lectio divina*, or sacred reading of Scripture, has been a significant catalyst for inner purification and change in my life. In an hour-long format, this exercise includes three readings of a passage, ample time for meditation between each reading, followed by twenty minutes of silence. This practice often leads to new insights as well as new power and conviction to act differently.

During one particular experience with lectio, the light of Christ and the purgative power of God's Spirit were intense. During the second reading of Mark 14:17–25, each of us in our little group was using our imagination to put ourselves at the Last Supper, where Jesus and his twelve disciples had gathered for one last meal before his impending arrest and crucifixion. I imagined I was one of the disciples who heard Jesus say, "One of you will betray me." In my mind, I responded with the others, "Surely, not I, Lord?"

Yet, my heart was fear stricken, wondering. Was Judas lying, or was he so out of touch with his heart that he didn't know that he would betray Jesus? I asked myself the same question, and suddenly I realized what I have not wanted to admit. I, too, could betray

Jesus. I did not have the power within me to assure myself or Jesus that I would not betray him by sinning. I pleaded for help.

I suddenly pictured a huge door separating me, in my inner darkness, from his light outside. The door to my mind began to open a crack. A brilliant light began pouring into the dark places. I started to cry. I could not stand the intensity of the truth. Tears were running down my face, and I tried to close the door. I cried out in my mind, "I can't stand it. It's too much!" Yet, I knew I needed to see the truth. The truth was my only hope of softening my hardened heart.

In that one powerful experience, I don't think I saw everything I need to see. Yet, I saw enough to know that I needed Jesus to purify my heart and shine his light into all of my dark places. Jesus was my hope of changing. I felt wounded and shaken.

I wouldn't want to repeat such a powerful experience very often. Yet through it, the work of transformation took another step forward. Though what Christ revealed pierced me, I realized how seeing the truth more vividly was helping me. That day I became committed at a new level to seeking God and opening myself up to Christ's purifying fire and healing touch. (See Eph. 5:13–14.)

Get practical about taking steps to change—and get help. Practically speaking, most of us need help in getting to a place where we are truly ready to make a change, let alone actually following through on our resolve. Most of us know what it is like to want to change but to fail trying, so we recognize that usually something more than good intentions and enthusiasm is needed. Here is where a concrete plan, including a way to hold yourself or to be held accountable, is very helpful.

As you become aware of impurity in your life, name it, renounce it, and take concrete steps to think and act differently. As one therapist pointed out in a newspaper article I read this past year, New Year's resolutions actually work more often than one might think, if certain conditions are right.[4] In my coaching work, I see clients make significant changes all the time, providing they are ready to change, take manageable steps, get adequate support from others, and allocate enough time and energy to devote to changing their life patterns. Why do so many people lose weight with Weight Watchers, for example? The conditions are right.

Classical spiritual disciplines can help create the right conditions for inner change. Fasting, silence, solitude, Bible reading, and prayer, along with other practices such as journal writing, *lectio divina*, small groups, spiritual direction, and honest accountability relationships are specific activities or associations that can help the purgative process. Regular participation in worship and Holy Communion can strengthen and revitalize you. Pilgrimage or any extended, physically challenging experience can particularly help you not only face reality better but also begin to produce changes within yourself.

Be confident about your own capabilities and realistic about where you need help at the same time. Of all the resources I draw on to help me grow, I find that just sitting with God, in stillness, is often the most powerful spiritual practice available to me. I will meditate on a Scripture passage, look at a statue of Jesus, stare out at the lake, or just sit in a comfortable chair and let my thoughts and prayers wander.[5]

With God's help, you are not powerless in the face of temptation. As Paul explained to the Corinthians, both warning them against arrogance and teaching them how to handle temptation, "No testing has overtaken you that is not common to everyone. God is faithful, and he will not let you be tested beyond your strength, but with the testing he will also provide the way out so that you may be able to endure it" (1 Cor. 10:13). Your job is to expect to be tempted, yet also to look for the way out God provides for you at the time—and to take it.

Be realistic about what you are up against. Since my intense encounter with the purifying light of Christ, I have continued to experience "fleshly lusts" waging war against my soul, to use Peter's language (1 Pet. 2:11 KJV). Sometimes, I slavishly give into their power or even fool myself and embrace the desires and impulses as if they are what I really want. However, I can also hear the inner voice of the Holy Spirit much more quickly and clearly, reminding me what is truly loving, good, and right for one who loves God and seeks to follow Christ. I am more astute about how easily I deceive myself or justify my self-indulgence. Now, I am much less likely to be fooled and much more likely to recover quickly from a temporary setback in the "battle."

Most if not all of us will struggle with sinful desires all of our lives, with more or less success, depending on many factors. All of us will continue to fail from time to time, no matter how pure and strong we may become. But the good news is that the Holy Spirit is stronger than any power or evil impulse (see 1 John 4:4), and purgation and inner change do happen over time for those who seek spiritual transformation with God's help.

Create helpful habits to stay pure. Here are some daily practices and strategies I employ in my own efforts to remain pure and to live in sync with the Holy Spirit.

- Read Scripture to divert your mind from yourself, and especially your impure thinking, to focus on God and on the truth God wants to reveal to you.
- Put yourself in places (nature, prayer, worship services) where praise and awe of God will well up within you naturally, and often the power of sinful desires will diminish. If you experience critical or impure thoughts filling your mind in the context of worship, ask the Holy Spirit to hold back the negative influences and to fill you with the love and light of Christ.
- Focus on Christ, and remind yourself what kinds of thinking and behavior would best serve Christ in the specific relationships or situations you are dealing with.
- Ask God to fill you in ways that diminish the temptation to get your needs met in unhealthy ways. Many of us know what is like to pray for God to change us, and then not experience any noticeable transformation. I recommend turning the prayer around. Instead of focusing on your weaknesses or failures, pray for an ability to focus on your strengths and for a greater ability to use them to do something constructive. Praying this way has often given me more positive energy to

move forward, distracting me from the temptation and directing me to something that truly can bring joy and satisfaction.

- Focus on serving others. Seek to act in ways you believe are truly in their best interests while relinquishing secret desires to serve others for your benefit.
- Learn to walk on by a temptation situation or to build barriers around yourself to make it harder to be seduced or drawn into sinful thinking or actions. At this point in your life, you probably know well what is life-giving and aligned with God's will and what isn't. Holding an internal debate about whether or not to indulge in sin is a waste of time and probably dangerous. Just keeping walking.
- Remind yourself that sinful impulses are not simply wrong but are actually waging war against us. They are our enemies. When contemplating indulging in sin (if it is truly sin), we are not debating whether or not we will "treat" ourselves. We are being stupid. If you are not sure whether something you want or an impulse you have is a good thing for you, then ask the Holy Spirit for wisdom and consult a wise counselor, but never forget what sin truly is: the enemy of your soul and of all that you hold dear.
- Seek refreshment from God. Experiences with the love and grace of God have produced the most powerful and satisfying inner change in my life. At times, just sensing God's love for me or feeling a strong desire to draw closer to God has motivated me to clean up my thinking or behavior. Also, when I am actively using my spiritual gifts, such as when I teach others, I feel a great deal of joy. I usually feel well-connected to God at such times, and the pull of sinful desires lessens. The more satisfied I feel in my relationship with God, the less interest I have in false substitutes.

The key to engaging wholeheartedly in the transformation process, though, is not to load up your life with spiritual activities. You have to choose wisely, based on your own time, energy, and maturity. What is most important is your openness to face the truth about yourself, take action where you can, develop your own habits and strategies to deal with your impurities and temptations, and learn how to flow better with the Holy Spirit's transforming activity in your life. When addiction is involved or you are dealing with deeply engrained, unhealthy ways of thinking that undermine your ability to function well in an area of your life, professional help and spiritual counseling also are often needed.[6]

A person will never be completely pure or free from the contaminating influences of sin, distorted thinking, and painful wounds in this life. However, by drawing on whatever appropriate means are available to you, you can daily experience cleansing from God and various degrees of transformation. In some ways, the mystics have it right when they emphasize purgation as key to spiritual growth: Purification with inner change is the pathway to greater spiritual insight and the deepest levels of communion with God.

For Further Reflection

SUNDAY, JUNE 25, 2006. DAY 2. Today, I was praying for clarity about my future when I heard a response in my head that seemed right: "This pilgrimage is about preparing you to hear your call—not to tell you what your call is." Yes, of course! Purgation precedes illumination. I don't like suffering any more than anyone else (I realize that some painful changes may await me), yet I am willing to do whatever it might take to move forward with my life. And if purgation could mean being freed a little more from the things that are holding me back, I am all for it. I am not seeking some magical, extraordinary spiritual experience as much as I just want God to use this special opportunity to set me a little more free and give me more insight into my purpose.

Though many of us like easy answers when they are available, we often have to undergo a process, sometimes lengthy, sometimes painful, of *first* being changed internally in order to be able to understand and, more important, to accept God's next call.

Reflect on the journal entry and comments above, and use the following questions to guide your own journal writing. Discuss your answers with fellow pilgrims in your spiritual community who are seeking inner change.

- How do I sense that God may be changing me in ways that fit my calling and purpose in life?
- What impure thought, attitude, or behavior is the Spirit calling me to confess and turn away from so that I may be cleansed and forgiven?
- What needs to change in my life *now*?
- What spiritual practice or new daily habits might help set me free to know, love, and serve God more fully?
- What help do I need from others to help me live a purer life? In order to get this help, whom will I ask for what? When will I ask?
- What other thoughts or responses were prompted by this chapter on seeking inner change? What specifically do I intend to do differently or more consistently?

In Pursuit of God

~

MONDAY, JULY 10, 2006. DAY 17. FROMISTA. *I finally got
extended time to walk alone today—two hours! I loved it. It was
great to just let my thoughts flow wherever they wanted to go. At
one point, I got into an internal dialogue about my relationship
with God. I was surprised by where I ended up.*

*The conversation began when I suddenly blurted out that I
was fairly satisfied with my spiritual life. I told myself, based on
what I know about God and spirituality, I would rate my spiritual life a nine out of ten. Sure, there is probably a tremendous
amount of knowledge about God available throughout the universe, but I suspect that most of it is well outside of my grasp. I like
where I am spiritually, and trying to increase my satisfaction level
probably wouldn't be worth the effort required.*

*In fact, perhaps my energy would be better applied elsewhere.
After all, isn't active engagement in the world more important
than personal spirituality at a certain point? I've already made
a huge commitment to my relationship with God. I'm here on pilgrimage, aren't I? When it comes to everyday life, don't the huge
needs everywhere call for Christians to roll up their sleeves and
devote themselves to action? After all, as the hands and feet of
Christ, isn't it up to us to attend to concrete, this-world concerns?*

*Made sense to me. Christians are needed everywhere to meet
human needs and to help develop solutions to local and world
issues. The more I thought about the scope of human suffering, the
more my answer seemed self-evident: stop worrying about becoming more spiritual and devote more time and energy to helping
out!*

*Yet, almost as soon as I reached this conclusion, something
shifted within me.*

Paul's words to the Philippians came to mind. He said that nothing mattered more to him than knowing Jesus Christ and the power of his suffering and resurrection (Phil. 3:7–14). Paul was actively involved in the "real world" as a church planter, evangelist, fundraiser for the poor, author, public speaker, and teacher. Yet, he insisted that his first priority was to be well-grounded in a solid relationship with God in Christ and then passionately pursue a deeper relationship with Christ on an ongoing basis.

His words struck home.

I suddenly realized that perhaps I was not engaged in simple introspection and reflection. Perhaps God was part of the conversation, too, and I was being led down this line of thinking for a purpose. I needed to think through what made sense to me logically, and then be redirected to a different conclusion.

Would God truly want me to risk "wasting" my life, my time, my energy seeking a deeper spiritual life, pursuing what is beyond me and may very well be unknowable? The answer that came to me was now clear: "Yes."

FOR THE FIRST COUPLE OF weeks on pilgrimage, a lot of my thoughts and conversations with others were centered on myself, my future, my family, my marriage, religion, and everything we were experiencing. On many days, though, just getting to our day's destination consumed most of my energy and concentration. Sometimes, especially on long, hot days, my mind seemed to be a blank slate on which nothing was being written or had ever been written! The more my feet or legs were already aching before we started out, the longer it took to reach our destination, and the hotter it got, the more I cared about just getting there. I would long to see our final stop rise up on the horizon or appear around a bend. When we finally saw the sign we had been waiting for—perhaps only two or three more kilometers (one to two miles) to the *refugio*—we would feel new inspiration. We knew we were going to make it. Whew!

Yet, as the days passed, I began to sense that something was missing. Surely the pilgrimage had to be about more than just getting there each day—beating the worst of the sun, getting a bed in a hostel, washing our clothes, taking a nap, shopping for food, eating food, showering, and going to bed early enough to start all over the next day! Even when I was able to think about myself or have meaningful conversations with others, I still felt something was getting lost—or, to be more accurate, *Someone.*

Now in retrospect, I realize that I was experiencing something on pilgrimage that has often been true of my life. I am rarely physically exhausted or in pain, as I was when walking on the Camino, but I often experience the same kind of preoccupation with myself or with what I am doing. My life is filled with so much activity, my heart with so much desire or anxiety, and my mind with so many thoughts and concerns that I can easily forget about God and lose a sense of connection to God. Even with all the work I do in ministry, spiritual coaching and teaching to help others, I can easily miss the most important thing—or, again, the most important *One.*

I forget about God, and then all of a sudden I realize that I miss him. I become consumed with pursuing my own goals and agenda, and I suddenly remember Jesus. I start to question the value of focusing on spirituality or some other aspect of the Christian life, and pertinent Scripture comes to mind. I feel lost or confused, and I will unexpectedly come across another person whose story or wisdom is just what I need to hear. I wonder if I am a fool to be devoted to Christ, and then I see someone whose disbelieving mindset and life choices remind me why I so highly value a close relationship with God and the wisdom and guidance found in the Bible.

Then I reach out to God—sometimes praying to the Father, sometimes to Jesus, other times to the Holy Spirit, often to "God" without trying to distinguish between Father, Son, and Spirit. Sometimes nothing seems to happen when I pray, and I may not feel much of anything. However, before I know it, something shifts within me. I may become more aware of the presence of God, gain a new perspective on something, or simply feel more peace. I rarely discover grand solutions to major problems just by praying, but I often gain insight or come to see meaning and hope in whatever is troubling me.

When I experience these kinds of inner shifts, I think the Holy Spirit has been at work. I am receiving answers to my sometimes spoken and sometimes unspoken questions or cries for help. I am being changed, at least for that moment, and I sense that I am getting back in sync with God and the Spirit's leading.

In pilgrimage language, the Spirit seems to be continually helping me remember why I am walking, reconnecting me with God on the path, and keeping me going in the right direction. On the road to Fromista, on Day 17 of the Camino, I was reminded that, above all, I am a pilgrim on the road to God, and, simultaneously, God is my best and constant traveling companion.

Seeking God—Father, Son, and Holy Spirit

By the time I arrived in Fromista, I was more committed than ever to seeking a deeper relationship with God. But how would I proceed? Should I seek to know some generic, vaguely defined god, so commonly referred to in our modern society? Just seeking "God" has the advantage of distancing spirituality from all the baggage and limitations of any particular religion, and the general reference may help avoid conflicts between different religions and might promote better interreligious dialogue.

Or would I pursue more deeply the God of the Bible? This approach had the advantage of allowing me to draw from a roughly four-thousand-year-old Judeo-Christian tradition. Also, as I was to learn when I interviewed Buddhist monks in Myanmar and Thailand the winter following the pilgrimage, dialogue partners from other religions don't want to discuss vague spirituality or intellectual musings about God with others. They want to talk with true believers who have great spiritual depth growing out of their own tradition. Plus, the truth was, over the previous thirty-five years the Christian Scriptures had led me in powerful ways to God the Father, Jesus Christ (God's Son), and the Holy Spirit. I decided to seek to know the God of the Bible in every way accessible to me.

My next question was, how would I differentiate between God the Father, Jesus Christ the Son, and the Holy Spirit? Of course, I knew the difference between them conceptually, but what about in experience? I wanted to know who (which person of the Trinity) was relating to me at any given moment, because I suspected that my relationship with Father, Son, and Holy Spirit could deepen better if I became more sophisticated in identifying who was who. I could easily pray to one or the other, but would it be possible to know the Father experientially in a way that was different from knowing the Son or the Spirit?

When I looked to Scripture for help with my questions, I noticed that even New Testament writers do not always clearly distinguish between the three persons of the Trinity. When New Testament writers simply speak of God they are typically referring to the Creator of the universe and Father of Jesus Christ. Jesus is God's Son, Savior of the world, and, as risen Christ, appointed Lord (leader) of all those who believe (and ultimately of the entire world). The Holy Spirit comes from God to fill believers and enables them to serve God's purposes in the world. Yet, these are not the tidy distinctions they may seem to be, and overlap is everywhere.

Some passages speak of the Son or Spirit helping with creation. The Holy Spirit is Christ's Spirit. When New Testament writers speak of the Lord God, sometimes they means God the Father and sometimes they means Jesus Christ. Their ease with equating the Son with the Father, and connecting the Spirit to both Father and Son, helps to explain why theologians eventually developed the concept of the Trinity. In the defining work of the Councils of Nicaea (AD 325), Constantinople (AD 381), and Chalcedon (AD 451), theologians refined concepts that are incomprehensible to most people: Jesus Christ was of one substance with the Father, he was both fully God and fully human, the Spirit proceeds from the Father and Son, and the Trinity represents one God in three persons.

As I thought about all this, I was still not getting any help to know how I was going to know the difference between Father, Son, and Spirit in my experience. I looked harder at Scripture and found some clues. For example, according to John, Jesus said, "I have come that they may have life, and have it to the full" (John 10:10

NIV). The Father is the one who prunes and sanctifies us (makes us holy; John 15:2; 17:17), and the Spirit makes us new and teaches us truth (John 3:5–8; 14:26). Jesus taught his disciples to pray to the Father (Luke 11:2) and to ask the Father for the Spirit (Luke 11:13).

In Paul's epistles, he regularly greets other Christians with the "grace and peace from God our Father and the Lord Jesus Christ" (1 Cor. 1:3; 2 Cor. 1:2; Gal. 1:3). He taught that "God sent the Spirit of his Son into our hearts, the Spirit who calls out, 'Abba, Father'" (Gal. 4:6 NIV). It seems we are to look to God the Father as the initiator who sends the Son and Spirit to us, while both Son and Spirit will lead us back to the Father.

I eventually concluded that, while the three persons of the Trinity are completely intertwined, each has different roles (even if there is overlap between some of them), and distinguishing between them does matter. They each have complementary roles in the lives of believers, and Scripture suggests that each member of the Trinity deserves our praise and thanks for different reasons.

I also suspect that one's felt needs may be met better by praying to one or another member of the Trinity in any given situation. Praying to God is praying to God, and the three are in complete harmony with one another. Yet, praying to one or the other might may make more sense to us theologically (intellectually) at times, or simply feel better for some reason. Perhaps we want to share something with our Divine Parent, or need to talk to our Savior and Lord, or want to be filled with the Spirit. Perhaps the praise we feel seems more naturally directed to our Creator, while at other times we want to express our love and appreciation for Jesus. Some Scripture suggests we can pray to our Creator directly; other passages suggest that prayer should be directed to the Father but in the name of Jesus.

Developing our relationship with each person of the Trinity helps us develop our relationship with God in general, because each member adds something to our understanding, appreciation, and experience of God. At the same time, however, we should rarely worry about which member of the Trinity is the "right" one to address because Father, Son, and Holy Spirit must surely work in concert with one another. Just praying to the biblical "God" is enough identification in many situations, while using any one of the many other names or titles suggested in Scripture for God—Yahweh, Provider, Lamb of God, Bread of Life, Good Shepherd, Counselor, Prince of Peace, Wisdom, and so forth—may actually be very helpful to us at certain times. Furthermore, because of our own weaknesses and needs, traumatic experiences with religious leaders or in our families of origin, or various intellectual issues, at times we may not feel comfortable praying to the Father, or saying the name of Jesus, or referring to the Holy Spirit. At such times, just calling out to the Creator, Divine Light, or Higher Power may be the best we can do until God leads us to a deeper understanding of who God is or helps us reclaim the biblical names for God.

What seems more important than being able to perfectly "slice and dice" the differences within the Trinity, or worrying about which person of the Trinity we are relating to at any given moment, is simply to be in a life-giving relationship with God—Father, Son, and Holy Spirit—and to accept the mystery of blurry distinctions at times. Yet, this is not a reversion to a generic God but a humble acceptance of our limitations in grasping the complexity and nature of a triune God, while at the same time seeking to appreciate the distinctions whenever possible and helpful. Biblical writers themselves seem less concerned with precise definitions of the three persons than they are with promoting a vital spiritual life that includes all three persons:

- Experiencing a restored, loving relationship with our Creator, God, the Father, which honors him as the one and only true God;
- Having faith in and allegiance to our Savior and Lord, Jesus Christ, God's Son, who shows us who the Father is and whose work on the cross provides a way for humanity to be reconciled to God; and
- Being filled with and led by the Holy Spirit, who draws us to the Father, helps us know the mind of Christ, ministers to us in our need, and enables us to live like Christ and serve God's purposes.

This fuzzy set of distinctions works for me pretty well, but occasionally I hear the voices of my theologian friends in my head. They remind me how complicated the whole notion of the Trinity is (as if I need to be told), and urge me to keep trying to go deeper in my understanding of what this phenomenon of three persons in one might mean for my spiritual life. While distinguishing clearly between the three members of the Trinity may not be critical, getting to know each person more deeply might greatly enhance my relationship with God.

In trying to help us understand and appreciate God better, theologians have grappled for centuries with affirming both the unity of God and the distinct persons of the Trinity, and they have consistently concluded that both affirmations are important to hold in tension as a paradox. To neglect the unity of God leads to polytheism, a belief in multiple gods consistently rejected in the Judeo-Christian tradition. To not recognize the distinct persons within God fails to do justice to the teaching of the New Testament and undermines a key theological insight: God is essentially relational and calls believers into the relationship that exists between Father, Son, and Holy Spirit.

The ultimate hope and purpose for Christians, according to biblical teaching, is to live in an intimate relationship with God that mirrors the unity that the Trinity now knows. Christ called his disciples into unity with God and one another, as he and the Father were already unified. As brothers and sisters of Christ who are being conformed into his image, believers will one day enter fully into the "interiority" of the divine fellowship, in which we join Christ, our brother, in union with God—Father, Son and Holy Spirit.[1] We will not ever become God (as Christ is) or absorbed into God (as some Eastern religions suggest) but will live forever as "one" with God, unable to be separated from God's love (Rom. 8:29–39; John 17:21–23).

The Practical and Spiritual Value of Pursuing God Now

Looking to the Bible and developing our relationship with Father, Son, and Holy Spirit, then, helps us grapple with the important philosophical and spiritual issues of life: who we are (ontology), how we know God (epistemology), how should we live (ethics), and what our purpose in life is. Instead of trying to figure out who we are by what we do, what others tell us, or what we create on our own, we can start our search by looking to our Creator. Who else would know better who we are and what our purpose is than the one who created us? According to biblical writers, God the Father has revealed to us that we exist to live in a loving relationship with God that honors and brings glory to God.

Our failure as human beings to honor God with our thinking and behavior undermines our ability to be in perfect fellowship with God and to live out our purpose in life. Biblical writers explain that God has taken initiative to solve the breach in our relationship with God by becoming incarnate as God's Son. In the form of Jesus of Nazareth, God became better known to humanity. Then, in Jesus's death and resurrection, God provided a way for our sins to be forgiven for all time. To know Jesus better helps us know God's character and the magnitude of God's love for us, exemplified in Christ's suffering and dying for us. Since Jesus leads us to the Father and shows us how to live as God's children, by knowing him better we can know the Father better, can understand the meaning of our life more clearly, and will be inspired to emulate Jesus.

The Holy Spirit, the Spirit of Christ, is perpetually being given to believers by the Father so that we may find healing and restoration in our relationship with God and be increasingly drawn into union with God. The Spirit also allows us to experience God's power at work within us to make us more like Christ and to enable us to live out our purpose by loving and serving one another. Knowing the Spirit better means learning how to be increasingly filled and led by the Spirit.

My spiritual life was significantly advanced first by developing my relationship with God, the Father. As a teenager, I felt distance from my own father, and God the Father filled a great void in my life. When I was in my twenties, I realized that I had been afraid of the Spirit and was now ready to let the Holy Spirit work in my life more fully. I wanted to experience more spiritual power and transformation in my life, and the Spirit seemed like the natural one to whom to turn.

Then in the mid-1990s I realized that I had been neglecting Jesus in my spiritual life. While I was in graduate school and meeting so many people who knew God in vague terms or who simply could not accept Jesus as God's Son, I started to think more about who Jesus was and what he truly meant to me. I knew him as my Savior and Lord, but I wondered if something was missing. So I started asking God to show me Jesus more fully, and I also prayed to Jesus for help to know him better.

I went on pilgrimage because I highly valued my relationship with God, but I was mostly concerned about my own future and how God might help transform me. While on pilgrimage, I once again came to the place where I knew I wanted to make pursuing a deeper relationship with God an ongoing, high priority in my life— just for the sake of the relationship. Because of how I had already grown in my relationship with each member of the Trinity, when I began praying that God would help me to get to know God better, I consciously focused individually on the Father, Jesus, and the Holy Spirit. The next three chapters describe some of the fruit of my efforts over the years, including on pilgrimage, to get to know God better in all three persons.

CHAPTER 5

Knowing God

~

FRIDAY, JULY 14, 2006. DAY 21. MANSILLA DE LAS MULAS. What can I actually learn about God while walking so many miles, day after day, in the countryside of Spain? Perhaps the best thing would be to ask God to teach me. Maybe God will show me something about the Father, Son, or Holy Spirit through what I have experienced so far or by leading me into new learning experiences.

Honestly, I'm a bit skeptical. I don't expect to come up with much. What can I know about God, the Father, by taking a long walk? What can I learn about Jesus the Christ that I don't already know from studying the Bible? Getting to know the Holy Spirit better seems more likely, but my list of questions seems to be growing longer, not shorter. Well, we'll have to see what happens. . . .

FRIDAY, JULY 21, 2006. DAY 28. VILLAFRANCA. I really enjoyed my mile and a half (2.5 kilometers) of solitude today. I especially liked thinking more about what it might mean for God to be Father. My mind immediately went to the experiences I'm having with my sons. For nearly a month, I have been trying to use this unique pilgrimage opportunity to become a better father. I don't have a checklist of do's and don'ts. I'm simply trying to stay engaged mentally with them—to pay attention to what they need from me and to what I most have to offer them. I don't want to call attention to what I am doing. I just want to be the best dad I can be. . . .

Makes me think, though. I wonder how God thinks and feels about "parenting" us? God doesn't fail as I do, but, I think it is safe to assume, so much of what I aspire to be as a human father,

God must do by nature as Divine Parent. God loves, forgives, serves, sacrifices for me, cares and loves in action, offers guidance and wisdom, invests in me, engages me, draws me close, and I'm sure many other things I cannot even imagine.

Funny, the more I reflect on these things, the closer I feel to God. I want to figure out other ways God is a good parent to me, and ways I can become more like God in my fathering. . . .

Then, the next day

SATURDAY, JULY 22, 2006. DAY 29. LA FABA. *Though Jill questioned my sanity, Tim (my elder son) and I took an alternative route over the mountains and met up with Dan and her twelve hours later. The scenery was spectacular. The experience was the best of the pilgrimage so far. Poorly marked trails; long, steep inclines; midsummer heat; and a painful, final stretch downhill all made for a fabulous, memorable adventure. Hours in silence or simple conversation, in such beauty and hardly seeing another soul, created a peaceful, joyful feeling that was so deep neither of us could imagine ever feeling otherwise.*

Yet, the best part of the day for me was simply being with my son. The joy did not come from what we did or said as much as it came from being in his presence. We both felt completely free to be ourselves and to enjoy the experience together. I watched as Tim stopped to photograph the sunrise slowly splashing light into the valley hundreds of feet below us. I smiled when I heard joy in his voice while he marveled at centuries-old tree trunks or stooped to pat a dog that ran out of nowhere to greet us. I laughed when we had to duck to get out of the way of a horned cow that suddenly took an unhealthy interest in us. I growled with him as we inspected our long scratches and bleeding legs. Treacherous thorn bushes had left their mark after we were forced off trail on our final descent into the third steep valley of the day's hike.

What a great experience! I cannot put into words the depth of the joy I feel. And I realized something about God the Father that had never sunk in before, too. If God loves me as I love my son, surely God delights in just being with me as I was delighting in being with my son. If I can feel such joy just seeing Tim so happy and peaceful, I have to think that God—whose parental love must far exceed mine—must be thrilled to be with me at such times, too.

Reflecting on the Journey

Somehow my experience that day on the Camino helped me believe that God delights in me, just because I am a child of God. I already knew from the Bible that God's love for us is like the affection, tenderness, and care loving mothers and fathers have for their children (see, for example, Ps. 103:13; Isa. 66:13). Yet, after spending time with my son with an open mind and heart toward God, praying for eyes to see something about God as I walked, God's parental love has become more real to me.

In retrospect, I recognize my experience as another instance of moving from *knowing about God* (based on a biblical faith statement) to *knowing God* better (through greater awareness or appreciation of God). I didn't sense God's delight in me personally at the moment, which would have been an even deeper level of knowing, but as a result of my experience, I became more convinced that what I read in the Bible about God was true. The notion of God tenderly and joyfully delighting in me suddenly seemed entirely plausible. I felt a surge of warm appreciation for my Father's love for me.

I had opened myself to a more mystical path of knowing God— seeking to know God better through intuition and experience—and new insights, deeper convictions, and greater love, joy, and peace started emerging. I wasn't learning something about God that Scripture didn't already teach. I was grasping and experiencing God at a deeper level within myself.

I had questions, too.

Knowing God through Experience

In seeking to know God better on pilgrimage, I found myself asking, how reliable are feelings, impressions, and interpretations of "spiritual experiences"? I wasn't asking, can we experience God? (I took that as a given, based on what the New Testament says about the Holy Spirit's presence in our lives.) Rather, I wondered, can we get to know God better from our experiences? That is, can our experiences help us understand, believe, or appreciate God better and lead us into a deeper relationship with God?

I know that for some people this question is absurd, since the obvious answer to them, based on their own interpretation of their experiences, is "Yes!" Their spiritual life includes encounters with God, a regular sense of God's presence, and any number of confirmations of what the Bible teaches about God. However, many others are not aware of God's activity in their life, or, if they suspect God is at work, they doubt their perceptions.

For some of us, the question of whether we can know God better through experience is troubling because we have difficulty trusting our (or anyone else's) feelings and experiences as reliable guides. Indeed, many believers and skeptics alike have raised serious concerns about relying on subjective, human experience to make any truth claims about God. We can't see God, and we can't make God prove his/her/its existence or our relationship with him/her/it. Further, we remind ourselves, any God experience we think we have might actually be due to chance, a psychological phenomenon, or some other natural cause. Thus, while we can talk about what we believe and feel, and make conjectures about what happens to us when we have unusual "spiritual" experiences, we wonder whether we can legitimately take the next step to make any definitive statement about God or our relationship with God.

Over the centuries, philosophers have wrestled with the question of how one knows God (or anything, for that matter). Some have concluded that there is no God, and others that we simply can't know whether God (or any nonmaterial entity) exists or what the nature of God might be. Different proposals to justify believing in God have been offered by various thinkers, but no "proof" of God exists in philosophy to settle the question satisfactorily for the skeptic.

Early on in the development of Christianity, theologians recognized that an undue reliance on human experience was potentially misleading and thus harmful to individuals and the church as a whole. While various individual congregations seemed to readily endorse special revelation to individuals through ecstatic experiences of various kinds, "orthodox" theologians generally rejected anything that smacked of such gnosticism.[1] First, they argued, when someone claims to have a revelation from God, we cannot be certain where the vision, ideas, or feelings are coming from, since they cannot be tested for their veracity.

Second, and even more important, when these revelations contradict or undermine teaching that was passed down from Jesus and the apostles (or radically reinterpret their teaching), one would then have to choose between tradition and the new revelation. Under such a scenario, the so-called orthodox (literally, *ortho* means "straight," or in other words, "right," plus *doxa* meaning "view") theologians insisted that primacy had to be given to apostolic teaching (later canonized in the twenty-seven books of the New Testament). Individual experience was still very important, since Christians receive grace and undergo transformation in various personal ways. However, theologians insisted that one's personal thoughts and encounters with God needed to be evaluated in light of Scripture and the history of interpretation of Scripture by church leaders and scholars, in order to guard individuals and congregations from being led astray by their transitory feelings and unique experiences.

Today gnostic-esque religions, which emphasize personal revelations from God and especially other spirits, are attracting interest from a growing number of people. Further, a discovery of gnostic literature at Nag Hammadi in the mid-twentieth century has spawned much speculation that the early church was more diverse than originally thought. Some scholars argue from these findings that we should not view gnosticism as necessarily misguided but as one of many alternatives to the views that eventually dominated the church (orthodoxy).

From my vantage point, these claims that early Christianity was so diverse that (the implication seems to be) we should not put so much stock in orthodox teaching are overblown and misleading. The discovery of gnostic forms of Christianity need not mean anything more than human beings are perpetually drawn to valuing their own personal experience in an intellectual vacuum. Gnosticism and gnostic-esque religions will always keep surfacing, in my opinion, because of the power of our personal experiences and our desires to know something unique about God. At the same time, such overly experience-oriented faiths will keep fading away (or will be rejected by thoughtful people), as they devolve from simply honoring one's individual experience (which is important to do) to building theological castles in the air, as they often do.

As I wrestled with these issues, I was having difficulty coming up with a satisfactory conclusion about whether I could get to know God better from experience. I wanted to make the most of my experience, but I didn't want to be naive about both my limitations and the dangers of creating my own theology. At the same time, I didn't want to overreact, as some have done, out of fear and mistrust and not leave room for God to reach out to me personally to show me more about the Father that would help me grow spiritually.

Knowing and Not Knowing God

The truth is, knowing God is problematic for any thinking-oriented person. We are dealing with issues of spirituality (relating to an unseen God), which leaves us to speculate about God and talk about what we cannot see or verify.

Scripture itself alludes to the difficulty of truly knowing and understanding God. Biblical writers teach that God is both transcendent (beyond us) and immanent (present with us and within us). God is not hiding to avoid us, but rather we are bound by the limitations of our own subjective point of view and creaturely minds. We are simply not capable of fully knowing something or someone outside of ourselves, let alone something (One) so infinitely greater than we are. Yet, at the same time, our subjective limitations do not preclude the possibility that God may reveal himself to us. We may not be able by our own effort to figure out, let alone prove, who God is, but God could help us come to know and love God better over time. This is the standard position of mainstream Christian theologians—

God has taken the initiative to reveal to us enough about the Father, Son, and Holy Spirit for us to know, worship, and love God.

Fifth-century theologian Augustine suggested that our hearts are restless until they find rest in God. In this view, God has put a longing in our hearts that may be fulfilled only in a personal relationship with God. While we may be unable to derive scientifically verifiable knowledge about God from our experience, God may have put enough awareness in our hearts that we can truly know God. And those who care deeply about their relationship to God will persist in their search for God as long as their felt need for God is left unsatisfied.

If God truly has revealed God's self, then we can acknowledge that God is knowable and at the same time admit that many aspects of God cannot be known or verified. Peter Rollins, postmodern philosopher and pastor among those who identify with the emergent church movement, talks about the paradox of knowing and not knowing God, and what that can mean for believers. He adapts a quote from Christian philosopher Blaise Pascal, who writes about what "reasonable people" might conclude about God and how they might live. Rollins says that truly reasonable people in the world are those who "serve God with all of their heart because they know him, all the while seeking him with all their heart because they do not."[2]

Thus, the God-generated longing in our hearts leads us to God. Then, whatever we know of God spurs us on to learn more about God, even while we continue to recognize that God is far beyond our complete knowing or understanding. Inasmuch as we have tasted the goodness, joy, and peace that come from a relationship with God in Christ, we hope for more of the same, while expecting to be surprised over and over again by what we did not expect and could not imagine.

A Middle Way

As I wrestled with all these issues on pilgrimage, I again realized that basing one's knowledge of God *primarily* on personal experience

or in a historical vacuum is problematic, not just to many philosophers and theologians but also to me. A middle way, between intellectual skepticism (agnosticism) and wholesale subjectivity, exists.
This way is grounded in the person of Jesus Christ; applies reason;
honors the time-tested, sacred writings of the Judeo-Christian faith;
respects tradition (the long history of reflection on and application
of Scripture); and honors personal experience. Scripture is the starting place, where we are taught that God has taken initiative to make
himself known and is actively at work drawing us to God and faith.
Once we are willing to accept (or leap to) this position of faith, then
we may use all the other available tools and resources (reason, tradition, thoughts and testimonies of others, and personal experience)
in order to learn more about God and come to know God personally. Whether we start with Scripture and look for God in our experience, or vice versa, Scripture provides language, concepts, and
guidance in developing our understanding of and relationship with
God.

Of course, we will never be able to eliminate the possibility that
we will delude ourselves or misinterpret our spiritual experiences,
but this multifaceted, balanced approach to knowing God is the
most solid method available for developing a relationship with God,
from a Christian perspective. By seeking God in these ways, we max-
imize the contribution of all of our faculties, including our ability to
experience phenomena that we highly value but cannot fully explain.
At the same time, we reflect on God within a broad community,
tracking back to Jesus and beyond (through ancient Israel), while
drawing on our best resources and maintaining checks and balances
along the way.

In language that may be uncomfortable to some, I consider my
views about God to be working hypotheses that are informed and
tested by Scripture, reason, testimonies of other respected men and
women over the centuries, and experience. I am continually seeking
to engage God personally—to enjoy and develop my relationship
with God, on one hand, and to refine my working hypotheses, on
the other. I trust that the Holy Spirit is very much part of this ongoing process of spiritual growth and will help steer me away from fantasy and self-deception along the way.

Scripture for the Journey

The time-tested, commonly accepted collection of sacred texts that tie back to historical prophets and apostles—our best information about ancient Israel, Jesus, and the first century church—is called canonical Scripture. While such agreed-upon authoritative texts are subject to multiple interpretations, they still provide a fixed point of reference for all theological conversation. As such, Christian pastors and theologians traditionally consider the Bible to be the best backdrop for assessing one's own experiences.[3]

Scripture does not offer deep philosophical or psychological answers to our questions about God. We find no intellectually satisfying, rational argument in the Bible about the existence of God or how post-enlightenment thinkers can know God. To look for such material would be anachronistic. The Bible was written in a different era, when spiritual truth was presented as revelation through testimony, narrative, teaching, and preaching. The various messages we find in the texts are usually held up as truth for readers to take or leave, to believe or reject, to act upon or ignore. (For example, see Ps. 19:7–11.)

So, how can the Bible help the modern pilgrim know God (better)? By inviting us to "taste and see" for ourselves that the God the writers present is "good" (Ps. 34:8). According to the Scriptures, spiritual pilgrims do not have to try to know God on their own or in a vacuum. God has been and is at work throughout history and within our own personal experience to lead us to true knowledge of God that transforms our life. As we seek the God of the Bible and respond to God's initiatives, we may come to know God.

Key to benefiting from what Scripture has to offer is to grasp the difference between knowing *about* God and knowing God. One has to do with information and assertions, the other with a personal relationship with God. The former might include being able to list God's attributes as delineated in Scripture, while the latter refers to perceiving God's qualities in ways that personally affect one's life. Knowing about God includes hearing testimonies on how God has worked powerfully in history, while knowing God means encountering God personally and being transformed.

Knowing about God

In general, Scripture teaches that we can know about God through God's self-revelation in multiple ways. Indirectly, we may learn about God through nature. For example, one of the psalmists saw the glory of God in the heavens, which pour forth "knowledge" (Ps. 19:1–3), and Paul said that all of God's invisible qualities can be discerned from creation (Rom. 1:20). Direct personal appearances of God are rare, but many instances are recorded in the Bible. God appeared, for example, to Adam and Eve in the Garden of Eden, to Abraham in his backyard, and to Moses at the burning bush.

We can also know about God by reading biblical narratives that describe God's actions in history. From beginning to end of the Bible, stories and prophecies tell of God's activity among humans. God delivers the people of Israel from slavery in Egypt, raises up King David to rule over Israel, works powerfully through the life and ministry of Jesus, and gives courage, produces miracles, and establishes churches throughout the known world through the apostles after Jesus's resurrection.

We can know about God through the teaching and sermons of the prophets, whose job was to declare God's nature and will. Prophets often spoke in the first person as if their words were actually the Lord's. Hundreds of occurrences of "thus says the Lord" can be found throughout the Hebrew Scriptures (Old Testament).

Six historical books of the Hebrew Scriptures (Joshua, Judges, 1 and 2 Samuel, 1 and 2 Kings) were designated by Jewish scholars as the writings of "former prophets." In addition, Israel's religious leaders assigned three books to the major prophets (Isaiah, Jeremiah, Ezekiel) and twelve more to minor prophets. The early church also regarded the twenty-seven books of the New Testament as inspired by God and thus reliable guides to knowledge about God. (See, for example, 2 Tim. 3:16; Heb. 1:1–2.)

Numerous attributes of God emerge when we look at various passages within the Bible. Depending on how God is responding to the Israelites at any given time in history, we may read a story of God's deliverance, retribution, testing, or consoling. At times God appears to be punitive and dangerous, at other times gracious and tender. Sometimes, God is intimately involved in human history, while in other passages God seems aloof and indifferent to human plight. If Jesus is telling a parable, we may learn of God's unconditional love, as in the story of the prodigal son (Luke 15:11–32), or God's fierce wrath, as in the story of the vineyard owner who severely punished the tenants who killed his servants and son (Luke 20:9–18).

Which is the true picture of God? Biblical writers do not try to answer that modern question as if one perfect composite description is possible, but assume that all of the stories and traditions taken together reliably portray God as best as we can know him. They appeared to be rarely concerned about how their writing might be in tension with another writer's portrayal of God. Rather, a much higher priority seemed to be to point people to the one true God (as opposed to idols and other false gods).

In general, throughout the Bible, God is consistently portrayed as a God of both mercy and justice, as one who makes and keeps covenants, and above all as a God of love (John 3:16; 1 John 4:7–8). A refrain repeated at least nine times in the Bible summarizes well the collection of attributes for which God was best known both to ancient Israel and Christians: "But you, O Lord, are a compassionate and gracious God, slow to anger, abounding in love and faithfulness" (Ps. 86:15 NIV).

Knowing God

Knowing about God represents a rudimentary level of spiritual awareness. Real spiritual vitality also requires grasping the reality of God and developing a personal relationship with God. Some come to know God in a deeper way through special personal encounters with God or by perceiving and responding to God's blessings in their life. As I will discuss at length in the next chapter, Jesus is the preeminent way we can come to know about God and know God. We can also come to know God better as we look within ourselves for signs of God's qualities and activity and we experience being filled and led by God's Spirit. In the following, I take a deeper look at each of these ways of coming to know God more personally.

Experiencing God. On occasion, some people come to know God through unique encounters with God. For example, when the Hebrew prophet Samuel was still a child, he was living in Shiloh with Eli, a prophet and priest of the Lord. One night he heard the voice of the Lord calling to him, but he didn't know whose voice it was. Three times he heard the voice, and each time he went into Eli, assuming it was he who had called. Eli eventually realized that it was the Lord who was calling to Samuel. He then was able to coach Samuel to help him interpret his experience in theologically sound ways; he taught Samuel to recognize the voice of the Lord (1 Sam. 3:1–10).

Certainly Samuel must have known a great deal about God, based on his Hebrew upbringing and time with Eli and the other priests, but apparently he did not yet know God. At the beginning of the story of Samuel, the narrator explains Samuel's misinterpreting his experience with the (audible?) voice as ignorance of God: "Now Samuel did not yet know the Lord, and the word of the Lord had not yet been revealed to him" (1 Sam. 3:7). We may infer from this comment that by the end of this encounter with God, Samuel had come to know the Lord through this experience. His connection to God had become personal.

A more common way to develop a deeper relationship with God through experience is to attribute something wonderful that happens to us to God. Giving God credit for something means we are choosing to look at the good in our life through the eyes of faith as blessings from God rather than good luck or chance. As we respond with praise, thanksgiving, or some other kind of appreciation, we are likely to feel closer to God. This phenomenon is like receiving an anonymous gift and guessing who the sender may be. We may not be able to prove that, say, Sandra, sent it to us, but once we consider the possibility that Sandra was the giver, we may start feeling warmer toward her. We may even start noticing other ways that our lives are better because Sandra is in it. We may start reaching out to Sandra more, and our relationship may grow through the process.

As a biblical example, when David escaped from Saul, who was trying to kill him, David was filled with joy and gratitude to God. Throughout Psalm 18, David talks about his love for God and how much he has learned about God from his personal experience of receiving God's help.

> I love you, O LORD, my strength.
> The LORD is my rock, my fortress and my deliverer;
> my God is my rock, in whom I take refuge.
> He is my shield and the horn of my salvation, my stronghold.
> —Psalm 18:1–2 NIV

The Lord is not, of course, actually a rock, fortress, or shield, just as God is not a fire-breathing dragon and does not surf the clouds on the backs of cherubim (18:8–10). In fifty verses, David effusively and poetically dramatizes his experience of God's intervention on his behalf and what he has learned about God through the experience. David does not literally see God, but his experience with God leads him to draw conclusions about the nature of God that he expresses metaphorically. From this experience and others, David learned that God was someone he could count on for strength and help in time of trouble. As a result, David loved and trusted God deeply.

Job's experience with God, on the other hand, was very different. The text tells us that Job was a righteous man, yet God allowed him to suffer great loss and pain (just the opposite of what David would have expected, based on his affirmations in Psalm 18). The story includes much dialogue between Job and his friends, who blame him for his troubles in order to justify God. Job will not accept their views and rails against God (without blaspheming) as he defends his innocence and decries the injustice of his suffering. Job assumed from his painful ordeal that God had wronged him.

In the end, God rebukes Job for thinking he can know enough to draw such conclusions about God. At the same time, God rebukes Job's friends for thinking that they can speak definitively about God. No matter what humans may think they know, God's perspective is beyond our capacity to understand. When confronted by God in the story, Job comes to realize that the creator and sustainer of the universe has knowledge, power, and understanding that far exceed his ability to grasp. In the face of this deeper knowledge of God, Job's only response is to become silent and to humble himself before God. (See especially Job 38:1–42:6.)

Samuel, David, and Job offer three very different experiences of God. None of them received a full revelation of God's nature. Yet each learned something through their experiences that they didn't know or realize in the same way before, even if their encounter with God was only a snapshot. They each drew conclusions that seemed true for them yet do not establish a standard for everyone in every other circumstance. On the basis of just this small sampling of biblical stories of encounters with God, we can conclude that God is beyond fully comprehending. Yet by God's initiative with individuals, humans can come to know God better than they would only by speculating about God or learning about God from others.

A skeptic might look at the examples of David and Job side by side as proof of human inability to truly know God, because they vary so markedly. However, biblical writers believed they show just the opposite—God can be and is known through human experience, yet we must remain humble, recognizing that however well we may know God, God may at any point act (or fail to act) in surprising ways for reasons only God knows.

Knowing God by knowing Jesus. According to the New Testament, the best way for anyone to truly know what God is like and to enter a relationship with God is through Jesus Christ. According to the apostle John, Jesus was the manifestation of the Logos of God in the flesh, "the glory as of a father's [God's] only son, full of grace and truth" (John 1:14). In Colossians, we find significant faith claims about Jesus that equate him with God as cocreator and identify him as the lynchpin in God's work to reconcile humans to himself.

> [Our Lord Jesus Christ, the Son of God] is the image of the invisible God, the firstborn over all creation. For by him all things were created: things in heaven and on earth, visible and invisible, whether thrones or powers or rulers or authorities; all things were created by him and for him. He is before all things, and in him all things hold together. And he is the head of the body, the church; he is the beginning and the firstborn

from among the dead, so that in everything he might have the supremacy. For God was pleased to have all his fullness dwell in him, and through him to reconcile to himself all things, whether things on earth or things in heaven, by making peace through his blood, shed on the cross (Col. 1:15–20 NIV).

Verses such as these greatly influenced theologians responsible for formulating official doctrinal statements about God—that Jesus Christ is God the Son and a full member of the triune Godhead, faith claims that have been passed down to us through the centuries. The basic message is this: if you want to know what God is like, look at Jesus in whom "God was pleased to have all his fullness dwell." Then, if you want to know God through Jesus, pray to know Christ personally. (See chapter 6.)

Knowing God within ourselves. Scripture teaches that God is not distant from us but is close at hand and actively at work in unseen ways to draw us closer to him. As Paul pointed out in his evangelistic appeal to the Athenians, while God desires that we search for him, he is not far from any of us. In fact, "in [God] we live and move and have our being" (Acts 17:27–28). The transcendent God who is far beyond our ability to ever fully know is also an immanent God who is close at hand and at work in our lives.

In the sixth century before Christ, Jeremiah wrote of a day when God would create a new covenant between God and humans that is characterized by knowing the Lord. When the new covenant is in place, "No longer shall they teach one another, or say to each other, 'Know the LORD,' for they shall all know me, from the least of them to the greatest, says the LORD; for I will forgive their iniquity, and remember their sin no more" (Jer. 31:34). Later, Christian apostles and prophets believed that Jeremiah's prophecy was fulfilled in the coming of Jesus, and the new covenant established through his death and resurrection. (See, for example, Heb. 8–9.)

Jesus said that people do not come to him unless the Father draws them (John 6:44), indicating that God is the one who opens our eyes to Jesus's true identity and the hope that is in him. According to Paul's teaching, the Spirit of God dwells within every believer and actively works within us (Eph. 1:13–14; Gal. 5:22–23). Likewise, Peter taught that Christians partake in "the divine nature" (2 Pet. 1:2–4).

All of these passages suggest that we can know God by looking within ourselves—listening for God's voice and noticing how the Holy Spirit may be transforming our minds and hearts, convincing us of wrongdoing, leading us to "right doing," leading us to faith in Jesus Christ, and helping us experience God's love and grace for ourselves and others. God's activity within us helps us perceive the reality of God, to have faith in God, and to become more like God.

Seeking God and living by faith. We can also know God better by actively responding to the Holy Spirit's call on our lives, pursuing a deeper relationship with God, and living in ways that depend on God to work in us and through us—even if we are at times quite limited in our understanding of God's ways. Isaiah wrote, for example:

> Seek the LORD while he may be found, call upon him while he is near; let the wicked forsake their way, and the unrighteous their thoughts; let them return to the LORD, that he may have mercy on them, and to our God, for he will abundantly pardon. For my thoughts are not your thoughts, nor are your ways my ways, says the LORD. For as the heavens are higher than the earth, so are my ways higher than your ways and my thoughts than your thoughts (Isa. 55:6–9).

Rather than trying to explain why bad things happen to good people (a preoccupation for many of us), Isaiah is addressing why good ("God") things happen to bad people (meaning, any ordinary sinner). His answer is simply that God is merciful, extending hope to undeserving people like us, who have at times turned away from God or acted in ways that are contrary to God's will for us. The way we come to know God as merciful and forgiving is by admitting our wrongdoing, submitting our wills to our Creator's, embracing the gift of Jesus Christ, and seeking the restoration the Holy Spirit brings. In other words, we will come to know God in these profound ways as we act in faith—not to earn God's approval (our doing enough good to earn it is not possible), but to seek what God is offering by turning to the Lord and receiving his inexplicable gift.

In the psalms we read invitations to more or less try God out. For example, at one point we read, "O taste and see that the LORD is good; happy are those who take refuge in him" (Ps. 34:8). God has initiated contact with us in many ways (through prophets, Scripture, Jesus, the Holy Spirit's prompting). At some point, it is up to us to respond if we are going to develop a relationship with God.

Likewise, Peter had to step out of the boat and begin to sink before he could experience Jesus's power to help him walk on water. The apostles and early believers had to witness to their faith, create churches, send missionaries out to the world, pray for one another, and perform any number of other acts of faith and love in order to witness God's transforming work through them. Even when they underwent terrible persecutions and apparent setbacks, they continued to actively live their lives by faith and eager expectation of experiencing God's love, faithfulness, and power.

Next Steps

To know God better as spiritual pilgrims, we may draw on Scripture, the testimony of others, and our own experience as guides. We do not know how or when God will respond to us, and often we will recognize God's activity in our lives only in retrospect. Our calling is to walk humbly by faith, trusting in God's activity in our lives, while recognizing our inability to ever control or fully know God. Our most dogmatic convictions are always, at best, faith statements, claims that cannot be proven objectively but that nonetheless guide us and shape our relationship with God. As spiritual pilgrims, we must trust that the Holy Spirit is in fact leading us to know God better along the way, while always leaving room for our ideas and convictions to be modified throughout the journey.

Practically, you can take many steps to come to know God (better) on pilgrimage. The best place to start is to read the Bible, looking especially for what you can learn about the character of God—so that you know better whom you are looking for! Then learn to reflect on your life through the eyes of faith. Pray for the Holy Spirit to reveal God's nature and activity within you and around you, both in your past and present experience.

Don't expect to suddenly discover new qualities of God that no one ever thought of before. On the contrary, the goal is to know better the same God that biblical writers have written about and deeply spiritual people have known through the ages. The goal is finding not something new for the world but something new or more profound for you personally or for your community of faith.

Look through Eyes of Faith

Whenever any of us reaches out to God, hears new religious ideas, encounters some unusual phenomenon, or experiences something that seems to point us to Something or Someone beyond ourselves, we are likely to wind up doing what religiously minded humans have always done. We try to put together the pieces of our experience by drawing on our head (rational thoughts), heart (emotions), and gut (visceral reactions) as best we can. As you do this, do so through the eyes of faith.

For example, one of the most formative experiences I had as a teenager was to pray to God to show me if he cared or not. As I knelt by my bed, praying earnestly for a sign, I saw in mind a huge hand extended through the clouds toward me, a gesture I inter-preted as personal concern for me. I knew at the time that I had probably created an image that fit with what I wanted to believe. Later, I also realized I was probably trying to fill a void I felt with my dad. For years I wondered, was I deluding myself that night or was God working through my imagination to lead me to a truth about God in a form that an adolescent boy could grasp?

As I tried to sort out what was happening to me in that moment, my mind leaned one way and my heart another. My mind doubted the authenticity of such a convenient image; my feelings of joy told me I was embracing the experience as true. Eventually, my gut prevailed by telling me, "Go with it. Some things you just can't fully understand." So I did. I accepted that God was communicating to me that he really did care about me and that pursuing a relationship with God was worth the effort.

Since then I have studied the Bible, talked to many spiritually mature people I respect, listened to the experiences of others, read what philosophers and psychologists think about religious experiences, and continued to reach out to God. Based on the teachings and testimonies from the Judeo-Christian tradition, I find it plausible that God would use whatever means necessary to help a young boy see God and move forward in his spiritual life in a way that fit his stage of development. The hand in the cloud may have been my invention (based on images I had been exposed to elsewhere). At the same time, I found in Scripture that David described God's intervention in his life with just such an image of God reaching down from heaven (Ps. 18:16). Further, as someone suggested to me, the Spirit may have used my creativity to convince me of a spiritual truth I needed help believing: God truly does care and will respond to my requests to help me grow in my relationship with God.

What have I done? *I have chosen to inform my thinking with Scripture and look at my experience through the eyes of faith.* I haven't tried to prove that God reached out to me that night. Instead, I have drawn on the best resources available and have used my head, heart, and gut to wrestle with my needs, desires, ideas, and experiences in relation to God.

Our experiences can motivate us to look more carefully for what God might want to show us, teach us, do within us, accomplish through us, or lovingly give to us. Then, through the process of embracing our experiences, reflecting on them, learning from them, experimenting with our responses to them, we will find that our beliefs, feelings, and gut instincts about God will be reinforced, challenged, or refined on a continual basis. We can seek to learn and grow in ways that satisfy our longing for God and spiritual sensibilities, while allowing all of our faculties to provide checks and balances on our tentative conclusions.

Look for God in Your Past

One of the main ways you can come to know God better is by stepping back and looking through the eyes of faith at the big picture of your life as well as the many significant turning points and experiences. As you look back, you will learn more about yourself, how you have changed and grown, and how the Holy Spirit may have been working in your life.

In looking to the past, I am not suggesting that you live in the past. In fact, as many wisely advocate today, we would all do well to learn how to live fully in the present, making the most of each moment of our life, neither dwelling on the past nor worrying about the future. Jesus taught, "Do not worry about tomorrow, for tomorrow will bring worries of its own. Today's trouble is enough for today" (Matt. 6:34). Living in the present helps you remain fully engaged in what is happening at any given moment, not get mired in past glories or failures, and not waste present opportunities dreaming about the future. At the same time, reflecting on the past can actually help you live more vitally in the present in anticipation of a more meaningful and joyful future.

When I look at my past through the eyes of faith, I can see how the Holy Spirit has worked through many significant events, people, and circumstances to shape who I am and my relationship with God. I meet someone special, take an incredible class, experience a great success or devastating tragedy, discover something profound or powerful in Scripture, use my talents in ways that open my eyes to meaning and purpose in my life, or make a critical decision with far-reaching consequences. Each experience then joins a whole train of other significant life-changing moments. While anyone can point to noteworthy "chance" encounters or "coincidences" that have altered one's life significantly, when you look at your life through the eyes of faith, you will see God at work.

> Reflect on your life through the eyes of faith. Where can you see God present or active in your journey? In what ways has your experience, or lack thereof, left you wanting something different in your relationship with God?

When I first made my list, six or seven memories or periods in my life jumped right out at me, times when I especially sensed God's working within me in powerful ways. The more I thought, the more my list kept growing. Here are some of the most significant moments from my list so far:

- Praying to God to ask him to show me that he cared about me as a teenager
- Submitting my will to God's after one particular evening of wrestling within myself
- Publicly declaring my faith and commitment to Christ in baptism at age sixteen
- Going on a service project as a teenager where I first learned that I loved teaching and that God could use me to help others through teaching
- Being mentored by Mike, a caring, older Christian
- Being exposed to myriad meaningful experiences at college, including spiritual emphases weeks and the example of godly, caring professors and administrators
- Taking summer school in the Middle East, followed by a few weeks exploring Europe with friends
- Being theologically and culturally stimulated at seminary
- Pastoring my first churches
- Getting and being married
- Having to face personal weaknesses, limitations, and failure in new ways in my marriage and professionally
- Struggling to overcome a life-threatening illness
- Grieving the death of our first child through miscarriage
- Rejoicing in the birth of two children and family life ever since
- Deepening and broadening through Ph.D. work
- Suffering through my mother's long, losing battle against Alzheimer's disease
- Experiencing the love and grace of God in ways that transformed me and my marriage
- Attending one site visit to a program for at-risk, troubled youth that dramatically altered my career path

- Serving as an executive in a growing nonprofit organization for ten years, an experience that taught me how to better deal with conflicts, to manage, to communicate, to promote, and to lead
- Choosing to leave a conventional career path to pursue my vision for a global teaching ministry, and creating a new nonprofit organization
- Interviewing Buddhist monks in Thailand, risking arrest or violence in dangerous Asian and African countries
- Teaching and coaching others in French-speaking countries

The longer my list grew, the more I felt grateful for how God has worked in my life in significant ways, transforming my relationship to God, my relationships to others, and my ability to serve and live out my purpose in life effectively.

Sometimes, though, in the midst of current frustrations, disappointments, suffering, aspirations, or unfulfilled dreams, we forget to look back to identify all the good in our life. We don't consciously acknowledge and appreciate the myriad ways we have grown and developed, experienced joy and meaning, and felt and received love. Often, we even fail to appreciate the good that has emerged from some of the most painful circumstances in our life. We become so focused on what is wrong or missing in our life that we forget to reflect on how God's hand may have been at work in our life, guiding or helping us.

Such remembering is worthwhile, though. Ignorance and spiritual amnesia of how God has been at work in our past can seriously affect our spiritual vitality in the present. Grateful awareness and appreciation, on the other hand, can be extremely comforting, encouraging, and motivating.

Each of us grows and changes in ways unique to us, each of us struggles with different blind spots and stubborn sins, and we all have ups and downs. At times we feel close to God, and other times God seems far away and we may languish in doubt, confusion, or emptiness. Nevertheless, overall, when you look back on your life through the eyes of faith, you will be able to see signs of God's active presence in your life—activity you would expect from a loving, giving, and forgiving God who works in and through you to accomplish good purposes that benefit you and those around you. Then, by reflecting on your life's experience through the eyes of faith, you will likely become more confident in your knowledge of God and trust more in the Holy Spirit. Your love for God will grow, and you will come to expect that the Holy Spirit will continue to work in you and flow through you in beautiful, joyful, and constructive ways.

Keep Seeking God

Keep looking for God within you and all around you in the present, too. If you feel yourself being drawn toward God, ask what the Holy Spirit is trying to show you or say to you. Look for signs of God's working in your life for good in the present. Even (especially) in the hard circumstances, look for what God may be trying to teach you. Open your eyes and heart to the opportunities that come to you to do good in the world. The Holy Spirit is inviting you to share in God's love, goodness, generosity, or some other virtue that will bring more joy to your life and help you see more clearly God's presence and activity in your life.

God is not playing a game of hide and seek with us. Not only can God be found, but God in Christ will find us before we find him. The Gospel story of Zacchaeus, the wealthy tax collector, illustrates both the importance of seeking God in Christ, and the reality that Christ is simultaneously seeking us (Luke 19). Zacchaeus, a short man, climbed a sycamore tree to be able to see Jesus when he passed by amid the throngs. However, when Jesus reached the tree, he called Zacchaeus to come down. Why? The passage says, because Jesus had already planned on spending the night at the house of this man, whom he had never met. What follows in the text is the account of Zacchaeus's dramatic conversion and repentance, leading to his making restitution to those he had wronged.

In case we miss the point, Luke records Jesus's words of self-understanding at the end of the story. Jesus said, "For the Son of Man came to seek and to save what was lost" (Luke 19:10 NIV). Gospel stories such as this one teach that no matter how far we may have drifted from God, how cold our spiritual life has become, how confused or disillusioned we may be, or how much our relationship with God has gotten off track, Christ has come for us and is actively seeking us. No matter how lost we may be, the good news is we need not stay lost. Zacchaeus's experience illustrates what Jesus also does for others: God is searching for those who are searching for him, and Christ will find us.

For Further Reflection

Tuesday, July 25, 2006. Day 32. Café at the end of the day. Today was glorious. Walked by myself most of the way, singing, thinking, and just soaking up the sun and countryside. I noticed an interesting shift that took place right after my midmorning break. As I resumed walking, I was in a more reflective, quiet mood. Gone was the high energy and ADD (attention deficit disorder). I suddenly thought to say to God, "If there is something you want to say to me, I'm ready to listen."

Hmmm. I wonder if God was patiently waiting for me to get ready to listen. I wonder how often God waits for me. . . . I think I may have just received another insight into God: "God is patient, waiting for us to be ready to listen."

"Thank you, Lord, for your patience with me. Help me to learn better how to be present with my sons and others while patiently waiting for them to be ready to listen to me."

Reflect on the words above. Use the following questions to guide your journal writing, and discuss your answers with other spiritual pilgrims who are seeking to know God better.

- If you had to explain God to someone who had never read the Bible, what would you say?
- What is your working hypothesis about God and how God relates to you? How are you testing it out in day-to-day living? Where is it working for you, and where isn't it working?
- How will you look for greater knowledge and understanding of God? How would you describe your level of biblical literacy, especially related to what the Scriptures teach about who

God is and how God works in human lives? What kind of experiences will you pray for in order to deepen your intimacy with God?

- What help or support do you need from others as you seek to know God better? Whom will you ask? When will you ask?
- What other thoughts and responses emerged for you from this chapter on knowing God? What specifically do you intend to do differently or more consistently?

CHAPTER 6

Following Jesus

≈

SUNDAY, JULY 30, 2006. DAY 37. SANTIAGO DE COMPOSTELA. *I'm sitting in the great cathedral, at the end of our walk—but not the end of our journey. The worship service just finished, but I couldn't understand a word of it. At one point, we passed the peace to others around us. My son Dan and I just hugged. I shook hands with and smiled at two strangers. I felt a surge of emotion. I realized how much it meant to me to be in a place of worship surrounded by other believers. One reason I believe in Christ is because of the inner peace I've experienced through faith, and the sense of peace I have often felt in the midst of other believers.*

Then came a big surprise. Mass was conducted, and all pilgrims were invited to participate, Protestants and Catholics alike. A priest came to the back where we were standing. He placed the wafer in my mouth, reciting something about "corpus Christi" ("the body of Christ," in Latin). I suddenly welled up with nearly uncontrollable emotion.

I moved as fast as I could to the nearest side chapel. Though barred from entering, I could see clearly through the gate. There was Christ hanging on the cross. Tears flowed from my eyes. I sobbed. My son just looked on, wondering what was happening to his dad. Questions were racing through my mind, too.

Why did this happen? What exactly was happening? I don't know.

The wafer was only partially eaten in my mouth. I was remembering Jesus and his death. Words of confession tumbled from my lips. "Lord Jesus, I believe. I believe. I do believe. I believe you are the Savior of the world, and there is no other." In that moment, every bit of doubt was completed erased.

WAS THIS A MINI-DAMASCUS road experience? What was so pent up within me? What released it? What happened to me? The only answer that makes sense to me is that I met Jesus, or rather, Jesus met me. My experience in the church was a divine encounter that dramatically brought my inner debate to an end. My renewed conviction blew past my skepticism, my cynicism, my arrogance, and all the other obstacles that had been cluttering my heart and mind and holding me back, on and off during the whole pilgrimage.

In that moment in Santiago de Compostela, the power of the experience was utterly compelling, even though I may not have fully understood it. I knew what I believed, perhaps more strongly than ever, and more involuntarily than ever. Finally, I blurted out while on my knees in front of the crucifix, "You are my only hope for eternal life!"

Then there was silence. There was nothing more to say.

Reflecting on the Journey

If you have ever had an unusually powerful spiritual experience, you probably know some of what I am talking about. Even if you can't point to one particular turning point in your faith, you can probably identify a stream of faith development in your life over the years.

> Take a moment for reflection. Was there a time when Jesus became more than a historical figure to you and became the object of your worship? If so, how would you describe the development of your faith before and since then? What are the most significant influences that have either helped or hurt your ability to know, love, and ultimately follow Jesus?

As I reflect upon my own spiritual journey, many significant experiences have helped me follow Christ better. When I was four years old, my mother taught me that Jesus died for my sins. I was raised to attend church and had a child's faith in Jesus, but I was more rebellious than most of my peers through my junior high years.

However, one night when I was maybe fourteen, I had an encounter with God that significantly altered my commitment to Christ.

One Sunday night my parents had left for church, only two blocks away from our house, walking ahead of me—or so they thought. Our church was so big that I could lie to them and tell them I was there, even if I skipped out. Instead of going to church, I sat on our front porch and had a cigarette. Ditching church, smoking cigarettes against my parents' rules, and doing it right on our own front porch without their knowing about it was a little thrill for me. It was also kind of stupid, because any of my neighbors could have seen me and told on me. But I wasn't thinking about that. I was just thinking about doing whatever I wanted to do.

It started to rain, and the same old empty feeling that had been bothering me came over me again. For some reason, I started talking to God. I said, "OK, God, if you want me to go to church, make it stop raining and I'll go." Well, it didn't stop raining. In fact, it started raining harder.

Then it hit me. Who was I to tell the Creator of the universe what to do? What right did I have to lay down conditions to God? Suddenly, I knew what I had to do. I threw down my cigarette. I walked the two blocks to church in the rain. By the time I arrived, I was soaking wet. I sat down in the back of the sanctuary just in time for the sermon.

That night the pastor preached a message about being a committed follower of Jesus Christ. He said he knew that someone was there who needed to respond to the message—a well-known rhetorical device for evangelists, to be sure. Nevertheless, I knew that someone was me. I had accepted Jesus as my Savior as a very young child, but that night I committed my life to follow Jesus as the leader, as Lord, of my life.

That experience was a significant turning point in my life. Instead of continuing to run around looking for new thrills, trying to make myself happy, I realized that life had a bigger purpose. I was tired of running from God and rebelling. I was lonely, empty, and longing for something more out of life, and I knew God was calling me to give my life to him. I knew I just couldn't say no to

God anymore. And, based on the preaching I heard, saying yes to God meant saying yes to Jesus.

My relationship with God changed that night, and my devotion to Jesus was sealed. I soon got involved in volunteer projects through my church, went to seminary after college, and have spent the past twenty-five years in full-time Christian ministry, teaching the Bible in college and seminary and now also writing and lecturing on Christian spirituality. Over the years, I have gone through stretches of doubting and questioning, especially as my study of philosophy and religion have opened my mind and given me alternative ways to think about God and human existence. Disappointing life experiences and personal suffering have confused me, challenged me, and caused me to rethink everything I took for granted as a teenager—from the reliability of the Bible to the divinity of Christ, the uniqueness of Christianity, the love of God, and the meaning of life. Yet, over and over again, I keep cycling back—not necessarily to the same exact beliefs, but to the same God. No matter how intriguing great religious figures from other religions or how much I respect the thinking of certain nonbelieving philosophers, I keep being drawn back to Christ. My faith has become more intellectually sophisticated and now fits better within a much broader worldview and understanding of faith development, but my heartfelt love for God and simple devotion to Christ keep being renewed at a deep level within me.[1]

If I had been raised a Hindu or Muslim or in some other culture or religion, I probably would have sought God through whatever vehicles were presented to me. However, I will never know what might have been. Instead, I know only how I have come to increasingly believe in, trust, and love the God of the Judeo-Christian tradition and Jesus, the one honored as the unique Son of God.

In Santiago de Compostela, my tearful confession of faith clearly fit into a stream of spiritual formation that had begun more than forty-five years earlier. Though not my first conversion to faith in Christ—I have had a series of significant spiritual turning points and reaffirmations of faith over the years—certainly it was one of the most powerful. I was seeing through the eyes of my soul, once again, that Jesus truly is the light of the world—the way, the truth, and the life for me. I was not simply coming to an intellectual conclusion about Christianity or reiterating an inherited faith. I was experiencing a compelling reaffirmation of my spiritual convictions, born from a lifetime of seeking God, studying Scripture and religion, and experiencing answers to prayer for greater wisdom, understanding, guidance, and transformation.

No one manipulated me. The setting was at first, actually, a bit off-putting rather than inspiring. To this Protestant, the sanctuary looked a bit like a pagan temple with statues of everyone but Jesus everywhere. I couldn't understand the speakers because they spoke in Spanish. The crowds and tourists were distracting. My tiredness may have made me more emotional, but my crankiness did not put me in a worshipful mood. I had simply been there, reading Scripture on the meaning of the Eucharist, and reflecting on some of the many issues I had struggled with over the previous five weeks on pilgrimage. Physically, I hardly participated in the service at all—I passed the peace and ate the wafer.

Surely psychologists could posit explanations for the various religious experiences I have had in my life. I have probably heard them all already. Ultimately, I must recognize that some of what I experienced was probably tied to my human frailty and the impact of seen and unseen forces at work in my mental and emotional state, dynamics I will never be able to fully comprehend. The rich symbolism of participating in a ritual honoring the life and sacrificial death of Jesus would have been very powerful at the end of a long pilgrimage and alone may have been enough to provoke my emotional response.

At the same time, my life experiences, my perception of reality, and my faith all suggest to me that more was going on in the cathedral than just a self-generated psychological phenomenon. At Santiago de Compostela, I believe I had yet one more encounter with the living God, and this God experience was linked in a powerful way to Jesus Christ.

Seeking Jesus, Finding Jesus

Prior to arriving in Santiago de Compostela, I had put much thought and prayer into my relationship with Jesus throughout the pilgrimage. Almost as an experiment, I had wondered while walking what I could do to better know and love Jesus Christ—as distinct from God as Father or the Holy Spirit. The more I thought about the question, the more I started noticing symbols of Jesus everywhere on the Camino—on hillsides, in the villages, around the public squares, and, of course, in every church.

Though in recent decades Spain has become decidedly more secular, it is still predominately a Roman Catholic country. James Michener, in *Iberia*, one of his several historical novels, discusses the thoroughly Catholic character of Spain. He focuses on the expulsion of the Moors in the fifteenth century through the mid-twentieth century, the time period covered by his book. I spoke to few individuals about their personal faith, but the many symbols and special rituals, alongside regular Mass and religious holidays, all suggest that Jesus Christ is important to the people of Spain, at least historically.

Christ's exalted status means, for example, crosses are displayed in public places in nearly every town. In some regions during Holy Week, elaborate outdoor rituals are carried on throughout the nights to express the meaning of Christ's passion and crucifixion. And in nearly every church, Christ is prominently displayed, hanging on the cross, usually in the front of the sanctuary, behind the altar, often above his mother Mary (who is regarded by Catholics as the Queen of Heaven and is usually depicted holding the Christ child on her lap). In addition, I sometimes found in a number of churches, when I poked around behind curtains and looked in various corners, a statue of the crucified Jesus in a glass casket affixed to poles and waiting for Good Friday when the people would parade it through the streets as a way to honor Christ and the extent of his sacrifice prior to Easter Sunday.

Everywhere I looked, symbols pointed me to Jesus Christ. Though in Catholic Spain he is depicted primarily on a cross, Christ is also portrayed in art, stained-glass windows, and sculptures. As is true wherever Christian symbolism is displayed, Jesus is held up variously as the judge of the world, the savior of those who put their faith in him, and the ultimate redeemer of the universe. As such, Christ symbolizes hope to believers, offering forgiveness for the past, guidance for the present, and promise for the future.

In many towns, I would spend time in the church there, sitting at length in front of the crucifix. The dark, cool sanctuary provided relief from the blistering midday summer heat. But even more, contemplating the visual depiction of Christ at the moment of his greatest personal sacrifice would powerfully engage my mind, my heart, and my spirit.

As a Protestant, I was used to seeing only an empty cross, symbolizing that the hope of Christ extends beyond his death for humanity to his resurrection. Yet Catholics portray Christ hanging on the cross to emphasize the ongoing power and benefit of Christ's sacrifice, which is ritually celebrated in the Mass. For me, both the empty cross and the crucifix move me similarly, because both communicate the extent of Christ's sacrificial love to me more than any other religious symbol. The visual depiction of his suffering and death, especially evident in the crucifix, reminds me that it cost Jesus a great deal to fulfill his purpose in life. By contemplating his sacrifice, made with real flesh and blood, I grasp better the extent of his love and devotion to God, whom he called Father. I can feel the intensity of his passion more fully. His commitment in the face of hostile opposition, culminating in his dying in order to remain faithful to God, overwhelms me—yet draws me to him more strongly than ever.

Thus, by contemplating the cross or crucifix, I move from knowing about Christ to knowing Christ better and loving him more. By reflecting on the many symbols and rituals found ubiquitously in Spain, I came to know Jesus more profoundly as hope—for all who put their faith in him and for me personally. On pilgrimage, I did not learn one thing about the Son of God that isn't already explained in Scripture, but seeking a deeper understanding and connection to Jesus through my experience profoundly deepened my appreciation and love for him and strengthened my devotion to him.

A couple of months after the pilgrimage, I had another powerful encounter with Jesus. I was visiting a Protestant cathedral in Lausanne, Switzerland. Built in the 1200s, it came under Reformed influence in the mid-1500s. I spent about an hour walking around looking at the stained-glass windows, thinking, and praying. I was about to leave when I realized that somehow I had overlooked the most prominently positioned window at the end of the church, behind the communion table. Under the figure in the window were the words, Jesus Christ Roi ("King," in French). Prominently seated on a throne, Christ was commanding the allegiance of believers.

I felt compelled to kneel and pray, "Lord Jesus, you are my King. What do you want me to do?" In the moments of silence that followed, I knew what I was being led to do. I experienced instant clarity and conviction. When I stopped making excuses or doubting myself, I felt strength and peace come from simply responding in obedience to my King.

What happened? I was seeking Christ by wandering through that sanctuary, and when I saw the image of Christ on the throne, I felt moved to specific prayer. I didn't come to know Christ better or love him more in this instance, as I had on other occasions. Rather, this time *my encounter with Jesus was helping me follow him better*. I was reconnecting with the Jesus I already knew and loved and contemplating his role as leader of my life. By opening my heart and focusing my attention intently on Christ in this way, a spiritual transaction took place. The Spirit drew me back to my calling and highest priority by reminding me of my priorities and encouraging me to stay focused. I gained new clarity and motivation to get back to my writing.

I am not on the Camino anymore, but I am continuing my spiritual pilgrimage. As I keep my eyes and heart open along the way, I keep meeting Jesus. I learn more about Jesus and come to know him better personally. My love continues to grow for him, and I am learning more about what following Jesus means. Even more important, the more I know and love Jesus, the more I want to follow.

Scripture for the Journey

When looking at Scripture both from a historical point of view and through the eyes of faith, which see the holy texts as inspired by God, the Bible is indispensable to knowing about Jesus, knowing Jesus personally, and following Jesus. The four Gospels in particular are our primary historical documents, albeit written in a first-century, pre-Enlightenment manner, which establish the historicity of Jesus and the beginnings of the early church. Furthermore, the various teachings and testimonies throughout the New Testament are foundational for Christian doctrine, moral living, spiritual growth, and the life of the church.

However, as New Testament scholar Wayne Meeks articulately points out in his recent monograph, *Christ Is the Question*, our available resources cannot provide enough information to gain a clear, consistent picture of Jesus.[2] All attempts over the centuries to create a biography of Jesus have failed. They always seem to reflect the biases of the writer and age in which they are written and depend on emphasizing some passages to the exclusion of others or on harmonizing differences in ways that do violence to one or more texts. Too many gaps and conflicts between especially the Synoptic Gospels (Matthew, Mark, and Luke) and John leave the historian and seeker alike with many unanswerable questions.

So, where do we go from here? Meeks argues that instead of relying solely on researching historical documents to know Jesus, each individual, community, and generation must engage personally in the question of who Jesus is for them. Coming to know Jesus is not an intellectual, historical research project but results from an ongoing, dynamic spiritual process, rooted in history as well as requiring personal and communal involvement. In other words, the biblical narratives and testimonies call us to seek our own personal connection with (knowledge of) Christ that goes beyond collecting facts and creating syntheses to engaging our hearts and loyalties.

When we look to Scripture for insight into Jesus and how we can know Jesus, we immediately discover that Jesus Christ is either the subject or the underlying assumption of the entire New Testament. A postmodern approach to Scripture helps us recognize Scripture as a pastiche of testimonies, which help us understand the meaning of Jesus's life and how people can relate to Jesus experientially. Rather than just reading biblical texts to try to piece together clues about what happened historically, then, we can look at the twenty-seven books of the New Testament as a collection of testimonials reflecting the thoughts and experiences of individual Christians and those of first-century Christian communities. The Bible, therefore, helps us not primarily by providing a collection of facts and ideas to be intellectually noted and subscribed to but by pointing us toward Jesus and helping us see what a relationship with God through Jesus might look like.[3]

Seeing Jesus

To appreciate the testimonies of biblical writers, we must try to see the Jesus they are portraying for us and what he meant to them. All of the Gospel writers, in particular, want their readers to know that Jesus was an extraordinary spiritual leader who fulfilled the expectations of the Hebrew Scriptures and reinterpreted contemporary understanding of how to love and serve God faithfully. He was devoted to serving God's purposes, was full of compassion, performed miracles, cast out demons, and taught with great authority. He came into repeated, hostile conflicts with the religious authorities and ultimately was put to death by the Romans. For each Gospel writer, the most amazing turn of events of all was that he was resurrected from the dead.

To signify Jesus's greatness and uniqueness, all four Gospel writers referred to him as the Son of God and Son of Man, probably allusions to Hebrew messianic figures. Jesus had a unique mission, which he fulfilled through his preaching, miraculous healings and other displays of power, death, and resurrection. The various writers' express this mission differently, with considerable overlap, too, but they all agree that he was sent by God to accomplish something very significant.

For example, both Matthew and Mark quote Jesus's saying, "The Son of Man did not come to be served, but to serve, and to give his life as a ransom for many" (Matt. 20:28; Mark 10:45 NIV). All three Synoptic Gospels describe Jesus's mission as primarily to the lost of Israel, and Luke expressly quotes Jesus as saying, "For the Son of Man came to seek and to save what was lost" (Luke 19:10 NIV). John, with all the other New Testament writers, clearly saw the resurrected Jesus as the Savior for the whole world and not only Israel (John 3:16; 4:42).

John poetically portrays Jesus's unique relationship to God and significant purpose by describing him as God incarnate (in the flesh), who brought divine light into the world and provides salvation for all who believe in him. He writes:

> The true light, which enlightens everyone, was coming into the world. He was in the world, and the world came into being through him; yet the world did not know him. He came to what was his own, and his own people did not accept him. But to all who received him, who believed in his name, he gave power to become children of God, . . . "For God so loved the world that he gave his only Son, so that everyone who believes in him may not perish but may have eternal life. Indeed, God did not send the Son into the world to condemn the world, but in order that the world might be saved through him" (John 1:9–12; 3:16–17).

In the experience of John and his community, no one was like Jesus or has done what Jesus does. Jesus said of himself in John: "I am the way, and the truth, and the life. No one comes to the Father except through me" (John 14:6).

When looking over all the testimony of the New Testament, we can see that in some way that exceeds our ability to fully grasp, the apostles came to view Jesus in a unique Father-Son relationship. In John's language, Jesus was God's "only Son"[4] (3:16). Though the title "the son of God" was used in ancient Israel at times to refer to a special regent of God, without reference to divinity, the early church ultimately interpreted "Son of God" to refer to Jesus's unique identity as both fully divine and fully human. He was more than the sum of the roles he played, commonly summarized as a combination of prophet, priest, and king. He was also divine and as such, to know Jesus is to know God the Father (John 1:1–3; 14:8–11; Col. 1:15–20; Matt. 11:27).[5] The apostles knew this Jesus as *the* Son of God and the Savior of the world who shows us the way, speaks the truth, and leads all those who put their faith in him to eternal life.

Knowing and Loving Jesus

We can also infer from the testimonies of Scripture that the apostles and other biblical writers came to know and love Jesus personally in profound ways. Matthew, for example, implies that by coming to know Jesus, believers came to know God the Father and found true rest for their souls. Matthew 11 records Jesus's words: "All things have been committed to me by my Father. No one knows the Son except the Father, and no one knows the Father except the Son and those to whom the Son chooses to reveal him. Come to me, all you that are weary and burdened, and I will give you rest. Take my yoke upon you and learn from me, for I am gentle and humble in heart, and you will find rest for your souls. For my yoke is easy and my burden is light" (vv. 27–30 NIV).

When we read Jesus's words also as the personal testimony of Matthew (and those who shaped his Gospel), we can infer that Jesus had an extremely powerful impact on those who put their faith in him. Similarly, in a verse in John that we just looked at, Jesus says, "I am the way, and the truth, and the life. No one comes to the Father except through me" (John 14:6). The style of writing is very different, but John is also communicating that in his relationship with Jesus, he has found what he was most looking for—the way, the truth, and life. Clearly, these early Christians wanted later generations to know Jesus as they knew him—as a source of spiritual rest who can meet their deepest needs and can reliably lead them to (eternal) life.

Not surprisingly, then, those who knew Jesus also loved him. We see this phenomenon expressed powerfully in 1 Peter, where we read how much love believers had for Jesus, even in the midst of suffering. Peter wrote: "Though you have not seen him, you love him; and even though you do not see him now, you believe in him and are filled with an inexpressible and glorious joy, for you are receiving the goal of your faith, the salvation of your souls" (1 Pet. 1:8–9 NIV).

Peter is describing knowing Jesus through both faith and experience. His readers had never seen Jesus, but they believed he came from the Father, died and was resurrected for them, and was their

Lord and Christ (Messiah). In their experience, God the Father had given them "new birth" leading to "living hope" and great joy (1:3–6). These beliefs and experiences naturally led to heartfelt love for Jesus Christ, as the story told in the Gospels of a woman who bathed Jesus's feet with her tears illustrates. She wept over him, and then wiped his feet with her hair. As Jesus explains, she loved him greatly because she had been given (forgiven) so much (Luke 7: 36–48).

Following Jesus

Finally, the testimonies of Scripture show us that as believers came to know and love Jesus, they also became devoted to him. They followed him by obeying him, serving God's purposes, and continuing his mission, even at great personal sacrifice (John 10:27; 12:26; 14:23; 17:1–26; 1 John 2:3–4).

Matthew expresses the extent of the apostles' devotion to Christ and the strength of their bond with him in the final words of his Gospel. From these three verses we can infer something about what spiritual faith and faithfulness was like for these early Christians: Jesus had become their ultimate authority, they were committed to continuing his mission in the world, and they were depending upon their ongoing relationship with him. Jesus said: "All authority in heaven and on earth has been given to me. Therefore go and make disciples of all nations, baptizing them in the name of the Father and of the Son and of the Holy Spirit, and teaching them to obey everything I have commanded you. And surely I am with you always, to the very end of the age" (Matt. 28:18–20 NIV).

Early Christians were so devoted to Jesus that they were willing to give up a great deal in order to follow him. The original disciples literally gave up most of their possessions, trusting in Jesus's promise of the kingdom of God and eternal life in fellowship with God (Mark 10:28–30). They also had to "take up their crosses," which probably involved daily sacrificial service and suffering.[6] According to tradition, ten of them ultimately gave their life too, being martyred for their allegiance to Jesus.

Whatever picking up one's cross might have meant in practice for any individual, we can discern a deeper spiritual truth in what the apostles are telling us by recording this portion of Jesus's teaching. By relinquishing all claims to their life and following Jesus, they discovered that they were really saving their life. Mark, along with all the Gospel writers in one form or another, recounts a teaching of Jesus to express this spiritual truth: "[Jesus] called the crowd with his disciples, and said to them, 'If any want to become my followers, let them deny themselves and take up their cross and follow me. For those who want to save their life will lose it, and those who lose their life for my sake, and for the sake of the gospel, will save it. For what will it profit them to gain the whole world and forfeit their life? Indeed, what can they give in return for their life?'" (Mark 8:34–37).

Thus, the early Christians are showing us that knowing, loving, and following Jesus involves a strange mixture of receiving life from him and giving up life to follow him. On one hand, being in relationship with Jesus leads us to know God the Father better and relieves our spiritual angst and weariness with life. On the other hand, following Jesus demands everything from us. We are offered what we most want spiritually and are called to give up everything else that we know and want to cling to inasmuch as it stands as a competitor to true allegiance to God and Christ. These two teachings may seem to be paradoxical, yet both are important dimensions of vital Christian spirituality.

For John, serving Christ is not in any way at odds with experiencing the spiritual blessings of knowing Christ. Rather, serving is inseparable from experiencing blessings. Following, obeying, and bearing fruit all flow from truly knowing and loving God the Father and Jesus (John 14:15, 21, 23–24; 17:3). In John 15, Jesus explains: "I am the true vine, and my Father is the vinegrower. He removes every branch in me that bears no fruit. Every branch that bears fruit he prunes to make it bear more fruit. You have already been cleansed by the word that I have spoken to you. Abide in me as I abide in you. Just as the branch cannot bear fruit by itself unless it abides in the vine, neither can you unless you abide in me. I am the vine, you are the branches. Those who abide in me and I in them bear much fruit, because apart from me you can do nothing" (vv. 1–5).

John is expressing spiritual truth he and the Christians of his community experienced. As they came to know and trust Jesus personally, they began to experience greater joy, love, and peace (see John 13:34–35; 14:27; 15:11; 16:33; 17:13). They also received new purpose in life—to serve Christ's purposes—and an ability to obey Christ's commands through their intimate relationship with God, the Father, Son, and Holy Spirit.

Jesus explained the relationship between abiding in him and obeying him this way: "My Father is glorified by this, that you bear much fruit and become my disciples. As the Father has loved me, so I have loved you; abide in my love. If you keep my commandments, you will abide in my love, just as I have kept my Father's commandments and abide in his love. I have said these things to you so that my joy may be in you, and that your joy may be complete. This is my commandment, that you love one another as I have loved you" (John 15:8–12).

John knew the love of the Father through the love of Jesus. However, he did not consider knowing Jesus and experiencing his love as an end in itself. We are loved that we may love. Perhaps John and the others learned from experience that when they did not let the love of God flow through them to one another, their experience of the love of Jesus for themselves was choked off. Perhaps he wanted readers to realize that in order to continue to experience divine love as God intends for us we must share that love with others.

In all, the New Testament is full of stories, teaching, and correspondence that tell us a lot about Jesus and about what early Christians experienced in their relationship with him. Their lives were transformed as they came to truly see, know, and love him, culminating in the ultimate reorientation in life—committing themselves to follow him. They believed that Jesus had a unique connection to God the Father and revealed the Father to us. They welcomed him as the one sent by God to bring believers into an eternal relationship with God. They found existential relief and peace with God through a relationship with Jesus and knew the love of God through Jesus's love. They followed him by placing allegiance to him above all other loyalties and by serving his purposes, sometimes even at great personal cost. They were filled with love and joy through their relationship with Jesus and lived fruitfully by maintaining a close relationship with Jesus. As they learned to let God's love to them flow through them to others, they continued to experience God's love in its fullness in their life.

Next Steps

Scripture shows us the way to Jesus and what a relationship with Jesus might look like. However, each of us must find our own particular path by following the signposts well marked out in the Bible, by listening to those who have known Jesus, and by picking up our feet to seek and follow Jesus ourselves.

Follow the Signposts

There is no substitute for reading Scripture in order to learn about Jesus from those who first knew him. Countless Bible study resources exist to help seekers and believers grasp the major teachings and testimonies of the Bible. Specific resources can easily be found in any Christian bookstore on the life and ministry of Jesus in particular.

The four canonical Gospels offer four different perspectives on the life and ministry of Jesus of Nazareth. Substantial agreement exists among the Synoptic Gospels, while John's Jesus speaks in metaphorical language, in long speeches, and seems at points to follow an itinerary different from the Synoptics. Other New Testament writers show hardly any interest whatsoever in Jesus's earthly life but focus on the meaning of his death, resurrection, and ongoing presence in the lives of believers through the Holy Spirit.

Academically, you can study the different ways the various writers of the New Testament portrayed Jesus as well as note common language used and important names, titles, and themes related to Jesus that keep reappearing. Then, in addition to gaining a solid intellectual knowledge of biblical stories and teachings about Jesus, what is most important as you read the biblical texts is to let God show you what you most need to see about him. You can pray for eyes to truly see Jesus in them and to see what God wants to reveal to you about him that may be particularly valuable, given your stage of spiritual development or particular needs and calling.

You will also get more out of the Bible if you try to understand both the author's intention in writing and your intention in reading. For example, as a unique genre of literature among ancient histori-cal writing, each Gospel tells the story of Jesus for a purpose: to lead readers to encounter the living, risen Christ and to faith and disci-pleship. Each writer in his own way wanted readers to come to know the Jesus that lived, died, and was resurrected in ways that would lead to personal belief in and devotion to him. John offers the clear-est explanation of his purpose in writing his Gospel when he con-cludes the account of Jesus's life this way: "Jesus did many other miraculous signs in the presence of his disciples, which are not recorded in this book. But these are written that you may believe that Jesus is the Christ, the Son of God, and that by believing you may have life in his name" (John 20:30–31 NIV).

In the epistles of the New Testament, most authors are writing to churches that need encouragement to stand strong in their faith, teaching to understand Christ and discipleship better, or specific instruction on dealing with various issues. Every writer refers explic-itly or alludes to Jesus, but none is interested in giving details about the earthly life of Jesus of Nazareth, referenced frequently in the Gospels and Acts. The writers of the epistles want to help their read-ers better know and follow Jesus Christ, the risen Savior and Lord. Through the letters the apostles wrote to various churches, you can learn a lot about the devotion early Christians felt to Jesus—who they knew him to be, what roles he played in their lives, and what putting one's trust in him truly means.

Knowing why you are reading is important, too. What we bring to the text often affects what we take from it. Ask yourself what you are looking for when you read. Do your goals line up with the author's intention, as best as you can determine it from the resources available to you? Are you open to the Holy Spirit surprising you with meaning that you might not have considered? Are you open to letting the Spirit speak to you very personally?

Listen to Those Who Have Known Jesus

In addition to listening to the testimony of New Testament writers, seek insight into Jesus Christ from those who have known him in past centuries and in the present. Especially seek out those you trust and who have shown in their lives signs of truly knowing and following Jesus.

One of the reasons I grew in my faith as a teenager was because of the influence of Mike, an older Christian, who shared his own faith story with me, reached out to me, and modeled following Christ for me. Since then, I have read many books, studied the writings of early church fathers and other theologians, and talked about spirituality with many people, all of whom have opened my mind to various possibilities of how one could relate to God and follow Jesus.

I don't expect to have the same experiences as everyone I meet. I also don't assume that someone's interpretation of his or her spiritual thoughts, feelings, or experience automatically gives me reliable information for my own relationship with Christ. But I listen. I reflect on what I hear. I compare what others say with what I find in Scripture. Some people inform me, some inspire me, some confuse me, some leave me cold, but regardless of my response to them, my encounters with other people of faith stimulate and enhance my own thinking and relationship to God in Christ.

Seek Jesus for Yourself, Then Follow

Ultimately, to cross the bridge from knowing about Jesus to knowing Jesus (which will lead to following him), you will need to be open to developing a personal relationship with Jesus. You will need to move from thinking about who Jesus was in history to deciding (even if provisionally) who Jesus is for you today. I have been finding my relationship with Jesus deepening as I have started asking the Holy Spirit to help me see Jesus for who he is, to draw me closer to him, and to lead me to follow him more faithfully.

Once when I was in my thirties, I had an extremely powerful experience of seeing Jesus through new eyes. I had been reading a well-known scholar's interpretation of who Jesus was. I was assuming, as usual, that there would be significant biases and limitations to his perspective, yet I let his words speak to me in the force of a personal testimony. This scholar portrayed Jesus as a sixties-style social activist who died because he stood up for justice and threatened the religious establishment.

What made this experience more than just learning about Jesus (or just learning about someone's opinion of Jesus) was that these words penetrated my heart in a deeply personal way. As I absorbed the Scripture-based picture that was being painted of Jesus's compassion, service, teaching, preaching, and giving of himself, culminating in the ultimate self-sacrifice, his own life, I suddenly felt completely unworthy of Jesus. The words had hit a nerve. I realized how very different Jesus was from me. Yet he was, at the same time, everything I admired and hoped to be as a spiritual leader devoted to God. In a new way, I was able to see his greatness that day. I saw that I could never be his peer (an absurdly vain thought, I know), and that at best I could worship him and seek to follow him in my own imperfect, stumbling way. I began to tremble.

Spiritual transformation was taking place; I was moving to a deeper appreciation of who Jesus was and is, and my devotion to him was instantly growing. I did little to make it happen but show up; my heart and mind was open to seeing Jesus in a fresh way, and I sat down to read the book. Through the eyes of faith, I recognized that the Holy Spirit was answering my prayers to help me see and appreciate Christ better. Ever since that moment, even in the midst of ongoing intellectual questions and ups and downs in my spiritual life, I have felt a deeper and more binding devotion to Jesus that has not gone away.

Sometimes the most important thing you can do to grow spiritually is to make the effort to show up—physically, mentally, and emotionally—where you can learn more about Jesus Christ, and ask the Holy Spirit to help you experience Christ in some way. Do you have a sense of what the next steps might be for you in developing your relationship and devotion to Jesus? I am not talking about trying to produce faith or control the encounter with him. I am talking about making a concrete effort to seek him in whatever ways draw you and to be open to new understanding, experience, attitudes, and responses.

For Further Reflection

Monday, April 21, 2008. Chartres, France. On the south side of Chartres Cathedral, a larger than life statue of Le Beau Dieu (The Beautiful God) is mounted on a pillar between two large doors, the middle set of three entrances. The figure is Jesus, holding a Bible near his heart in his left hand and holding up his right hand to bless others. Alongside him are twelve apostles (less Judas, plus Paul), six on each side, each holding the instrument of his martyrdom, except for John who was not killed for his loyalty to Jesus. Most days while we're here, I pause at this spot to contemplate the beauty and greatness of Jesus and the devotion and sacrifice of the apostles. Sometimes I just stand there in silence, waiting for whatever I might think or feel because I opened my heart to Christ in that moment. Sometimes I pray, asking Jesus to help me see something I need to see, to answer a question that is troubling me, or simply to draw me close to him. I may stay only a few seconds, rarely more than five or ten minutes. Often, I leave inspired or encouraged. I'm always glad I've been there.

Use the reflection above and the following questions to guide your journal writing. Discuss your thoughts, feelings, and intentions with some fellow pilgrims from your spiritual community who are seeking to know, love, and follow Jesus better.

- How much do you know about Jesus? How would you describe your relationship with Jesus? Which of the following statements best fit you:

  I know about Jesus.
  I know Jesus through personal experience.
  I am devoted to Jesus in my heart and mind.
  I love Jesus and want to know and follow him better.

- What significant experiences have you had that have helped you know Jesus better? If you haven't had any or many, how would you like to know Jesus?
- What ways to know Jesus better are you drawn to? What are you going to do to respond to the desires of your heart and questions of your mind?
- What help or support do you need from others as you pursue a deeper relationship with Jesus? Whom will you ask? When will you ask?
- What other thoughts or reactions were prompted by this chapter on knowing, loving, and following Jesus? What specifically do you intend to do differently or more consistently?

CHAPTER 7

Spirit-Led Living

~

WEDNESDAY, JULY 19, 2006. DAY 26. FONCEBADON. Today we walked nearly thirty kilometers (eighteen miles) to Foncebadon, a small, decrepit village on the side of a mountain. Not a very exciting destination. Nor was it a very good day from the outset.

We had just come off a wonderful few days of walking, but this one did not start out well. My family was already calling me Mr. Grumphead behind my back before we had walked even a few blocks. I had slept terribly all night long, tossing and turning due to light shining in my eyes. The heat was oppressive and I was self-conscious, sleeping only in shorts in a room full of people in close proximity. Then when it was time to leave in the morning, Jill and one of my sons got mad at me because I wasn't ready precisely at the time agreed upon. Instead of appreciating that I had been delayed by helping my other son and paying for the breakfast, they were mad that I was holding them up. I felt judged and under-appreciated. Rather than try to explain, I began sulking and walking by myself.

Then it started raining. By the time we got to our attic room at the end of the day, in a nearly deserted, broken-down village— seemingly ready for demolition—I was tired, sore, wet, hungry, and crabby. The day had not been very fun, and we were stuck in place with lousy food and uncomfortable accommodations. However, it could have been much worse.

Along the way, something significant happened that changed my perspective considerably. As I walked in solitude early in the day, I had asked God to help me connect to the Spirit better. I asked for grace to let go of my anger and to be filled with more love, joy, and peace. I felt so miserable, I was desperate for God's intervention. So I asked for help.

And it worked! Or something worked.

My anger somehow dissipated. I stopped getting rained on, even while my clothes were getting completely soaked. And through the experience of shifting winds and moods, rain spurts and dry spells, I think I gained new insight into how the Holy Spirit works.

As I trudged along in the drizzle and rain, I noticed times when rain clouds were quickly swept away from us by the wind, and it stopped raining. At other times when the wind was quiet, rain clouds hovered overhead and the rain kept falling on us. I started to look forward to when the wind would blow because I knew it might bring relief from the rain.

As I observed the different weather patterns, it hit me. The Holy Spirit is a lot like the wind and the rain clouds like my own self-oriented and counterproductive impulses and emotional reactions. When I ask God for help with an open mind and heart, the Spirit just might chase away my anger and foul mood. When I don't pray or I want to nurse my angry or hurt feelings, there is no movement of the Spirit. The clouds hang there and I get more and more wet and unhappy.

Reflecting on the Journey

My encounter with the rain, the wind, and the Spirit taught me that God can be truly present to me in my distress and anguish and can transform my heart and mind. However, I cannot control the Spirit any more than I can control the wind. At times I experience the fruit of the Spirit—love, joy, peace, patience, kindness, goodness, faithfulness, gentleness, and self-control—and at other times one or more these qualities seems completely absent. I don't seem to permanently possess these attributes, but they come and go depending on the quality of my connection to the Spirit at any given moment.

How have you experienced the Holy Spirit working in your life? Not, what have you read or been taught about the Spirit of God, but when and how have you actually sensed that God was producing something in you that was not your own creation? When did the Spirit seem most powerful or most helpful?

In Spanish art, as elsewhere, the Holy Spirit is often depicted as a dove. The image comes from the Gospel stories of Jesus's baptism. In all four accounts, the evangelists describe the Holy Spirit's descending in the form of a dove and alighting on Jesus. The dove represented both God's approval and God's filling of Jesus with the Spirit. As a result of such biblical narratives, the Holy Spirit is often thought of as the dove of God's presence, internal peace, love, presence, forgiveness, or approval.

I also experience the Spirit as the powerful wind of God. I cannot see it or control it, but I can sometimes feel the Spirit's presence. Sometimes I can see the effects of the Spirit, changing the mood of a group or leading us to consensus or new insight. Jesus likened the Spirit to the wind that "blows where it chooses" to explain how people are spiritually renewed and led to eternal life (John 3:6–8). He seemed to be saying that the Holy Spirit is God's wind of change to transform our heart, our mind, and every other aspect of our life, which flows according to God's will, in God's timing, with purposes that are often beyond our ability to know or understand. The result is eternal life for believers, but the process and experience often seem mysterious.

As I walked across Spain and thought about the Holy Spirit, I couldn't help but notice the gap between the transformation through the Spirit that Scripture seems to promise us and what I could actually see in my life. Worse, no matter how strong my faith, at times my sinful impulses and the weaknesses of my personality not only are alive and well but also feel like the strongest forces in my life. If the Spirit is powerfully at work in me, then why do I feel so disconnected from the Holy Spirit at times?

I am not alone here. No matter what moments of spiritual inspiration or transformation any of us have experienced, most of us, day-to-day, feel very, well, normal. As far as I can tell, most Christians I know (including myself) act and react more or less like everyone else, believer or not. Now, I have witnessed significant devotion to God and others in people of faith, sometimes over a lifetime and sometimes in moments of self-sacrificial action, generosity, compassion, or tremendous grace in the face of unfair or even cruel abuse from others. Yet, sometimes, these same exemplary individuals also seem capable of degenerating to the same selfish or unkind behavior that any of us displays in our weakest moments. I find myself wondering, what *ongoing* difference does the Holy Spirit really make in the life of a follower of Christ? Is Spirit-led transformation illusory or real? If real, are the Spirit's effects transitory or cumulative?

When I start paying attention to all the pain and suffering in the world—what we bring on ourselves and what we cause others—I realize how important these questions truly are. Our ability to be the people we aspire to be, to create and maintain loving relationships, to grow, and to contribute meaningfully to the well-being of others—and to stop contributing to the pain and suffering of others—depends on coming to grips with human capacity for evil and on understanding how the Spirit truly works (and doesn't) to help us be at our best.

The Depth of the Problem

When I think about all the literature I have been exposed to, I realize how often writers grapple with good and evil. From ancient times, story after story, historical account after historical account, poem after poem portray our ability and inclination to hurt one another and ourselves. Tales of the struggle between good and evil, whether tragedies or comedies, are popular because they portray what each of us lives every day, both within ourselves and in our relationships with others. We can identify with the powerlessness, fear, and horror often associated with the inter- and intrahuman struggle, and we love a happy ending that gives us relief or hope for ourselves.

Furthermore, watching my mother lose her battle with Alzheimer's, friends succumb to addictions, and caring individuals have affairs and leave their spouses, I have been especially frightened by how much humans can degenerate. In *The Metamorphosis*, Franz Kafka depicts how normal human beings who are not paying attention to their life choices can actually devolve over time. In this novella, Gregor, the protagonist, wakes one morning to discover that he has been transformed into a hideous bug of some kind. The story has been interpreted variously, but no matter what the author intended, Kafka has vividly depicted how human beings, through a series of choices made over time, can eventually become something quite repulsive to themselves and others.

In an even more disturbing way, Joseph Conrad raises the specter of human capacity for evil in his disturbing novel, *Heart of Darkness*. In the story we learn that Mr. Kurtz had gone as an idealist to what is now known as the Democratic Republic of Congo. When he left, he was a sick, degenerated, savage man who had become captive to his evil impulses. The story explores the evil (the darkness) that lies within even the most noble of human hearts and what can happen when it is left unchecked. Given the right conditions and lack of safeguards, Conrad seems to be saying that humans will degenerate morally and spiritually, doing abominable things to one another and to themselves. As Kurtz lay dying on the boat heading home from Africa, he summed up the depth of the dreadfulness he had experienced and participated in, in his now famous words, "The horror. The horror."

Sadly but not surprisingly, history is full of dark moments when suddenly an individual or whole community "snaps" and brutal genocide, cruel abuse, or greed-inspired exploitation takes place. In just the past couple of decades alone, the world has seen the horrors of genocides in Serbia, Rwanda, and Sudan; the vicious raping and mutilations in Sierra Leone, Congo and other African countries; terrorism in the United States, Europe, Africa, and Asia; and the use torture. We all recoil from such atrocities, but we must face the fact that human beings have been doing the same kinds of things since the beginning of history, and incidents of great hatred, violence, and cruelty keep occurring in various parts of the world with no end in sight.

In our more honest moments, many of us can see how capable of wrongdoing and evil we ourselves are. We may not have participated in egregious acts of violence against others, but all of us struggle every day with impulses, reactions, desires, attitudes, and choices that are self-serving, punitive, judgmental, hateful, or simply contrary to the life of love, joy, and peace that Christ envisioned for us.

I don't paint this sobering picture of the human condition out of pessimism or to discourage anyone, but to be honest about what is real in human experience. On pilgrimage, even with the best of intentions, I often disappointed myself by how I was acting and reacting. We had a great trip, but over and over again I saw in myself and others selfishness, lack of compassion, harshness, greed, jealousy, envy, anxiety, irrational fear, self-indulgence, and any number of other attitudes, actions, or reactions that seemed contrary to the leading of the Holy Spirit. There I was, a highly educated, Bible-believing, Spirit-indwelled, well-meaning follower of Christ who nonetheless kept being tripped up by the same human foibles as everyone else.

Side by side within me were joyful and surprising gifts of the Holy Spirit and experiences of my same-old, same-old self. While walking, I found myself spending a lot of time looking at what was really going on in my heart, mind, and life. To be honest, I was also trying to figure out if there was any hope for me, or anyone else, for that matter.

Scripture for the Journey

Scripture has a lot to say about the inner conflict between good and evil that we all experience. Biblical writers help us understand humans' propensity to be self-defeating and hurtful to others, while at the same time they hold up the mysterious and transforming work of the Holy Spirit as the one great source of hope for humanity.[1]

On the positive side, the outpouring of the Holy Spirit on a group of gathered believers in Jerusalem on Pentecost (Acts 2:1–21) signaled a new era in God's way of relating to human beings. Salvation was no longer only a future hope but was a present reality through the baptism and indwelling of the Holy Spirit. The Holy Spirit cleanses us from sin and enables us to resist temptations and to live a more righteous, fruitful life. Through the Holy Spirit, believers are given divine power to actually live more like God.[2]

Yet, at the same time, no matter how powerful one's encounter with the Spirit, there is always room to experience the transforming power of the Spirit in greater degrees. Thus, Paul frequently prayed for fellow believers to keep growing spiritually. When writing to the Ephesians, for instance, he asked that God's Spirit would strengthen them and increase their knowledge of (meaning "experience" of) Christ's love. He wrote: "I pray that, according to the riches of his glory, he may grant that you may be strengthened in your inner being with power through his Spirit, and that Christ may dwell in your hearts through faith, as you are being rooted and grounded in love. I pray that you may have the power to comprehend, with all the saints, what is the breadth and length and height and depth, and to know the love of Christ that surpasses knowledge, so that you may be filled with all the fullness of God" (Eph. 3:16–19).

So, with all this going for us through the Holy Spirit, why do we still seem to have so much difficulty experiencing a transformed life? If the Holy Spirit offers believers fellowship with God and divine power, why do believers so often just plod along exhibiting only modest signs of transformation and even periodically showing signs of regressive behavior?

Why Is Being Led by the Spirit So Hard?

In a word, the biblical explanation for our lack of Spirit-led living is *sin*—the cause and persistent effect of a world gone wrong, as played out in individuals, families, communities, and nations. In discussing the power of sin, the apostle Paul explains that our "flesh"—all the normal, self-centered, God-resistant, harmful impulses known to humanity—undermines our ability to live by the Holy Spirit. Paul explains that apart from the help of the Spirit, we are at the mercy of sin's power (Rom. 7:14–23). With help from the Spirit, we can say no to sin, though we still may succumb to its allure (Rom. 8:1–14). The result of sin's influence, the more we yield to it, is that we are dragged further and further away from God and the life Christ envisioned for us.

Further, Paul explains, the whole human race has reaped the consequences of our ancestors' rebellion against God. As a result, human beings have every kind of "wickedness, evil, greed, and depravity. [We] are full of envy, murder, strife, deceit and malice.

[We] are gossips, slanderers, God haters, insolent, arrogant and boastful; [we] invent ways of doing evil; [we] disobey [our] parents; [we] are senseless, faithless, heartless, ruthless" (Rom. 1:29–31 NIV).

Likewise, in his letter to the Galatians, Paul wrote about some of the more obvious acts of the flesh: "sexual immorality, impurity and debauchery; idolatry and witchcraft; hatred, discord, jealousy, fits of rage, selfish ambition, dissensions, factions and envy; drunkenness, orgies, and the like" (Gal. 5:19–21 NIV).

Here is the point: While Paul teaches that the power of sin was broken through Jesus's death and resurrection and that through faith in Christ and the indwelling Holy Spirit believers are no long slaves to sin (Rom. 8), we are still human beings, affected by the same contaminated spiritual DNA passed down to us through the generations, and we still live in a world thoroughly saturated by sin. Scholars differ as to whether the Holy Spirit restores believers to their original, pre-sin condition (like Adam and Eve before their fall into sin) or simply cleanses us from the consequences of sin before God, making us both justified and still sinners simultaneously.[3] In either case, while the Holy Spirit gives us the power to live new lives, the old life keeps calling to us every day, and we must continually deal with the ongoing psychological, emotional, and social effects of our sin-tainted upbringing and the world in which we live. Add to these factors the reality of spiritual warfare, which Paul describes as a battle waged by invisible, external evil forces—rulers, authorities, cosmic powers of this dark world, and spiritual forces of evil in the heavenly realms—against believers and all of creation (see Eph. 6:10–20), it is no wonder we struggle.

So what does all this mean for the those of us who want to live by the leading of the Holy Spirit but are continually struggling with sinful instincts, personal failure, inconsistency, and lack of spiritual vitality, in a sin-contaminated world? First, being torn between two instincts means we are normal. There are no Christians who do not have the same struggle. Second, our predicament throws us upon the grace of God as our only hope for forgiveness, salvation, spiritual growth, and personal transformation. Third, as we discussed in chapter 4, we must come to grips with what we are up against—our sinful nature and the forces of darkness in the world—and take seriously the challenge we face in trying to change our lives and in following the Spirit's leading. Then we need to adjust our expectations of how the Spirit works in our lives and do our part to make the most of what the Spirit offers.

What Can We Expect from the Spirit?

At one point in my life, I supposed that having the Holy Spirit meant that I would be magically delivered from the temptations of sin and the forces of evil in the world. I assumed I could live a holy and Spirit-filled life and would become completely transformed.

I never actually thought about my expectations in this way, but perhaps I thought that being a Christian meant that my life experience would be just the opposite of Gregor's in *The Metamorphosis*. Instead of degenerating to become an insect, I would experience not only regeneration but complete transformation to become like Christ. Perhaps I expected that although I had begun my faith journey as a fallible, corrupted human being, I would become, over time, less and less of a person until I finally became, well, what? What is not a person but really, really good, perfect, and wonderful? A god? I would never have said that I expected to become a god or the same as God, but what was I really expecting when I prayed to be filled with the fruit of the Spirit day after day? I wanted to be completely and irrevocably transformed.

Indeed, complete transformation into the image of Jesus Christ is the ultimate goal of the Christian life, according to the apostle Paul (Rom. 8:29). The problem is, none of us experiences that in this lifetime. It is an unrealistic expectation.

What is realistic, then? That you, I, and the rest of the human race will continue to be human as long as we live. That means we will continue to be subject to all the forces that Paul warns Christians to guard against. We may certainly expect our lives to be different because of the presence of the Holy Spirit—but, and here is the main point, *the new life available to us stems from the Spirit, not from us*. Apart from the Spirit's ongoing filling and leading, and our receiving and following, we will sink back into the same normal human life we have always known—for better and for worse.

Normally, people change slowly, if at all, throughout their lifetime. Human beings are capable of change; with God's help some of us make very significant changes, while others change more modestly or in the wrong direction. We may refine our style, with some becoming more polished, others more vocal, others courageous, and so forth. Some of us may mellow and become less abrasive, while others may learn to stand up for themselves better and actually become more willing to confront others when needed. Sometimes we become more forgiving and understanding, sometimes less so. In any number of ways, we can observe changes in ourselves and others, while at the same time be struck by how little some things and people ever change.

Furthermore, as we age, we also can observe that sometimes positive changes seem to reverse themselves. Hardening of the arteries, mental deterioration, loss of impulse control, and other types of deterioration commonly occur in one form or another, sometimes affecting our ability to experience or display the fruit of the Spirit. Such regression does not necessarily indicate a moral fault or spiritual deficiency but is simply a phenomenon of human existence. Some Christians become even more saintly in old age, others more brittle and cranky, but all of us are limited by our human frailties that may affect the vibrancy of our spiritual life. And in the end, we all die, because that is what human beings do.

Paul taught that in the end our bodies will go to the grave "in dishonor" and "weakness" in the hope of being raised in "glory" and "power" by God in the next life (1 Cor. 15:43). We are made of dust and will return to dust. By God's grace and Spirit, we taste the divine nature in this life and experience a measure of transformation, yet we are continually hindered by our limited, dying, and decaying bodies, which affect our thinking, feeling, and ability to relate to others.

Peter's image of the flower that blooms and then decays portrays well the evolving and devolving nature of human potential. He writes: "All flesh is like grass and all its glory like the flower of grass. The grass withers, and the flower falls" (1 Pet. 1:24).

What does all this mean for people who want to keep growing as Spirit-filled and Spirit-led followers of Christ? For one, it means that human development is not linear, with an ever-upward movement. We may very well be at our best physically in our twenties, peak mentally in our thirties or forties, become our wisest and most relationally astute in our fifties and sixties, and yet experience decline in various aspects of our life before we die. While some great saints seem to keep growing and becoming more Christlike until their dying breath—which is my personal goal—many of us experience physical deterioration that takes its toll on our ability to experience love, joy, peace, patience, kindness, gentleness, and self-control. Further, while some elderly Christians may become especially effective in their use of their spiritual gifts at the end of their lives, for others of us, our ability to use our spiritual gifts may very well suffer as our memory fades, our ability to recall key words declines, and we simply cannot handle the conflicts and stresses of daily life and ministry in the ways that we once could.

While we are right to hope and trust we will be completely transformed some day, we get only a taste of being like Christ in this life and may even lose some ability to function in the fullness and power of the Holy Spirit for various reasons due to human frailty. We may experience real change that seems permanent at one point in our life, but only when we are resurrected from the dead and given a new spiritual body will we be fully and permanently conformed to the image of Christ (1 Cor. 15:49; Rom. 8:29).

What expectation can we then have for Spirit-filled and Spirit-led living? Thinking of the Spirit as the wind of God may help us here. The work of the Holy Spirit is often to blow through us, transforming our thinking, feeling, and behavior even while our basic nature remains flawed and limited. Spirit-led living means just what it implies: *we live out our God-given purpose in life by virtue of the Spirit's ongoing work within us, as we follow the Spirit's leading, and not by becoming permanently and irrevocably transformed*. Our basic human nature is not changed as much as we are enabled to grow in our ability to let the Spirit have its way in us and to keep in step with the Spirit's prompting. We do in fact mature, but we never stop being human beings with many limitations.

If, on the other hand, I unrealistically expect my basic nature to change by the presence of the Holy Spirit in my life, I may set myself up to be perplexed, disappointed, and possibly deceived when my sinful impulses keep asserting themselves and I am not ready to handle them. The transformation Christians should seek, then, in this life, is not to become a god but to learn how to draw on the Spirit for power to say no to ungodliness and worldly passions and yes to all that is truly life giving (Titus 2:11–14). We may hope to act in godlike ways, which is what godliness means, but we will always be dependent on the Holy Spirit's activity within us to produce the fruit.

Further, when we understand Spirit-led living to be yielding to the Spirit's impulses within us (rather than being permanently changed), we will remember our utter dependence on the Spirit at all times. We will expect to be prompted by our old self-seeking and self-serving nature, and we will take seriously the power of unhealed wounds and our lack of wholeness to negatively affect our ability to relate well with others. At the same time, we will also increasingly go to the Spirit for power to resist our sinful inclinations and to want to act in ways that mirror God's character.

We can also expect to grow in our ability to please God by our behavior. Paul told the Thessalonians, for example: "Finally, brothers and sisters, we ask and urge you in the Lord Jesus that, as you learned from us how you ought to live and to please God (as, in fact, you are doing), you should do so more and more" (1 Thess. 4:1). He also taught the Romans to expect to grow through their suffering and life experiences (Rom. 5) and urged them to be transformed in the renewal of their minds (Rom. 12:2).

Over time, our renewed minds will more quickly recognize the influence of sin in our lives. On one hand, we will develop a more critical reaction to sin and greater distress over its presence in our life and society; while on the other hand, we may also become more gracious toward ourselves and others, accepting our human limitations better. We will more regularly draw on the Holy Spirit to move us away from sin and toward love and goodness instead. We will learn how to become more attentive and responsive to the Spirit's prompting and leading, more helpful to others, and, as a result, more fruitful in our ministries. Spirit-led living provides us with a way to move *from* sin and unhealthiness *to* the life God intends for us—again, not as a permanent, complete transformation but as a tool for rising to our best self in the moment.

Next Steps

While we cannot control the Spirit and we cannot stop the deterioration of our bodies, we can grow significantly in our relationship with the Spirit in ways that transform us, our relationships, and all that we seek to do for Christ. Some concrete suggestions to help you more fully and regularly experience Spirit-filled and Spirit-led living follow.

Be Open to the Spirit

Are you ready and eager for the Holy Spirit to fill you and lead you into the full life that Christ intends for you? Or are you afraid of God's having that much influence within you?

When I was a teenager, I was afraid of the Holy Spirit. I didn't want some powerful force that I couldn't control inside of me! I knew better than to try to tell myself that I didn't need to worry and that the Spirit was safe. The Spirit certainly was *not* going to be safe. I could only expect that my world would be seriously disturbed if I put down my defenses and let the Spirit go to work.

If you are feeling a little nervous at the prospect of the Holy Spirit's active working in your life, you may be afraid for other reasons, too. You might fear learning something you don't want to know or hearing something you don't want to hear. You may fear being told to do something you don't want to do. You may be afraid that the Spirit will ask you to give up something that you want to hold on to.

Rest assured, all your fears are likely to be realized. However, as scary as that might sound, the Spirit rarely overwhelms or overpowers us. Even more important, the Spirit's disrupting activity is also our best hope. Without disruption, there is no transformation, and without transformation, there is no abundant living. In my case, the Holy Spirit kept calling to me. I realized that I simply would not keep growing closer to God or fulfill my purpose in life unless I became more open to the Holy Spirit.

Ask the Spirit for Filling

After becoming more open to the Holy Spirit, actively reach out to the Spirit, listen for the Spirit's voice, and learn how to better recognize the Spirit's promptings. No how-to manual for Spirit-led living could help you as much as simply practicing sitting with God and listening to the experience of others. Regularly engage in spiritual practices, such as worship, reading Scripture, prayer, and seeking the counsel of Spirit-filled, gifted Christians. Create space in your life to listen to the Spirit by taking time for solitude, quiet, and even absolute silence. Specifically, pray to be filled with the Holy Spirit and ask others who seem to be Spirit-filled people to pray for you. You may have a dramatic experience with the Spirit, or your filling may be more subtle. What matters most is that the Spirit gives you divine power "to will and to work for [God's] good pleasure" (Phil. 2:13).

Over the years, whenever I have prayed to be filled with the fruit of the Spirit—love, joy, peace, patience, kindness, goodness, faithfulness, gentleness, and self-control (Gal. 5:22–23)—I have never suddenly been transformed on the spot. In fact, at times I have been disappointed and discouraged at the lack of this fruit in some of my relationships. In spite of my prayers, I consistently seemed to be annoyed instead of patient and harsh instead of gentle with certain people. Too often, I have been self-indulgent rather than self-controlled. When faced with uncertainty, it's easier for me to feel anxious instead of peaceful.

There is hope, but no change happens as if by magic. The fruit of the Spirit is generally cultivated over time, as we increasingly learn from our experiences to recognize the impulses of the flesh versus the prompting of the Spirit and to respond more readily to the latter while rejecting the former. Most important is that we continually seek to cultivate a more consistent connection with God, who is the true source of our ability to be the person we have been called to be.

For the past couple of years, I have been experimenting with a new method for connecting daily to the Holy Spirit. Every day before getting out of bed I pray, "Lord, please help me to live fully, love deeply, and give freely so that others may know and experience you through me." While walking on pilgrimage, I realized that I didn't fully understand what I was asking for. So I started asking God to help me know what each phrase truly meant in its depth, beginning with "to live fully." I had in mind the abundant life Christ promised (John 10:10), but I sensed something more might be involved.

Then one day on the Camino, about six months after I first began offering this prayer, a clearer meaning came to me. A full life is a Spirit-filled and Spirit-led life. Apart from the Spirit, I often try to fill my life with many thoughts, work, diversions, food, and drinks that tend to leave me feeling empty later on. On the other hand, when my thinking or activities seem to flow from the Spirit working within me or through me to serve others, I often feel a tremendous peace and joy. I have little desire to sin or to act in my normal self-serving ways. I often feel more love and patience. It is easier to be kind and gentle. I feel satisfied with my life, and I don't feel as if I need anything else. I feel "full," and in those moments my thinking and activity are much more Christ centered.

The difference between asking the Spirit to fill me with the fruit of the Spirit and praying for a full life led by the Spirit is that in the latter case, I am asking to be filled with the Spirit, not with fruit. You can certainly pray for specific fruit, such as more love, more patience, more kindness, and so forth; but the most important prayer is for the Spirit to fill you in a powerful way with a manifestation of God's presence within you. Rather than just focus on the desired characteristics (the fruit), focus on connecting with God—not only intellectually but with an open, submissive, expectant heart. Seek and wait for the Spirit. Look for the Spirit to be leading you and working through you, and see if the fruit of the Spirit doesn't follow naturally.

Use Your Freedom to Follow the Spirit

In his letter to the Galatians, Paul graphically reminded readers that Christ was crucified so that we could be free from the power of sin and free to love others by the Holy Spirit. At one point, he said, "You, my brothers [and sisters], were called to be free. But do not use your freedom to indulge the sinful nature; rather, serve one another in love" (Gal. 5:13 NIV). Then toward the end of his argument, he said, "Those who belong to Christ Jesus have crucified the sinful nature [our 'flesh'] with its passions and desires. Since we live by the Spirit, let us keep in step with the Spirit" (Gal. 5:24–25 NIV).

The alternative to living in Spirit-led freedom is to go back to the old way of thinking and living in slavery to sin. The result of that choice is death. Paul put it starkly when he said, "To set the mind on the flesh is death, but to set the mind on the Spirit is life and peace" (Rom. 8:6). The implication seems clear: the way forward is to stop trying to control your own life and living out of your own power and will when what you want is at odds with what God wants. As long as you continue to ignore, resist, or reject the movement of the Spirit within you, death works in you, destroying your peace with God and your ability to serve Christ effectively. As Jesus explained in the parable of the sower, worries, pleasure seeking, and the pursuit of wealth and material things choke out the gospel seed and hinder your ability to blossom and bear fruit (Matt. 13:22; Mark 4:19; Luke 8:14). This is simply how sin works in anyone's life.

When you are led by the Spirit, on the other hand, you renounce sin and selfishness, not by your own willpower but by exercising the freedom that comes from the Spirit's presence in your life. You repent, consciously turning away from what you know is wrong and turning in the direction God wants you to go. By confessing the sin in your life and seeking God's forgiveness, you can experience cleansing, new freedom from the sin, and greater ability to live by the Spirit. As always, hope comes from the presence of the Spirit in your life—not to magically change you but to experience afresh God's grace and prompting to show you the way to go. As you exercise your freedom in Christ to listen and follow moment by moment, case by case, your life truly does change for the better in many ways.

Ask the Spirit to Lead You

As you continually open yourself to the Holy Spirit and seek to be filled with the Spirit, you will be led by the Spirit. It also helps to specifically ask the Spirit to lead you, which is to say, pray for the ability to sense how the Spirit is leading and for the grace to follow.

Sometimes, I actually picture hoisting a sail to catch the wind of God when I am trying to get ready to meet someone, discern God's leading, or go into a ministry situation. One time, for example, I was going to meet a Muslim friend of mine. I had been frustrated with our conversations and wanted God to speak to him through me. I didn't know what else to say to him that I hadn't already said.

As I walked the several blocks from our apartment to the coffee shop where we were meeting, I prayed almost desperately for God's help to know how to share Christ with him in a way that he could appreciate. I suddenly remembered the Holy Spirit as the wind of God. The image of a sailboat popped into mind. My hands began moving involuntarily, mimicking the pulling of a rope to hoist the sail. I am sure I got a couple of strange looks from others on the street, but I didn't really care, because I was immersed in prayer. I was physically, mentally, and emotionally asking the Spirit to fill my sail and lead me where I needed to go.

I could not have made a better decision. (Well, I could have skipped the hand gestures in public.) When we finally met, I was able to relax and let go of trying to orchestrate the conversation. I let our exchange flow wherever it went. I followed my instincts to bring up significant topics of conversation (politics, family, life's purpose, values) and found myself quoting Jesus, without worrying what he might think, because the words flowed naturally within the course of the conversation. I felt prompted to affirm qualities that I was seeing in my friend. I challenged him to seek out friends who could truly support his efforts to improve his circumstances and to set goals to better his life—not in a paternalistic way but from the heart of a caring friend. We never talked about Christianity explicitly that day, but I am 100 percent sure that the Holy Spirit was guiding the conversation. I felt much love, joy, peace, patience, kindness, goodness, faithfulness, gentleness, and self-control throughout our time together. I was my best self—precisely because I was not trying to accomplish an agenda but was free enough to follow the Spirit's prompting. I would like to learn to live this way all the time.

The church also needs to cultivate a better ability to let the Holy Spirit lead and guide us as a body.[4] As an example of Spirit-led leading in a congregation, a pastor friend of mine, Ed, received some insight after his church struggled for two years trying to find a suitable church building. As Ed reflected on their discernment process, he noticed that while their first choice seemed to some people (at least to one man who claimed to have what he called "the gift of faith") to be the perfect place, there was much division in the church. The second choice seemed to produce little emotional energy, yet there was peace and unity among the congregation. He learned from that experience to trust the Spirit to lead them to the right answer and to fill them with the fruit of the Spirit, if the congregation is patient enough to listen to one another and to wait for unity to emerge. His experience does not mean that every Spirit-led decision in the church will produce love, joy, and peace for everyone, but when the Spirit is at work, believers will often see the fruit of its activity.

Asking for leading is a good daily practice for Christians and for congregations, but just asking does not guarantee how and when the best answer will emerge. If you have ever tried to sail a boat, you know how tricky it can be. So it is with the Spirit. Catching the holy wind when it blows and learning how to best go with its flow takes time and experience.[5] We also need to learn to differentiate between flowing with the Spirit and flowing with our own ambitions, drive, or overzealousness. Learning how to get out of the way of the Spirit while staying fully engaged with the Spirit takes practice.

Eagerly seek and gratefully embrace those moments when the Spirit seems to be working—bringing insight, comfort, strength, conviction, direction, hope, assurance, correction, wisdom, or some other valued gift. Yet embrace the Spirit as one embraces the wind. Let it blow across your face to delight you with God's presence or assure you of God's care. Let it fill your sails to give you wisdom, motivation, or power to go forward boldly. Do not for a moment think you can hold it, control it, or bottle it for future use. The Spirit comes when God wills, and your opportunity is to go with its flow.

Daily, the best course of action is to simply do what you already know God wants every Christian to do—to love God, others, and yourself with all of your being. Faithfully fulfill your responsibilities and honor your commitments to others. Seek the Spirit's wisdom, guidance, and empowering so that you can do what is most needed when it is needed and how Christ would do it. When you do suddenly experience Spirit-prompted love, joy, peace, or some other fruit of the Spirit, embrace it as a divine gift for the moment, because it is likely to disappear rapidly without notice. And when you are given the grace to savor an abiding sense of the Spirit's presence, enjoy the thoughts and feelings, humbly express your gratitude, and ask the Spirit to let God's love flow through you to others as purely and fully as possible.

Know and Use Your Spiritual Gifts

Sometimes when we don't feel or perceive the Spirit's presence, or when we feel overwhelmed by negative influences in our life, one of the best things we can do is to look for ways to serve God's purposes by using our spiritual gifts. Some of the most powerful and joyful times in my life are those when I am using my spiritual gifts in teaching, preaching, coaching, or consulting, because the activities coincide with how the Holy Spirit works through me to help others. Many times as I exercise my gifts, a new insight, idea, method, or illustration will pop into my head that seems especially useful. Certainly, many people experience creativity under a wide variety of circumstances, but when I see how the inspiration of the moment is so pertinent to someone else, I suspect the Holy Spirit was at work. Likewise, whenever I suddenly have a change of heart for the better, feel new motivation to serve Christ, gain special insight or wisdom, feel a surge of love, or hear words flow from me that are very meaningful and helpful to others, I trust that the Spirit has filled and led me in that moment.

Do you know your spiritual gift(s)? (For some biblical lists of various Spirit-endowed abilities, see Rom. 12:3–8; 1 Cor. 12:4–11; Eph. 4:11–16.) If not, ask your pastor or check online for a spiritual gifts inventory, and find out as soon as possible how God may have gifted you to serve others. If you don't know what names to give your abilities, just identify the things you like to do that could contribute to the church and world. Get feedback from knowledgeable individuals to confirm your greatest gifts and contributions. Then seek opportunities to get training to effectively use your gifts in Christian service, both for the sake of others and for you. Your spiritual vitality will often increase greatly as you use your gifts in the strength of the Spirit.

Whatever your gift(s) may be, the Holy Spirit intends to use you to serve God's purposes. The Spirit may simply work through your natural talent, or the Spirit may give you some special gift for the moment. You will not always know how the Spirit is working in or through you at any given moment, though you are likely to feel power, confidence, and joy. In this instance, Spirit-led living means trusting that the Spirit wants to work through you, and is in fact doing so, and then doing all you can to flow with the Spirit. Exercising your spiritual gift(s) is one of the chief ways you can fulfill your purpose in life.

Use Your Spiritual Gifts Wholeheartedly

Once you are sure what your spiritual gifts are, put your heart into using them to best of your ability. Do you have the gift of leadership? Then step up and lead. Do you have the gift of service? Then be on the lookout for those who need help, and give of yourself generously. Do you have the gift of encouragement? Then be ready to offer comforting or challenging words to others, even to strangers, as needed and appropriate. Do you have the gift of prophecy (you can cut through all the garbage to see what is real and what is needed now)? Then find ways to speak the truth and bring to light what the Spirit has enabled you to specially see. (Just be humble enough to recognize that discerning God's will for others and for your church may require more than just your voice and insight; others will usually need to participate in the discernment process before decisions should be made.) Do you have the gift of wisdom? mercy? administration? healing? giving? Whatever your gifts may be, own them without embarrassment and use them boldly and intentionally to serve Christ.

Peter urged believers to use their Spirit-given gifts wholeheartedly when he wrote: "Like good stewards of the manifold grace of God, serve one another with whatever gift each of you has received. Whoever speaks must do so as one speaking the very words of God; whoever serves must do so with the strength that God supplies, so that God may be glorified in all things through Jesus Christ. To him belong the glory and the power forever and ever. Amen" (1 Pet. 4:10–11).

Are you using your gift(s) as fully and wholeheartedly as possible?

Pray for the Spirit to Work through You

Serving God requires our full engagement, and yet no matter how much of ourselves we put into whatever we are doing, the Holy Spirit is still the most important ingredient in a fruitful ministry. Another one of my morning rituals is to name three of my chief spiritual gifts (inspiration, teaching, and encouragement) in a prayer, asking for God to use me specifically through these gifts each day. The basic form is, "Lord, please use me to inspire, teach, and encourage others to realize their God-given dreams and fulfill their purpose today." Often I will substitute "others" with the specific names of people I am going to be meeting. Other times I change the last part to fit with my writing and teaching goals. I will say something like, "Lord, please use me to inspire, teach, and encourage others to develop a more vital spiritual life and to serve Christ more effectively." Over and over again, God seems to answer this prayer in little and big ways, and praying about every aspect of my life seems to be bringing the Holy Spirit more and more into the fabric of my life.

If you were to weave your spiritual gifts into a daily prayer, how would you express your intention to serve God's purposes with your life? What would you ask God to do through you in the various aspects of your daily life—including today? Make your prayer fit with your giftedness, passion, calling, and opportunities, and pray it wholeheartedly.

Seek the Spirit in Community

One of the biggest crises in much of the Western world today is the decline of interest in church affiliation among those who still consider themselves highly interested in spirituality. However, many people don't want anything to do with the church—for good reason. As my pastor said recently, one of the biggest hindrances to furthering the gospel and helping Christians grow has been the church. Yet, he went on to say, at the same time the most effective means of furthering the gospel and helping Christians has been the church.

God never intended for believers in Christ to go it alone or to live in a spiritual vacuum. We need each other, in spite of our individual differences and the challenges of community life. Together, we need the church for teaching; encouraging one another; sharing in each other's joys and sorrows; giving as well as receiving; attending to multigenerational, community needs; and serving Christ more effectively. According to Scripture, Jesus is present where two or more are gathered in his name, and the Spirit works powerfully when Christians assemble to worship God and serve one another with their spiritual gifts. Paul called the church the body of Christ and taught that each member needs the others.

Are you regularly gathering with other Christians to worship, learn, support one another, and serve Christ in various ways? Are you relying on the Holy Spirit to equip you for works of service through others who have the gifts of preaching, teaching, leading, pastoring, encouraging, and so forth? You can read Scripture, pray, and seek to be filled with the Spirit all on your own, but Christ had a different vision for us. As imperfect and flawed as Christians and churches are, we simply need one another because that is how the Holy Spirit works to minister to and equip us. The Spirit works through each of us to equip and strengthen one another in various ways, so that together we will make up the body of Christ—in small communities that are microcosms of the church as a whole. (For more on the contribution of a spiritual community, see appendix B, "Giving Up on Finding Christian Community?")

The Horizon Ahead

Most of us would like to be fixed permanently by the Spirit, but God has not chosen to work this way. Paul explains, "We have this treasure in jars of clay to show that this all-surpassing power is from God and not from us" (2 Cor. 4:7 NIV). Instead of becoming completely transformed, our sinful nature is always lurking in the shadows looking for opportunities to influence us. We must grapple with issues of maturity and other personal limitations that make it difficult for us to live out of our best selves. We live in a sin-contaminated world, which sometimes seduces us and sometimes abuses us and often runs contrary to the Spirit.

Spirit-led living is the best and only hope for a better life that honors God and brings the joy and fullness you desire. The Spirit must live through you, filling you with fruit and leading you in the ways God wants you to go. Spirit-led living requires that you continually (re)connect with God, reject the impulses of the sinful nature when it shows itself, confess sins and receive forgiveness, and seek to recognize and respond to the Spirit's prompting as a way of life. You cannot control the wind of God, but you can learn to catch it when it blows and flow with it better.

Practically, as we have discussed, you will experience the Spirit more powerfully and regularly if you are open to the Spirit, seek the Spirit's filling and leading, use your freedom to follow the Spirit and not your sinful self, use your spiritual gifts wholeheartedly, pray for God to work through you, and seek to live a Spirit-filled life in Christian community. The more you learn to "keep in step with the Spirit" (Gal. 5:25 NIV) daily, the more you will discover power to overcome sin and sinful tendencies in your life. You will also better fulfill your God-given purpose to love God, others, and yourself with all your being.

For Further Reflection

To set the mind on the flesh is death, but to set the mind on the Spirit is life and peace.

—Romans 8:6

Reflect on the verse above. Choose any of the questions in "Next Steps" or some of those listed below to guide your journal writing. Discuss with a small group of people in your spiritual community who are also seeking to be Spirit-led pilgrims.

- When are you most aware of the Holy Spirit's influence and leading in your experience? What difference did your experiences with the Spirit make in your mood, your attitude, your behavior, or some other aspect of your life?
- As you think back on times when God felt closest, most powerful, or particularly helpful or active in your life, what did it feel like? Were you permanently changed, or was the experience transitory? What encounters with God have had the most long-lasting effect on you?
- How does the Spirit speak and minister to you through others?
- How does the Spirit seem to work through you to minister to others? How could you more wholeheartedly use your spiritual gifts?
- How do you sense the Spirit is currently speaking to or leading you in your life?
- What help do you need from others? Whom will you ask? When will you reach out for help?
- What other thoughts or reactions were prompted by this chapter on Spirit-led living? What specifically do you intend to do differently or more consistently?

CHAPTER 8

Crossing Bridges

∽

July 20, 2006. Day 20. Ponferrada. Meltdown. At lunch,
Jill snapped. After the boys left the restaurant, she burst into tears.
She was suffering from great physical pain and exhaustion. Worse,
she felt abandoned by me when we rendezvoused at the café, nine
kilometers into a twenty-six kilometer (sixteen-mile) day.

Dan and I had arrived much earlier than she and Tim.
When she hobbled in the door, I could tell she was not having a
good day. Dan and I were eager to get going, and she seemed very
needy and would be taking a long break. I thought I had expressed
my concern for her before setting out again, leaving her in the
care of our older son. However, she felt I had no idea how much she
needed me. In her words, I didn't "see her." I didn't appreciate the
extent of her distress and need for support from me. If I had truly
seen her, she reasoned, surely I would have changed my plans and
stayed with her.

Sadly, the problem was not so much lack of sight, but failure
of will. I didn't want to deal with what I saw. I wanted to go on
and not be trapped by her frailty. I couldn't stand the thought of
repeating yesterday's experience, when we inched along for miles
while the sun got hotter and hotter. Slowing down to go at her
pace felt frustrating and exhausting for me.

Still, what did yesterday have to do with today?

I now realize that Jill not only needs to know that I truly see
her—what is real for her. Even more, she needs me to care enough
to act on what I see. Caring means loving, and loving means
action. If she is going to be honest and vulnerable with me, I must
treat her with love and be trustworthy.

I think I'll offer to ride the bus with her if she wants me to. (I
hope she says, "No!")

Reflecting on the Journey

I had prayed quite a bit for God to use this pilgrimage to transform me. Yet, when my opportunities to think or act differently came, I often would miss them or would fail to take advantage of them. I wanted a better marriage, and yet I kept missing chances to respond to conflicts or needs in loving ways. I said I wanted to become more like Christ, but I seemed unwilling to make personal sacrifices to follow Christ's teaching and example.

Something was missing in my mentality. I could create a picture in my mind of what a transformed life might look like, but I seemed to lack an awareness of what I needed to do to cross over to that new life. I could imagine living in love and harmony with everyone and fruitfully using my gifts and resources to serve Christ, but sometimes I couldn't see what it would take to move from my current reality to get there. Or, if I did know what to do—not run away from a conflict, reorder my life in some way, face the pain of change, make personal sacrifices, let go of the past or of cherished habits, accept the reality of the present, reach out to someone I cared about—too often I seemed to choke in the face of opportunities to take action that could very well lead to significant transformation. Whatever the reason—ignorance, cluelessness, unwillingness, fear, laziness, distraction—I regret not seizing more transformative opportunities on pilgrimage and throughout my life, when fully engaging thoughtfully and constructively with someone or something could have made a significant difference in my life or theirs.

When we fail to take the necessary steps to move toward our visions, our paralysis or unwillingness to act is like wanting to hit homeruns but not swinging at the pitches. It is like asking a friend to come over to help you plant a garden but not answering the door when she knocks. It is like wanting to paint a beautiful picture but spending your money on desserts rather than on lessons, brushes, and paint. It is like planning a vacation of a lifetime but not making plane reservations to get you there.

We can dream all we want to about what might be, but we have to be willing to do the necessary work to realize our dreams. We have to face our fears. We have to make choices. We have to line up our values, our visions, and how we actually spend our time and resources. On one hand, we have to not run away from conflicts and unexpected difficulties but try to use them as a means to reach our dreams. On the other, we have to resist the impulse to pulverize opponents or thrash through obstacles so that when we reach our objective, we have not caused a lot of unnecessary damage getting there.

I realize now that on the Camino, God was bringing me to numerous little "bridges" to help me move from one way of being to another. Yet God was also helping me see how often I fail to cross the bridges I encounter—not to discourage me or make me feel bad about myself but to awaken me to the plethora of opportunities before me every day. I slowly began to realize that no matter how much I prayed to be transformed, nothing was really going to change until I crossed the bridges in my life. God was helping me right and left by giving me opportunities, but unless I took them, my life was going to be same-old, same-old.

When have you had a vision for some aspect of your life but a gulf separated you from the realization of your vision? Perhaps you saw a bridge that might take you closer, but you were struggling with actually crossing over? What did it feel like not to cross over? In those cases when you finally started moving, what did becoming "unstuck" feel like? If you made it to the other side of the bridge, what happened and what were your feelings once you got there?

Could you think of times when you saw what changes were needed in your life and you made them? Perhaps you had a vision for being a healthier person, and you decided to stop wishing and start taking concrete action to change your lifestyle. Perhaps you had a dream for mastering a skill or earning a degree, and you made the necessary sacrifices to do it. Perhaps you had a deep desire to make a difference in the world, and you finally altered your priorities so that you could commit more of yourself to others, and now you can see how they are truly benefiting. Maybe you have wanted to feel better about how you are relating to others and made some choices to stop doing some things and to start doing others, and now you feel more pleased with your interactions with others. Perhaps you have wanted a deeper relationship with someone and finally accepted that you had to stop hiding or avoiding conflict, and your honest interactions have produced more pain and yet, at the same time, a more satisfying, closer relationship with that person.

The possibilities are endless, yet every path to a transformed life leads across a bridge of transition from one way of being to another. We may not always be aware of crossing a bridge, and may only in retrospect discover that we have changed. However, if we look carefully at the path that took us to the transformative moments, we can often discern a decision we made or series of actions we took that brought us there.

The truth about transformation is simple: *if we want our lives to be different, we have to be willing to do what it takes to get there.* I am not saying that we can always make it happen by sheer willpower and effort, because sometimes we can't. Or that we won't need a lot of guidance and support in some circumstances, because we often will. Or that we will even understand how our transformation came about in many circumstances, because often we are changed on a subconscious level over a long period of time by a complex of unseen forces. Rather, I am making one critical point that is too often overlooked by those who dream about better relationships, more satisfying work or service, a healthier body, greater financial security, a closer connection to God or any other value of theirs: *unless we are ready to move forward on the path and to cross the bridges as we come to them, not much is going to change in our lives.*

In biblical language, we cannot be conformed into the image of Christ and fulfill our purpose in life unless we change, and change requires being responsive to the leading of the Holy Spirit. We must first face the truth the Holy Spirit shows us about ourselves and others around us, *and* then we must follow the prompting of the Spirit to take whatever action is needed.

We can all look back to important decisions we have made and actions we have taken that have made significant differences. If we would stop and look carefully at what is happening in our life right now, today, we would also see many transformative opportunities on our path. These are the bridges God has led us to. By God's grace, we can—and must—cross them if we are going to continue to experience transformation in our life and relationships.

Our Best Self

In my life, one kind of bridge keeps showing up over and over again on the trail. I am talking about the bridge from my lesser self to my best self.

In any given situation, we can describe our mood, thinking, attitudes, or behavior, while at the same time envisioning a different collection of moods, thoughts, attitudes, and behavior that fit with our idea of the person we would like to be or who we are when we are at our best. Crossing over from one way of being to the other is transformative, both for ourselves and for those who benefit from the changes we are making.

For example, just last night we were coming home from a special ecumenical worship service. I was disappointed (comparing it to Chartres, France, where I had spent the previous month) and feeling a little critical of some of the people I had seen there. I wanted to make jokes at other people's expense. Then I remembered my best self accepts people for who they are, builds them up, and looks for the good in any situation. He is genuinely grateful for his blessings and opportunities and chooses not to focus on unhelpful contrasts and comparisons.

In that moment, I was standing at the foot of a little bridge—a transformative opportunity. I could stay where I was or I could cross over to be the person I most wanted to be. I am not talking about faking it or turning a switch to magically become a different person. My opportunity was to remember who I wanted to be and to let the Holy Spirit take me over the bridge to that better place. I simply made a choice to let go of the criticism I was feeling and redirect my focus to what I was genuinely thankful for that evening—an opportunity to sit quietly, worship, and talk with a pastor I hadn't seen in several years.

The inner transformation was almost immediate.

Crossing over is sometimes very hard emotionally, especially when we get a payoff from staying put (for example, temporarily feeling better about ourselves as a result of complaining, criticizing, or indulging ourselves in some way). I have also experienced a lot of difficulty being my best self when I am around people with whom I have unresolved conflicts or when I feel a lot of pain from past hurts in our relationship. Yet, even in difficult situations, we can go part way across the bridge by moving away from being our worst self and doing what we can to let the Holy Spirit work through us constructively, even if all we can do is pray.

For example, I sometimes feel as if I have almost no power to feel love for certain people, and am afraid that I might even lash out when I see them. At those times, I keep praying, "Lord, please change my heart toward [someone], guard my lips from speaking out of anger, and help me get out of the way so that your love can flow out of me. Please do in me what I am not capable of doing on my own today."

In general, our best self is the one who embraces God, love, and all else that is good, right, and true and who freely flows with the Holy Spirit's leading in our life. We have all experienced being Dr. Jekyll in one moment, only to turn into Mr. Hyde the next, or vice versa. But I am not only talking about moving from our worst self to our best self, I am also talking about moving from our OK self to our best self. I am talking about realizing that we often have a transformative opportunity whenever we notice a gap between who we are at any given moment and who we would like to be. At the point of awareness, we then cross the bridge when we say yes to the Spirit (who has shown us the opportunity, given us the vision of our best self, and gives us the will and ability to cross over) and no to Mr. Hyde or any of his more subtle personas.

Our best self, then, is who we are when we are Spirit-filled and Spirit-led—loving God, ourselves, and others; valuing what God values; and living out God's will and calling for our life. Our best self also grows out of our unique personality, strengths, gifts, and passions. We know we have the right vision for our best self when the person we see in our mind inspires us, makes us smile, and helps us feel confident, grounded, and simultaneously humble and powerful.

We will be able to access our creativity and draw on our many resources to tackle life's challenges, fulfill our responsibilities, and pursue our dreams. We will be freely and joyfully offering our unique contributions to others and to the world.

Crossing Over

Living round-the-clock for thirty-seven straight days with my family members in stressful circumstances certainly did not always bring out my best self. Yet, I started to notice something I have experienced often throughout my adult life. The more I paid attention to what was "real" for them and me and the more I was praying and thinking about being a loving person, the more easily I could recognize a bridge when I came to one and the more eager I was to cross over to my best self.

For example, on pilgrimage, after that fateful day on the road to Ponferrada, I tried to watch for how Jill was feeling and listen for clues she would give me about her need for rest and support. On my own, I might be tempted to minimize her struggles in order to justify my going off on my own or pushing her to go farther than was good for her. Yet, the more I tried to tap into my love for her and God's love within me and to face the truth about her reality, the easier choosing to act in her best interest seemed to become. I had been saying I wanted a better marriage and wanted to be a more caring husband. When I started to look for transformative opportunities, I often realized, *here* was my chance!

With my sons, I noticed that I wanted them to be curious about all the religious symbols everywhere and to *want* to sit for hours in the church with me to write in their journals. Yet they often wanted to use their spare time to play cards, be alone, or sleep. When I stopped focusing on what I wished were true, I began to see what was real for them; and when I reminded myself that love means considering what is truly in the best interest of others, I became more receptive to the Spirit's leading. My facing the truth and connecting with godly values set the stage for me to make different choices in how I related to them. I began to see what their faces were expressing (because I was actually looking at their faces) and to hear what they were not saying with words. Then, as I gave up wanting them to have the same experience I was having, I started to be able to accept one son's fear and distress and the other's boredom and longing. I could notice what they truly enjoyed and appreciated as opposed to what I wanted them to care about and value. I was crossing bridges.

What I did, based on what I was noticing, varied depending on the situation. Once on the other side of the attitudinal bridges, I had more bridges to cross. How would I respond constructively to each one out of my best self rather than my reactive, judgmental, or thoughtless self? I would ask God to show me what I still needed to see about each one and for wisdom from the Spirit to know how to best respond. Sometimes they needed me to pretend I didn't notice their unhappiness. Sometimes they needed sympathy and encouragement. Other times they needed a firm prod to change behavior or accept a new challenge. I often needed to give them freedom to pursue their own interests while I pursued mine. I frequently needed to insist that we all sit down together to work out whatever the issue was.

As is often true in life, I couldn't determine ahead of time what action was needed. I had to assess each situation moment by moment, case by case. The important thing was to be ready to recognize when I was at a bridge and then cross it with the help of the Holy Spirit. The more I acted from a grounded, loving perspective, the more real transformation started taking place in my relationships with my family and in my ability to give to them what they most needed from me. We often felt closer, we laughed and enjoyed each other more, they seemed more nourished and relieved, and somehow the whole journey felt more joyful and worthwhile for all of us.

Scripture for the Journey

To help us recognize the various bridges God leads us to in life, Scripture offers a big-picture perspective on spiritual growth. Biblical writers call believers to continually seek and embrace transformation in their relationship with God and with their fellow human beings as God's will for their lives. The apostle Paul put it this way: "Do not be conformed to this world, but be transformed by the renewing of your minds, so that you may discern what is the will of God—what is good and acceptable and perfect" (Rom. 12:2). Scripture, then, gives us a map of sorts—not of the particular experiences we are going to have, but of the kinds of crossings (types of transformation) most of us will be given the opportunity to make in order to become more like Christ.

Most transformation called for in Scripture comes down to learning to become a more loving person—able to receive God's love, to return love to God, to love ourselves as God loves us, and to love others as ourselves. When Jesus names the two greatest commandments—to love God with all of our heart, soul, mind, and strength and to love our neighbor as ourselves (Mark 12:30–31)—he is telling us that love is the most important characteristic of a transformed life. Thus, we can expect that over and over again, day after day, we will come to a bridge that will lead us in some way to better love of God, ourselves, or others, if we will just cross it.

The Bridge of Repentance

True religion, in the Judeo-Christian tradition, has never been just about right beliefs, an individualistic relationship with God, or getting blessings from God for ourselves. What God wants from us is to create loving community marked by justice and mercy, which reflects God's character and values. However, no matter how nice we may be, most of us by nature tend to serve ourselves and use others for our own purposes. This reality requires that we change (in biblical language, "repent") to make love the highest priority of our lives, if we want to be aligned with God's will.

For example, any of us can say we are devoted to God and others, and even feel warmth for God or compassion for someone else, but the real test of love comes when we are given concrete opportunities to show our love. In 1 John we read, "Dear children, let us not love with words or tongue but with actions and in truth" (1 John 3:18 NIV). Love in action is true love; love in thought and feeling alone is likely to be self-deception.

Scriptural writers, especially ancient Hebrew prophets, insisted that the quality of our relationship with God was seen in how believers respected and attended to the needs of others. Hebrew prophets especially called long and loudly for justice and mercy to be the hallmarks of society. For example, Micah challenges those who satisfy themselves simply by offering the prescribed number of sacrifices each year. Instead, he argues, they should be more concerned about how they treat others and the attitude of their heart toward God. He writes:

> He has told you, O mortal, what is good;
> and what does the LORD require of you
> but to do justice, and to love kindness,
> and to walk humbly with your God?
> —Micah 6:8

Justice calls for treating others fairly and doing what is right. Mercy goes even further, to offer a helping hand to others, especially the widows, orphans, poor, and needy. (See, for example, Deut. 16:19–20; 24:17, 19.) The reason biblical writers say so much about these subjects is that human beings keep forgetting, refusing, or otherwise failing to live in humble submission to God and to act in loving ways toward others. Even religion can sometimes collude with our self-centered instincts and tendency to harden our hearts and perpetuate selfishness by guiding believers to focus on the wrong priorities or to justify themselves at the expense of others. When this happened in ancient Israel, the prophets became especially incensed.

For example, Jesus lambasted the hypocritical religious leaders of his day who did not understand (or were unwilling to accept) these spiritual truths that we have been talking about. He called the leaders "blind guides" who established religious practices that circumvented the obvious will of God and kept people from responding fairly and mercifully to the needs of family and other community members. (See, for example, Matt. 23:16–28.) He even warned his disciples to have nothing to do with those who refuse to see the truth, let alone act on their teaching, because disaster awaits anyone who follows such people (Matt. 15:14).

All biblical preachers agree that the only solution when our lives are so out of whack with God's will is to repent—or make a radical shift in our way of thinking and being. Jeremiah urged the Israelites to repent of their idolatry and hardened hearts and to stop acting in ways that would guarantee unfruitfulness and disaster. Using ground imagery, he commanded them in the Lord's voice, "Break up your unplowed ground and do not sow among thorns" (Jer. 4:3 NIV). Hosea prophesied likewise: "Judah must plow, and Jacob must break up the ground. Sow for yourselves righteousness, reap the fruit of unfailing love, and break up your unplowed ground; for it is time to seek the LORD, until he comes and showers righteousness on you. But you have planted wickedness, you have reaped evil, you have eaten the fruit of deception" (Hosea 10:11–13 NIV).

The cost of failing to do the good that we know to do, and can do, is that the ground of our life will grow hard and become unfruitful. Breaking up unplowed ground and planting the right kind of seed—acting justly, loving kindness, walking humbly with our God—is the only solution.

To return to the bridge metaphor, when any of us fails to act in a loving way in any given circumstance or when we have clearly rebelled against God in our hearts, we have come to another bridge—the bridge of repentance. We can stay where we are, on the side of self-centered instinct and behavior, and alienation from God's Spirit, or we can swallow our pride, confess our sin, submit our will to God's, and cross over to a place of compassion and loving action. The bridge of repentance takes us back to the true path where we can once again seek to live out of our best self—our Spirit-led self.

The Power to Cross Over

While crossing over the bridge of repentance and living out of our best self might sound like something we do out of our own will and action, scriptural writers also teach that God is intimately involved. In our experience, we may feel the need to submit our will to God's or to make the effort to do the loving thing in any given situation, but God is actually the unseen force at work in our lives who makes such repentance and obedience to the Holy Spirit possible.

In the New Testament, we find many indications that God has engaged in a lifelong process of calling us, planting seeds, and nurturing us, all to draw us closer to God and to enable us to live out God's purpose for us. God draws us to Christ, gives us faith, and prompts us to keep moving forward on our spiritual journey. Paul assured the Philippians that the One "who began a good work in you will carry it on to completion" (1:6 NIV). Those who have a relationship with God through faith in Christ can expect that God will continue to work in and among them to lead them to greater spiritual depth and maturity over time. God plants a seed of spiritual life within us that leads us to faith and then brings about, in powerful, experiential ways, growth and fruit marked by qualities such as wisdom, love, insight, purity, righteousness, and greater knowledge of Christ (see Phil. 1:9–11; 3:8–14).

The pilgrim's part, on the other hand, is to respond to the urging and leading of the Spirit in our lives to seek a deeper connection to God and to live out our callings more fully. Paul expressed this practice as "working out your salvation." He also said they should do so with "fear and trembling"—that is, they were to obey God's prompting with an earnest, sober realization of who is at work in their life (Phil. 2:12). Such teaching is not to terrify pilgrims but to wake them up to the true goal and nature of the spiritual journey and to who it is that journeys with them. We are in this world to serve God's purposes at God's initiative and by God's power.

On spiritual pilgrimage, then, we are not off on a lark or casual stroll simply to satisfy our own desires and interests. Neither are we taking a victory lap, simply celebrating all that Christ did for us on the cross, as joyous as salvation by grace through faith truly is. Rather, we are engaged in the most important dimension of human existence, the fulfillment of our divinely given purpose to become more like Christ, to serve God's will, and to keep moving closer to union with God in perfect fellowship with God. This purpose is so important that God is actually intimately involved with its fulfillment by changing our hearts and giving us the ability to act on the Spirit's prompting. Paul expressed this spiritual reality by saying, "It is God who works in [us] to will and to act according to his good purpose" (Phil. 2:13 NIV).

Next Steps

To seize transformative opportunities often requires thoughtfulness, spiritual vitality, and decisiveness. You need to give thoughtful consideration to how you are going to live, by both reflecting on biblical principles and listening to your feelings and instincts. You need to maintain a solid connection to the Holy Spirit. And you need to be prepared to act, because the quality of your life depends upon your making choices that are in sync with your faith, values, commitments, and the Holy Spirit's promptings. Your (in)action in critical moments of opportunity can have significant ramifications for your life and relationships. We sometimes take action as part of a long-term pursuit of a dream, vision, or calling. Other times, we have only seconds to respond, and in the moment we may scamper over the bridge of opportunity or stay stuck on the other side, missing our chance to do something to make a difference.

On the Camino, challenges, conflicts, and new situations were continually giving my family and me opportunities to deal with an issue or else suffer unpleasant or disappointing consequences within hours. If we pushed too far, we would exhaust or possibly injure ourselves. If we didn't stop crabbing at each other, we would become more and more alienated from one another. Likewise, we also could see the benefits of making certain changes almost immediately. By allowing time for a long break, we got the rest we needed. By taking a chance on a less traveled trail, we often discovered great beauty and solitude. When we did the work needed to resolve a conflict, we suddenly were able to relax and able to draw close to one another again.

In normal life, however, it is sometimes easier to avoid what you don't want to face, and many transformative opportunities are missed. Other times, because of ingrained habits or blindness to spiritual or relational realities, you may not realize a change is needed. Often, a person is inexperienced at following the Spirit's lead or simply lacks energy or motivation to cross the bridges in life that need to be crossed.

Consequently, you may proceed in life without seriously questioning your ways of relating to God, yourself, or others—that is, until something goes wrong. Perhaps an illness, a breakup of an important relationship, a setback at school or in business, an unexpected death of a friend or loved one, an encounter with a devout follower of a different religion, or some other experience jars you awake in a new way. Then, perhaps, you may be willing to reexamine your thinking and life. Perhaps.

But why wait? Why wait for something to go seriously wrong before considering how you might more fully experience the abundant life Christ spoke of (John 10:10)? Why wait for more pain and suffering before accepting the biblical invitation to learn more about the breadth, length, and depth of Christ's love for you and for the world (Eph. 3:17–19)? Why delay experiencing God's transformation of you into a more loving person, one who lives and serves Christ in the world from wisdom and personal depth (Phil. 1:9–11)? God certainly uses suffering as a means to transform us (Rom. 8:28), but why not get ahead of the curve and seek out personal and spiritual growth as a way of life when times are relatively good as well as when life is painful or difficult?

Why not set your intention on becoming a more thoughtful, Spirit-filled, decisive, action-taking person?

Set Your Intention

Those who grow deeper in their spiritual life and experience real transformation rely on God's working in their life, guiding them, changing them, prompting new thoughts, and leading them to new commitments, new relationships, new perspective, and new ways of being in the world. At the same time, such transformation often comes especially to those who highly value personal growth, who actively pursue a deeper relationship with God, and who seek to live out their purpose in life as fully as possible.

I attribute my changing my mind and finally reaching a point of readiness to go on the Camino to the Holy Spirit's transforming work within me. At the same time, I was making a conscious decision to pursue further transformation.

Reflect on your life for a minute. Think about a time when you did an about-face, changing your mind to do something that you didn't think you would ever do, in order to further your spiritual life. How do you think the Holy Spirit might have been working to lead you through the process? Where did your response have a decisive effect on the outcome? If you can't think of one particular event, how have you been generally aware of an interplay between the Spirit's working in your life and your own role in responding (or not) that has affected the quality of your relationship to God and others?

One of the ways the Holy Spirit works in us is to lead us to increasingly give higher priority to seeking God and God's vision for our life. As we become more conscious of God's values, and our desire to please and serve God grows, we will become more intentional with our choices and priorities. Even when we decide not to plan any particular act of devotion or service but just "go with the flow" of the Spirit, that decision in itself is setting an intention. In other words, the more God works in us, the more proactive we will become to work with God to foster spiritual growth and transformation, and to seek to live out our purpose.

Dallas Willard, noted author and professor of philosophy at the University of Southern California, offers helpful counsel for those of us who want to become more intentional in our personal growth. Willard argues that transformation best occurs when we have a vision for the change desired (V), set our intention on pursuing that vision (I), and then take advantage of the means of transformation (M).[1] His VIM paradigm is a helpful way to think about and pursue spiritual growth.

From a biblical perspective, the fundamental Christian *vision* is to become more and more like Christ—by living in perfect communion with God, by loving others as ourselves, and by humbly serving God's purposes for our life, whatever they may be. Jesus expressed this vision for spiritual vitality and maturity by praying that his disciples would become one with God and one another and by teaching the priority of loving God, self, and others with all of our being (see John 17:20–21; Matt. 22:36–40). Jesus modeled his devotion to God and serving God's purposes by his self-sacrificial life of ministry and service (see Phil. 2:5–11; Heb. 12:2–4). The rest of the New Testament writers affirm the same vision in various ways, while Paul summed it all up by portraying the ultimate goal as

becoming completely like Jesus himself (Rom. 8:29; 2 Cor. 3:18)—
a goal unattainable in this life, but one that will be fulfilled when we
are resurrected from the dead (1 Cor. 15:44–54).

The *means* of being transformed to become like Jesus is every
grace and resource God has given us. We have been given Scripture;
forgiveness of sins; the presence and activity of the Holy Spirit in our
lives; other Christians who help us, support us, teach us, and show
us the way; and the church as a whole and all that is available to us
through it. Spirit-filled and Spirit-led believers, in communion with
other Christians and grounded in the teaching of the Bible, have at
their disposal the grace and power needed to become more like Jesus
and to live out Jesus's vision as he did.

The piece that is often missing in an individual's life is the middle piece in Willard's trio: *intention*. As he puts it, "The problem of
spiritual transformation among those who identify themselves as
Christians today is not that it is impossible or that means to it are not
available. Rather, the problem is that it is not intended."[2] Once you
have the vision, you need to make it your intention to pursue it with
the means at your disposal. Even with intentionality, change is sometimes frustratingly elusive or slow to come. But without it, vision is
useless, and the means of being changed will be largely irrelevant.

Cross Over to Your True Self

Your life will also change for the better the more you face truth
about yourself and act in ways that are well-aligned with your interests, abilities, and opportunities, as opposed to acting in ways that
are aligned with your desires but not your capabilities. We may shy
away from such candid self-appraisal. After all, who wants to admit
their limitations or weaknesses? Between our pride, the pressure of
others, or some other unhealthy driving force, admitting that we
have unrealistic goals, we are in the wrong job, or simply don't have
what it takes to succeed in something we value can be really tough.

Yet to keep suffering because you refuse to deal with issues and
problems that you pretend not to see is not fun either. Instead, when
you face what is real and then take whatever steps naturally flow
from seeing the truth, you will be much more able to create a bet-

ter reality. Improving yourself; being strengthened; experiencing significant shifts in your work, ministry, and relationships; and helping make the world a better place for someone else are all examples of the kinds of transformation that can flow from facing the truth about yourself, listening to what the Spirit wants to say to you, and then taking action to follow the Spirit's prompting in sync with your capabilities and resources. Here I am thinking about taking a long-term perspective on personal transformation, and the bridges that are crossed slowly over time.

Alcoholic Anonymous's success grows out of insisting that those who want to live a better life first admit that they have a problem that they can't solve on their own. Facing truth like that is hard sometimes, but what makes such a confession so powerful is that it finally gives addicts firm ground to stand on while they are seeking to change their life. Not every issue requires admitting a high degree of powerlessness. But honestly assessing what is and what is not within your power is an important step toward creating or finding the resources you need in order to make needed changes in your life. The simple truth is that the more you face what is real, the easier it is to find a firm (not illusory or weak) foundation—be it God, the strengths and skills you have at your disposal, others and available resources, or all of the above—to begin building a better life, relationships, ministries, and anything else important to you.

Thus, a good alternative to living in denial and to fearfully avoiding conflict truly exists, despite how natural it may feel to dodge a painful realization, conversation, or confrontation. If you do what it takes to become more grounded in your connection to yourself, God, and others and refuse to live in Fantasy Land or to view yourself either as a superhero or as a victim of life, you will start to see more clearly what can be done to improve your life. Your energy and confidence for tackling challenges will increase. Over time, you will also discover more joy from living life by your values from a grounded, Spirit-led place.

Thus, acting on the reality the Holy Spirit reveals to you is also key to realizing your dreams. Once you allow yourself to see what is true about your present reality, you will be better prepared to identify stepping stones to reaching your vision. When you sit down to think about your life, the questions, who am I? (at the present moment) and, who might I become? (in the future) should rarely yield the same answers. Each question needs to be asked precisely because the answers produce different perspectives. The first tells you about your life today and the second about what your life might become in the future. By honestly facing the realities that come from exploring the first question, you have a better chance of creating a more satisfying answer to the second question. Usually, the more we can face what is (providing that we do not let reality bog us down or discourage us), the more we can pursue what might be—and thus embark upon a process of real transformation.

For years I had a dream of a global teaching ministry, offering inspiration, teaching, and encouragement to motivated people of influence. For a long time, I was frustrated that few seemed to recognize what I had to offer, and no one was inviting me to speak at conferences or pastors' retreats. Then I realized that who I was and the course I was on did not line up with who I wanted to become. In my heart and mind, I saw myself as a highly capable teacher and coach, but in my work and behavior my life was filled with other priorities and activities. My job focused on youth staff, nonprofit management, and fundraising. The one book I had published was in an academic field rather than geared toward pastors and other leaders. I had developed almost no network among those who conduct conferences, retreats, or educational events for the people I most wanted to serve.

Until I faced the truth about where I was, I could not see what I needed to do to pursue my dream. Getting more grounded in what was real led me to change jobs, publish new books, make a new set of friends, pursue ecumenical relationships with other pastors and church leaders, take initiative to offer leadership and pastors' seminars in Bulgaria, Myanmar, and Africa as well as in the United States. I committed myself to acquiring additional formal and informal training and accreditation and to launching a spiritual life-coaching practice. Now, I am experiencing greater joy as I am realizing my dreams, and I believe the kingdom of God is being better served. Thus, acting on the reality the Holy Spirit helped me to see has been helping me not only to realize my dreams but also to lead, teach, and serve better; use my gifts more effectively; and encourage others more passionately and powerfully.

Alternatively, when we refuse to face and act on truth about ourselves, our relationship to God and others, or the work we are trying to do, we are more likely to be frustrated, unfruitful, and ultimately unsatisfied with our life. We may really want things to be different, but they won't be what we envision or hope for unless we are willing to open our eyes to see what we need to see and to yield our wills to however the Spirit may be prompting. That is, we need to be willing to change in order to experience change. We need to actually choose to act differently before we can expect to see different outcomes. Often, we may need to set out on a different path, even before it feels right or comfortable, before we can experience a more permanent shift that we desire within us or in our relationships, work, or ministry.

On pilgrimage, though I often did not like to face reality, especially when my weaknesses or character flaws were exposed or something was demanded of me that I didn't want to give, facing the truth was well worth the pain and effort. The more I did, the more insight I gained, the better choices I made, and the happier I became in the long run—and the happier others often were, too.

At times, though, the changes you make will not make others happy, because they have something invested in the old you. Other times, those close to you can see something you can't. You need discernment to know when the objection of others is their self-centeredness or lack of understanding, and when it is a red flag you should be taking into consideration.

In other words, be sure that you are thoughtful and prayerful about choosing which bridges to cross and where they lead. We all know stories of midlife crises that bring newfound freedom, pleasure, and "love" that also leave in their wake broken marriages, devastated family members, loss of trust, ruined reputations, or trashed careers.[3] Sometimes the stirring for change within you needs time to incubate until you have enough wisdom to know how to honor the calling while still honoring your commitments and other practical responsibilities, or at least lovingly care for others affected if you conclude that you must change course.

To intentionally mix metaphors, the pilgrim's way requires learning how to stay well-grounded while you keep moving down the path and over the bridges God leads you to. In spite of how being well-grounded might sound, I do not mean being "stuck in the mud" or passively accepting the status quo or sitting around waiting for God to do something. Rather, to be well-grounded means to have both feet solidly on even ground, seeing and accepting what is real about yourself and your circumstances, while also being sure-footed and ready to act on what you see.

Spiritual transformation, then, entails *becoming more fully cognizant* of your physical environment; body, mental and emotional state; quality of relationships; and your connection to God and personal calling and capabilities *as you proceed* down the path, living out of this knowledge in ways that fit with your faith, values, and commitments and in step with the leading of the Holy Spirit. You simultaneously become better at seeing what you can know about your present reality, while you keep moving toward what you do not yet know. Being well-grounded helps you better recognize and cross the important bridges in your life, as you walk in faith out of faithfulness.

For Further Reflection

Postpilgrimage reflection. Fall 2006. Spiritual pilgrimage is a lifelong process of seeking God and personal growth and of depending on God to transform us in God's timing, in God's way, over the course of the journey. Over the years, I have spent a fair amount of time, money, and energy with family members, friends, pastors, therapists, colleagues, students, and others from different denominations and faiths. I have spent countless hours learning by reading, studying, journaling, confronting, experimenting, failing, starting over, and the like in order to better face what is real and to seek to become more stable and healthy in the various dimensions of my life. I have experienced so many good changes in my life over the years, and yet some days I feel as if I have just begun the journey. In the end, I am left to set my intention and keep walking as best I can, while depending on God's grace to pro-

duce the fruit that fits with God's intention and will for my spiritual pilgrimage.

Use the reflection above and the following questions to guide your journal writing and discussion with a small group of fellow spiritual pilgrims who are looking for God's bridges in their life.

- What are the most significant bridges I see in front of me right now? How do I feel about the transformative opportunities I see?
- What am I going to do with my transformative opportunities?
- What is my *vision* for my relationships: with God, my spouse or significant other (if you have one), my children (if you have them), my coworkers, my friends? What is my vision for other aspects of my life: my work, service, health, finances, recreation, and personal fulfillment?
- What *intention* do I have in each of these areas? That is, what specifically do I intend to do to pursue my vision for each area of my life?
- What *means* are available to me to help me pursue my vision?
- How would I describe my best self? What can I do to cross the bridge to live out of my best self more often?
- Whose help do I need to take concrete action and stay committed to the path of transformation I see before me? What will I ask for from them? When will I ask?
- What other thoughts or ideas were prompted by this chapter on crossing bridges? What specifically do I intend to do differently or more consistently?

Staying the Course

~

I WAS GETTING ANGRIER by the minute. The more I thought about everything that was wrong with the world, the more upset I became. The more I wondered why God wasn't doing more to make life better for the billions of suffering people, the angrier I got.

That day on pilgrimage I had been walking alone for several hours in the midsummer heat. Jill and my sons had decided to hike together, leaving me to cross the open countryside observing and ruminating on my own. The day started great, and I was enjoying being out in the open air by myself, but I was tired and my attitude toward God started to deteriorate.

Walking fifteen miles per day, often without shade from the sun, was starting to take its toll on me. The physical hardships alone kept me focused on survival needs and sometimes made it nearly impossible to even think about God, let alone work on deepening my relationship with God. Who could think much about God when your feet were aching, the sun was blazing, and you were worrying about finding a place to stay, drinking enough water, and getting enough sleep? Then when I did think about God, at least on this day, questions about the impracticality of devoting time to God and God's seeming apathy or impotence in the face of human suffering starting bubbling up. I was getting crabby.

As the day dragged on, these questions began to intensify. Soon I was wondering about the meaning of life and the role that God plays for the average person. While walking, I didn't have to worry about earning money for food that day, maintaining a home, or dealing with other demands of normal daily life, yet my concerns for physical relief, food, drink, shade, and shelter often distracted me from God and the needs of those around me. I wondered, if I am having such a hard time focusing on God, how would others who have far more to deal with each day find time or emotional energy to attend to their relationship with God? If I, with all of my biblical knowledge and theological training, am questioning my faith from a position of privilege and relative comfort, what must those who are suffering or have less spiritual training than I do think about God and God's involvement (or lack thereof) in their life?

As some of these thoughts were swirling around in my head, a peasant in tattered clothing passed me. He rode in a medieval-looking cart pulled by a single horse. He was on his way to till his garden with a primitive hoe. As he struggled just to survive from day to day, did he have time to think about God or develop his spiritual life? Did he care about his relationship with God?

I grimaced recalling another man—and many others like him—whom I had met the day before. He had been sweeping out the church. His teeth were clearly rotting from never having brushed them. I suspected he had never been to a dentist and probably had other problems, too. The quality of his health appeared to mirror the quality of his life. What relevance did faith in God have for him? I mean, God may exist and love him, but what difference did that fact make in his daily life?

Then there were the hopeful teenaged girls whose destiny seemed to be heartbreak, exploitation, and disillusionment. I felt angry thinking about any number of girls I saw in many of the villages we passed through, who were all dressed up and just sitting in the plaza, hoping some boy would notice them and love them. Yet, according to stories I read and heard, many would likely settle for some man who would only exploit them. They would probably marry eventually and have a bunch of kids, but their husbands would soon acquire a mistress or two while they would be left at home to care for the children and household. Did these girls think about God and believe that God had a good purpose for their life?

My mind quickly went to the millions of people who regularly suffer from exploitation and abuse. What about those who have to work two or three jobs just to make ends meet? What about the single parents, even in affluent countries, who feel overwhelmed with trying to meet the needs of their children, let alone their own? Then there are the millions of displaced people in the world, fleeing from marauding bands of soldiers who may rape, maim, or kill them or members of their household. The questions multiplied in my head as fast as the scenes of suffering humanity flashed across my mind.

I was not having a good day.

The more I reflected on my own suffering and the suffering of others, the more despair I felt. Then came anger. What must all these people feel? Forget the impracticality of carving out time for God. Why would anyone *want* to devote themselves to seeking God if this painful, disappointing, pathetic life is what God willed or permitted for them?

Fontaine, one of the protagonists in *Les Miserables*, a nineteenth-century novel by Victor Hugo that was turned into one of the most popular musicals of all time, sings a poignant song of disillusionment and despair that mirrors some of what I was feeling in those dark moments on the Camino. Fontaine's own dreams had been crushed when her lover abandoned her, pregnant and without means to support herself. In time, she had been forced to entrust her child, Cosette, to an unscrupulous, abusive couple. She felt helpless to do anything to recover her lost love or to find forgiveness. She slaved for long hours just to feed herself and send a little money to the couple, who, unbeknownst to her, were keeping the cash for themselves instead of properly caring for Cosette.

Fontaine's song captures well the grief and bitterness of lost dreams, which have dissolved into disappointment and pain, and of shame from poor life choices:

> I dreamed a dream in time gone by
> When hope was high and life worth living.
> I dreamed that love would never die.
> I dreamed that God would be forgiving.

> *   *   *

> Then I was young and unafraid,
> And dreams were made, and used and wasted,
> There was no ransom to be paid,
> No song unsung, no wine untasted.

But the tigers have come at night
With the voices soft as thunder
As they tear your hope apart
As they turn your dream to shame.

* * *

I had a dream my life would be
So different from this hell I am living
So different now from what it seemed
Now life has killed the dream I dreamed.[1]

Many of us have not known the horrors experienced by the characters in *Les Miserables*, but even the most privileged or successful among us often suffer from pain hidden from others. How many of us agonize over great loss, bitter disappointments, grief, shame, personal failure, or some other physical or emotional distress? This is simply the way life is in a world contaminated by sin. Alongside whatever joy, love, satisfaction, or happiness we might feel at times, no one escapes the depths of pain that life can inflict on us.

On pilgrimage I was facing these facts of life on a new level. I didn't know it at the time. I just thought I was wondering about the meaning of life for others less fortunate than I. But in truth I was finally letting myself feel the depth of my distress and despair over the injustices of the world, the suffering of great masses of people, and God's seeming inactivity.

I don't want life to be full of suffering, but it is. I don't want to watch loved ones suffer and die, but I have had to. I don't want to accept that sometimes I am falsely accused or mistreated by others, and no remedy emerges. I don't want to feel the pain of failure, rejection, or unrequited love. And I don't want to have to face that I have disappointed myself and others—worse, hurt myself and exploited, mistreated, and neglected others—in so many ways, but I have.

Out on the long, lonely roads of Spain, I began wondering, if life is so miserable for so many people, what is the point of it? And if God doesn't seem to save us from our misery, why spend time or energy trying to develop a relationship with this God? And what business do pastors, priests, and other spiritual leaders have calling people who are consumed with surviving or are stricken with disillusionment and heartache to worship and serve God? Can they afford to devote precious time, energy, and attention to deepening their spiritual life when they need to pay attention to themselves and those who are dependent on them?

Today I realize that beneath these questions lay a deeper issue. What I really wondered was, in light of the brutal realities of life, who would have *the heart* to seek after God? Do not the pain, suffering, and disillusionment with life kill our hearts for God as Fontaine's deep disappointments killed her dreams? Who would *want* to pursue a God who appears at times to be so indifferent to the human predicament? I certainly know how motivated I can be to pray when I feel needy or desperate, and I can imagine how a hungry or frightened person would seek God for food, for healing from sickness, or for victory over invaders or enemies. I understand prayers of desperation! But why would we want to persistently love God with all our heart, mind, soul, and strength, as Jesus taught? What would truly motivate us to put all our eggs in God's basket, given all we have to deal with in life? How could we trust, and how could we continue to care?

But so many can, and so many do.

A Heart for God

I remember the first time I was exposed to Christian communities in developing countries. I was visiting a poor congregation in Mexico City. The year was 1980 and I had taken a team of youth on a mission trip there. We were going to help dig latrines and paint churches and never dreamed that the people of the congregation would have such a profound effect on us. There in the midst of great poverty I experienced greater happiness among the people than I knew back home, and worship was more vibrant and heartfelt than any I had ever experienced in affluent suburbia. I was so surprised. I didn't know that I had been assuming people could only be happy and praise God if they were financially secure and lived a fairly comfortable life.

I couldn't have been more wrong.

Since then I have had many opportunities to meet deeply spiritual and religious people who highly value their relationship to God in the midst of much suffering and deprivation. I recall many individuals I have met while teaching and ministering in Eastern Europe, Africa, and Asia. While their cultures varied considerably, what they had in common was not only poverty and a history of hardship but also deep trust in God and gratitude for all their blessings.

For example, in just a ten-year period in the Democratic Republic of Congo (DRC), beginning in 1996, more than five million people died from war, hunger, and disease; now thousands more continue to experience vicious crimes of mutilation and rape. In the fall of 2007, I led a pastors leadership conference in Goma (a key city on the eastern border of DRC and Rwanda) and was startled by the deep faith I discovered among the people. While I naively expected many to turn away from God in anger or disillusionment, I witnessed just the opposite. Many were clinging all the more to Christ and to their faith.

A few months ago, a friend of mine returned from visiting AIDS orphans in Africa feeling sheepish. While there he had come upon a tiny home whose walls were sheets of aluminum. He had been shocked to find inside a grandmother, a couple of siblings, and five grandchildren—all orphaned. As the elderly woman told her story, she was smiling because she was so grateful for the ways God had provided for her little family. In light of all they had lost and how little they had, how could she say that? Yet she did, and she believed it. Even more, she was living out her faith and gratitude in ways that gave her daily strength and hope as she cared for these children and helped out others in her church and community when possible. My friend had gone to help these impoverished people only to discover the impoverishment of his own soul.

I am surprised it took me so long on pilgrimage to remember a simple spiritual truth that should have been readily available to me: *spiritual vitality isn't a luxury, it's a lifeline.* I must have heard dozens of sermons on the subject, and I have given a few myself. I even learned how important leaning on God was while watching my mother die of Alzheimer's disease over an agonizing, faith-testing fifteen-year stretch. I also learned the vital importance of daily reaching out to God for perspective and encouragement when I battled a terminal disease that was diagnosed the day after my first son was born in 1986, and from which I was healed several years later.

For some reason, however, my circumstances on pilgrimage were causing memory failure. A little physical hardship made me realize how privileged I am in my normal life and how greatly many people struggle just to survive. Seeing impoverished people and their living conditions brought up all my old doubts about God's presence and love. What I was really feeling was frustration, sadness, and distress that life is so difficult for so many people and God doesn't seem to be helping more.

What I was forgetting is that dissatisfaction with life or disappointment with God doesn't remove one's longing or need for God. And busyness or preoccupation with survival doesn't make a relationship with God unimportant or unattainable.[2] Connecting to God cannot wait until our lives are in order or we have extra time; we must seek God *in the midst* of our struggle.

And why would we want to?

Because no one loves us as God does, there is no greater power for forgiveness and inner healing, and no greater source of hope than the Holy Spirit's working in our hearts and minds in the midst of our suffering, loss, and grief. We may often want more from God than is forthcoming, but what God does give cannot be found anywhere else.

Human suffering raises troubling questions for believers in a good and loving God, yet at the same time, suffering can drive us to God better than can comfort, ease, and affluence. The more we are stripped of our illusions about what this life can provide for us, the more ready we are to look beyond ourselves for meaning and purpose. The meaninglessness, seeming absurdity, and pain of daily life can help us get in touch with our heart's deepest longing for God and the meaning that comes from giving of ourselves to others. Human suffering has the potential to lead us to the one true source of eternal healing and hope that otherwise we might never seek, let alone find.

The Power of Pilgrimage

Pilgrimage was exposing how shallow my spiritual life and love for others can be. A little pain, a little anxiety, a little conflict and I could marginalize God and others in my thinking and daily life. Then when life didn't go the way I thought it should or the way I wanted it to, I could easily blame God and justify my anger or withdrawing from God.

At the same time, it wasn't long before my initial reaction of pulling away from God and others in my distress began to reveal to me how much I truly valued my relationship with God and those I love. The more I focused on my personal struggles and myself and the more I began to lose a conscious connection with God and those around me, the more empty and dissatisfied with life I felt and the more I unconsciously hungered for God and spiritual nourishment. My agnostic friends would counsel me to forget about God and move on, but I knew that they didn't know what they were missing.

Thus, while the physical and environmental demands were threatening to undermine the power and gift of the pilgrimage, the Holy Spirit was using them as a catalyst for deeper reflection, insight, and longing for God. I came to realize in a more profound way that my *response* to my physical reality—not the experiences themselves or what God was or was not doing—was determining how relevant my relationship with God was to my life. Each day I had a choice: I could seek God, deeper meaning, and love in the midst of my pain and suffering or I could get swallowed up in myself and my problems. Pilgrimage was helping me see that my anger with God only proved how much I believed in God and highly valued my relationship with God. The truth is, in spite of my tendencies to wander away from God and the frustration and disappointment I sometimes feel with God, I love God deeply and want nothing more than to maintain a close relationship with God.

Spiritual Spiraling

As I went from being happy walking alone on a country road in Spain to feeling distress, disillusionment, and doubt; to reawakening my longing for God; to a renewed faith and love for God, I was reenacting an old pattern in my life: on good days I call it "spiritual spiraling" and on others "sheer madness." I have a tendency to repeat a cycle, beginning with enthusiasm about my faith and serving God, moving to doubt and frustration with God, then drifting mentally and emotionally, and eventually seeking help from God. My search is usually rewarded with answers to prayer, new insight, encouragement, divine surprises, or some other shift that leads me to become enthusiastic about God and serving God wholeheartedly once again. The cycle looks something like this:

Enthusiasm

Seeking God

Doubt

Drifting

I call this phenomenon spiritual spiraling, because when I return to enthusiasm after a sojourn through doubt, drifting, and renewed seeking, my faith is often stronger and deeper. On the surface one might think that I am just going in circles, but each cycle only appears to mimic the previous one. Usually, I am actually growing spiritually, even if at times in the spiraling I may feel as if I am moving away from God for a while.

On the other hand, sometimes this spiraling is simply sheer madness because letting my faith go into a tailspin often seems quite counterproductive, at least in the short run. In spite of long-term growth that can come from the cycle, entertaining serious doubts about God after so many years of experiencing God's faithfulness to me usually doesn't serve me well, because I tend to waste time and energy before coming back to my faith once again, and my wandering undermines the vitality of my ministry to others.

Perhaps I will one day stop doubting, but until then, when I realize that I have started going into a tailspin, I have learned what to do. Either I need to get right to seeking God and asking for help—bypassing hours, days, or weeks of brooding—or I will have to wait until my drifting becomes so unsatisfying that I am motivated to cross back over the bridge to faith in God once again.

I realize that not everyone may be able to relate to my spiritual highs, just as not everyone struggles as much as I do with doubt, anger, or frustration with God or drifts in their conviction and commitment to Christ, and thus may not be able to relate to my lows. Yet I suspect that nearly every Christian experiences a waxing and waning of their spiritual vitality from time to time, in some form or another. The question is not, do we doubt or drift at times, but do we remember to keep getting back on the path that leads to God?

Staying the Course

Though at one point in my life I couldn't imagine ever going on pilgrimage, and in the middle of the trip I questioned our sanity at times, my summer journey was one of the most profound transformational experiences of my life. My extraordinary summer in Spain was filled with questions, reflection, exploration, experimentation, physical exertion, sacrifice, and discovery that I simply could not have experienced in my "normal" life. Yet at the same time, my going on pilgrimage was simply one more Spirit-led adventure— one more step—in a lifelong process of spiritual growth, through which I keep learning more about myself, drawing closer to God, making changes, and having other changes forced upon me.

What I didn't realize at the time was how challenging reentry was going to be once the pilgrimage was over. On the Camino, I knew clearly how important maintaining a spiritual life was to me. Once home and back to the demands of starting up a business and new ministry, negotiating family relations, reentry to American culture, spending time with friends who had not had the same experience, and a whole host of other stresses, distractions, and discouragements, staying on course was challenging.

Almost right away many of the old temptations of my comfortable life at home—old ways of thinking and being in the world that had been challenged on pilgrimage and even replaced at times with much better ways—started calling to me. I could feel the tension, even if I didn't always know what was out of place. I didn't want to lose the gains of the summer: greater simplicity, a slower pace of life, extended time alone with God, significant times with my family, and a stronger resolve to face reality and to deal with issues in a straightforward manner. Yet American culture so prevalent in the fabric of our life and relationships doesn't always support these values. I was resolved to keep going with the flow of the Spirit in my life, but I didn't realize how hard doing so was going to be at times.

When we live as spiritual pilgrims, pursuing God and transformation as a way of life, often the changes that take place within our lives happen little by little over time. When we make such incremental changes, the internal shifts are often subtle, and we may not experience a major clash with our culture, at least not until the changes we make force us to make uncomfortable choices that affect others. At other times, a significant transformative experience (such as pilgrimage, a spiritual retreat, some other powerful event, or a major decision we make) may bring about deep change in the way we think, in our relationships, in our work or some other important aspect of our life. At times, the sheer power or implications of our change propels us, though the changes made may be undone if we do not reinforce them by continuing to take action in ways that are aligned with our new way of thinking and feeling.

To not lose the gains from the summer, as well as to keep flowing with the changes that were unfolding in my life, I needed to make a plan to stay on course. I had crossed many bridges, and I didn't want go back. I wanted to continue growing and following the path as God revealed it to me. I wanted to keep going on my spiritual pilgrimage.

One Step at a Time

As I reflect on the past couple of years since walking to Santiago de Compostela, I know better why I went on pilgrimage and how I have been changed. I realize transformation was taking place through the process of deciding to walk the Camino and throughout the five-hundred-mile journey, and that it continues as I act on the insights and experiences of the pilgrimage now that I am back. Further, I find that the more I view all of life as a spiritual pilgrimage, the more I expect God's transforming work through all that happens in my life, and the more I intentionally seek to make a solid connection to God each day and live out of an ongoing sense of God's presence.

My yearning to stay on track has led me to seek the Holy Spirit's leading in every aspect of my life. I have become more diligent about carving out time and emotional space to listen for the Spirit's voice, and I am consciously trying to rely on the Spirit for guidance as I integrate the learnings from the pilgrimage with the rest of my life. I have been praying for the Spirit to fill me and lead me as I set my personal and professional goals and order my priorities for the day, week, month, and year(s) ahead. I don't mean I put a blank sheet of paper in front of me, close my eyes, pray, and ask God to direct my hand, as some might think relying on the Spirit might entail. Rather, I have been starting each day by sitting quietly, opening my heart and mind to God, and waiting until I sense that I have truly welcomed the Holy Spirit and submitted my will to God's. Then I can work on my other priorities and respond to the challenges and interruptions of the day from a place of spiritual groundedness and sensitivity, continually reaching out to the God who is close at hand for guidance, strength, courage, and encouragement.

I am also taking time to periodically reflect on my life to see what is real in my relationship with God, work, service, relationship with my wife and sons, extended family, friendships, health, finances, and personal needs and desires. I ask the Spirit to show me what I need to see, to reveal changes I need to make or actions I need to take to help me to be more loving or to live better by godly values in each area. I ask for wisdom, especially in the difficult challenges or conflicts I may be facing so that I can gain a godly perspective. I also pray for grace to let go of the attachments I have to the approval and acceptance of others so that I can be freer to love them as unconditionally as possible. I don't want to fall back on old ways of grasping and reacting or criticizing and judging. I want to keep growing in my ability to live out of my best self as often as possible.

To help me, the Holy Spirit has been teaching me to *let go* of my instinctive reactions to situations or normal ways of approaching life in order to *take hold* of the opportunities and gifts before me and adopt God's perspective and motivation. Because my strong emotional impulses and reactions sometimes bring out my worst, I have to let go of them at times before I can be free to see people and situations through God's eyes (inasmuch as that is possible) and to respond in godly ways. In many cases, I don't need to be taught how to be polite or to say the socially acceptable thing or to avoid doing the wrong thing, but what is my motivation? Often, I don't want to alienate, I don't want to hurt someone's feelings, I want others to think well of me, I am afraid of the consequences of acting on my impulses, and so forth. While these are not necessarily poor motivations, there is a better one: love.

The more I read Scripture and pray, the more I witness the painful and sometimes violent conflicts that go unresolved in every sphere of human relationships, and the more I witness the huge disparity and injustice in the world, the more I sense that the Holy Spirit is prompting me to become a person of greater love. The Spirit has been showing me how important it is to listen and to consider the interests of others as well as my own, especially in situations where I have a great deal of personal interest. I feel compelled to stand up more courageously and vocally for those who are being hurt, neglected, or exploited. I feel led to let my assets shrink if need be in order to give more generously to the needs of others. I also sense a nudging to love the world enough to call and work for policies that truly benefit humanity as a whole. I don't take credit for any of these personal developments but simply point to the Holy Spirit, who seems to be transforming my mind and heart to better serve God's purposes. The more I let myself be led by the Holy Spirit, the more love seems to emerge.

Spirit-led living, then, takes us from the *good*, whatever we may be inclined to do out of our self-interest to help others, to *God*, who leads us away from serving ourselves to truly loving others for their sake. As we move from good to God, we go beyond just following well-intentioned rules for society to becoming the most loving persons we can be and doing the most loving things we can do. None of us is changed once for all time, but the more we yield to the

Spirit's leading to cross the bridges of opportunities when we come to them, the more our lives will reflect God's love and our relationships will be transformed.

I have so much to learn about recognizing the voice of the Spirit and responding more quickly and confidently. I often question the small voice in my head and ask myself, "Was that the Spirit, my own wisdom, or some other desire or impulse?" But as difficult as discerning whose voice we are truly hearing may be, it is the right question to be asking and one we need to keep raising over and over again.

As far as I can tell, the spiritual journey must be walked one step at a time as the Spirit shows us the path and gives us courage, strength, and grace to take the next step. I am learning to let go of my need to see two, three, or ten steps down the road and to let the path appear in God's timing. My job seems to be a combination of creating vision for my life, setting goals, and pursuing God and my dreams with intentionality, all the while focusing on the present moment, living as faithfully as possible with my current responsibilities and opportunities, and seeking to be my best self in every interaction with others.

I am on an ongoing journey of spiritual growth, and while I have a long way to go, I have come a long way already. I am a spiritual pilgrim in pursuit of God, seeking to follow Christ and be led by the Holy Spirit, one step at a time. Just as the Camino took us over mountains and into deep valleys, and at times on many circuitous trails, I do not expect to follow a linear course. I will continue to experience spiritual spiraling, I will need to stop and rest periodically, and I may even retrace my steps on occasion when I doubt myself, get confused, or lose heart. Yet, over all, I trust that the Holy Spirit will continue to lead me forward. I have been changed, I am changing, and I look forward to all the changes still ahead. This is the path I am on, and by God's grace I hope to continue on it for the rest of my life.

I welcome you as a traveling companion.

APPENDIX A

The Holy Spirit
and Believers

~

THE HOLY SPIRIT COMES from God and Jesus Christ and is known to Christians as the third member of the Trinity. New Testament writers in general do not always clearly differentiate between God (the Father), Christ, and the Spirit. When Paul refers to God, he usually means the Creator of the universe and Father of Jesus Christ. Jesus is God's Son, Savior of the world, and appointed Lord (leader) of all those who believe (and ultimately of the entire world). The Holy Spirit is God's (and Christ's) Spirit who fills believers and enables them to serve God's purposes in the world. Yet, these are not tidy distinctions and overlap is everywhere, a fact that helps explain why theologians eventually developed the concept of the Trinity—three persons in one.

While the three persons of the Trinity are completely intertwined, biblical authors will emphasize one or the other person depending on context. Paul, along with all biblical writers, is less concerned with precise definitions and more with promoting a vital spiritual life, marked by a restored, loving relationship with God (the Father); by faith in and allegiance to Jesus, God's Son, who shows us who God is and whose work on the cross provides a way for humanity to be reconciled to God; and by being filled with and led by the Holy Spirit, who ministers to us, helps us know the mind of Christ, and enables us to live like Christ and serve God's purposes.

Here, in this appendix, I am going to focus on the Spirit in order to provide further biblical and theological background for Spirit-led living. Numerous books and other resources are readily available on the Holy Spirit. The following is a simple overview of many of the chief biblical teachings on how the Holy Spirit interfaces with those who worship God and follow Christ.[1]

The Spirit's Role Prior to Christ

One of the most significant changes from Old Testament to New Testament times has to do with the role of the Holy Spirit in the lives of ordinary believers. Prior to Christ, the Holy Spirit spoke only occasionally through special individuals. For example, Joseph's unusual ability to interpret Pharaoh's dreams was attributed to the Spirit of God dwelling within him (Gen. 41:38). At times the Spirit of God would literally compel individuals, usually only the ancient Hebrew prophets, to prophesy (utter words from God to address issues of their day or on occasion foretell events) and then leave them again.

One time, for example, God made Saul suddenly enter into a "prophetic frenzy" with a group of prophets who were prophesying. The reasons for this extraordinary phenomenon were to change his heart through the experience and to give him a sign that he had been chosen to deliver his fellow Israelites and to become their king (1 Sam. 10:1–13). Other times, a "spirit of wisdom" would be given to great leaders, such as to Moses or Joshua, to enable them to lead wisely (for example, Deut. 34:9). Similarly, Solomon was given a great, wise, and discerning heart to lead the people (1 Kings 3:5–13). The Spirit also put ideas into David's mind about what the temple would look like and contain (1 Chron. 28:11–19).

Other times, individuals were imbued with the Spirit in order to serve some special divine purpose, from conquering enemies to crafting furnishings for the tabernacle (Ex. 31:1–5; Judges). However, in general, as far as we know, the average person was not filled by the Holy Spirit or led by the Spirit. The norm seemed to be that individuals and the community as a whole had God's laws and were expected to follow them in their own strength, with the support of the community.

The Spirit's Role Since Christ

Since Christ's resurrection, beginning with the outpouring of the Holy Spirit on a group of Christians gathered in Jerusalem on Pentecost (Acts 2:1–21), a new relationship with the Spirit was inaugurated. God began to pour out the Holy Spirit on all believers, regardless of status in the community, gender, or age, as had been anticipated by the ancient Hebrew prophets Joel and Jeremiah. They had looked forward to a day when a new covenant was in place, when a new level of intimacy with and knowledge of God would be created by God within the heart and mind of each believer (Joel 2:28–32; Jer. 31:31–34). Jeremiah expressed the words of the Lord this way: "But this is the covenant that I will make with the house of Israel after those days, says the LORD: I will put my law within them, and I will write it on their hearts; and I will be their God, and they shall be my people. No longer shall they teach one another, or say to each other, 'Know the LORD,' for they shall all know me, from the least of them to the greatest, says the LORD; for I will forgive their iniquity, and remember their sin no more" (vv. 33–34).

These prophecies, combined with extraordinary experiences such as those at Pentecost, became the grounding for early Christian teaching that every believer in Christ was sealed with the Holy Spirit permanently (Eph. 1:13), though some branches of the church have taught, based on a few narratives in Acts and personal experience, that believers must be specially baptized in the Spirit to experience the full power of the Spirit. As time went on, the dramatic displays of the Spirit became less frequent in most congregations, and the net effect of the Spirit's activity in the life of the believer and community became most important.

Believers Are Baptized by the Spirit and Receive Eternal Life

In all four Gospels, the Holy Spirit figures prominently as the source of power in Jesus's life and the gift of Jesus to believers. John the Baptist declared that when Jesus came, he would baptize believers, not with water but with the Holy Spirit.[2] According to John, Jesus taught that with the bestowal of the Spirit of God came eternal life, which is evidenced especially by faith in God's Son and in love for God, Christ, and others.[3] Eternal life refers to both quality and quantity of life: it includes forgiveness of sin and a renewed relationship with God; it begins now in this life and extends for eternity. In order to experience eternal life, we must be born again of the Spirit (John 3:3).[4]

The Spirit Leads Us to Spiritual Truth

Jesus had told his disciples, according to John's Gospel, that he would send the Spirit to guide them "into all truth" (John 16:13). For those who never meet Jesus in person, the Holy Spirit does the job of convincing people of their need for Jesus Christ as Son of God and Savior of the world (John 16:5–11; 1 John 4:2–3, 14).

In explaining the mystery of faith, Paul explains to the Corinthians that God is not known by human beings reasoning their way to belief but through the proclamation of the Gospel. "For since, in the wisdom of God, the world did not know God through wisdom, God decided, through the foolishness of our proclamation, to save those who believe"(1 Cor. 1:21). Preaching focuses on the foolishness of salvation through Jesus Christ and his death instead of trying to persuade through human logic and insight. Then, in the context of proclamation, nonbelievers come to faith through a powerful experience with the Holy Spirit (2:1–5). Thus, in the end our ability to know God and Christ depends on God's gift of the Spirit, who reveals to us what we cannot know on our own (2:6–16). Further, only by the Holy Spirit can anyone acknowledge Jesus as Lord (1 Cor. 12:3).

The Holy Spirit does not only bring people to faith in Christ, however. Believers also depend upon the Spirit to continue to grow in wisdom, power, and knowledge and understanding of God and Christ. Thus, we find several biblical examples of prayer for eyes to be opened or for insight, power, or love to increase. God produces such growth and transformation through the Spirit.[5]

The Holy Spirit Encourages, Empowers, and Renews Believers

The apostle Paul taught that believers are sealed with the Spirit as a guarantee of their eternal inheritance (Eph. 1:13–14). The Spirit equips and enables believers in Christ to resist temptations and to live the righteous, fruitful life Christ intends for his followers (Rom. 8:13–14; Gal. 5:16–23; see, too, Titus 2:11–14). When Jesus breathed the Spirit into his disciples, he was giving them power to do the work of God (John 20:19–23). Believers are called to respond to the Spirit by setting their mind on the Spirit and keeping in step with the Spirit's leading, in order to benefit fully from God's presence and power (Rom. 8:6; Gal. 5:24–25).

The Holy Spirit is also a great source of encouragement and help to believers. Jesus said that the Spirit produces "rivers of living water" that nourish, renew, and empower believers (John 7:37–39). The Spirit also helps us pray when words fail us (Rom. 8:26).

The Holy Spirit Enables Believers to Do Fruitful Work in the World

The Holy Spirit is also indispensable for the church as a whole and for empowering believers to serve God's will and fulfill their purpose in life—the "good works" that God has in mind for each of us (Eph. 2:10). The Spirit's role is to give various gifts (abilities) to believers, who will in turn help other members of Christ's body become equipped for works of service (1 Cor. 12; Eph. 4:11–16; Rom. 12:3–8). As we exercise our gift(s) and carry out the good works God intends for us to do, we will become more like Christ (becoming spiritually mature), and together the full body of Christ more closely resembles Christ. Paul explains this phenomenon this way: "It was [Christ] who gave some to be apostles, some to be prophets, some to be evangelists, and some to be pastors and teachers, to prepare God's people for works of service, so that the body of Christ may be built up until we all reach unity in the faith and in the knowledge of the Son of God and become mature, attaining to the whole measure of the fullness of Christ" (Eph. 4:11–13 NIV).

As individuals and local churches, believers in Christ will naturally express the love of God in various ways to members of their own congregations and others in their communities. Paul suggests that the Holy Spirit helps here, too, when he prays that God would give believers strength to fulfill the good intentions in their hearts (2 Thess. 1:11).

The Spirit Transforms Us Over Time

Over time, with God's help, Christians develop perseverance, character, and hope through suffering (Rom. 5:3–5). Likewise, James saw that Christians developed perseverance and maturity through their suffering (James 1:2–4). Peter explained that suffering tested the genuineness of faith and implied that the testing made one's faith more vibrant (1 Pet. 1:7).

In other words, when the Holy Spirit uses our experiences to change us or leads us to truth we need to face, and we make changes, transformation has taken place. If we move from disbelief to trust in Christ, our worldview and outlook have been fundamentally altered. When we stop doing something that we know is wrong, because the Spirit convinced us through guilt or inspiration to change our behavior, our lives have been at least partially transformed. When over time we start sharing more, giving more, or serving more, we are being transformed. When we experience forgiveness and are set free from guilt and shame, we have been transformed.

Now, we will all surely sin again and again by impure thoughts, overt acts, resistance to God, or sins of omission. Yet, our weaknesses, failures, and spiritual immaturity do not negate the reality of the changes we have already experienced or how far we have come in other ways. They simply confirm our ongoing need for grace and the renewing work of the Holy Spirit. Paul said that while our physical bodies are dying, our inner selves are being renewed every day and we are being transformed into the image of Christ (2 Cor. 3:18; 4:16–18). Real transformation is taking place in those who are believers in Christ through God's work in their lives by the Holy Spirit. Yet at the same time, believers will always remain dependent on the Holy Spirit for daily forgiveness, renewal, filling, and leading.

APPENDIX B

Giving Up on Finding Christian Community?

~

I N A CULTURE where individuality, self-reliance, and self-confidence are so prized and where disillusionment with the Bible or established religion have pushed so many out on their own, a special word about our need for one another and Christian community may be helpful. Spiritual pilgrims must walk their own paths, but wise pilgrims seldom if ever try to go it completely alone. We need each other for support, for wisdom, for perspective, for accountability, for encouragement, for help, and for prayer. Though each of us has our own unique perspective, we need to know the views of others to help us navigate our way.

Community may be defined and experienced very narrowly, such as by our best friends, family, or small group; as it is most commonly, such as by our classmates, others in our town, or those who attend our church; or very broadly, such as by others within our state or nation or even fellow human beings throughout the world from different cultures and religions. We may regularly spend time face-to-face with a set group of people or enjoy a network of relationships via the Internet with people we have never seen, though most of us will always want some physical touch and to be physically present with our friends to feel satisfied in our relationships.

When we were on pilgrimage, walking fifteen miles a day for five-and-a-half weeks, we felt a sense of community both among the walkers and with the many hostel hosts and greeters along the way. Our journey was enhanced by each member, including those who caused conflict or bothered us, because they helped us learn more about ourselves and forced us to adapt, change, and seek God in new ways, or else continue to suffer. Our deepest sense of community, however, came from those we walked with for the whole journey.

The keys to a vital community, however formed and defined, are connection and communication along with commitment and caring. The best community experiences include openness, acceptance, humility, and grace. From the anonymous co-pilgrim encountered on the path to interactions with beloved companions along the way, even to annoying fellow pilgrims, we can benefit greatly from interactive relationships with others. In community, however defined, we can share our experiences with one another, and in the process open ourselves up to learning from, being influenced by, and influencing one another. Wherever we may find them, we will benefit greatly if we can accept that we need people who have complementary gifts and personalities, and if we seek out those who have something special to offer us and commit ourselves to offer our gifts, time, and energy to those who need us.

We will also grow spiritually if we find ways to connect with those who have extraordinary experience, insights, or gifts. Some of these people will be in our Christian community or church. Others we will only know through their writing, art, architecture, songs, or some other expression of their unique contribution.

Further, for Spirit-led pilgrims to keep growing, our conversation with others also needs to extend backwards throughout recorded history. As we draw on the wisdom of the ages and the experiences of our forebears, including the writers of Scripture, we will be much more knowledgeable, grounded, and wise. Similarly, the conversation also needs to look ahead by imagining the kind of social, religious, and political world that we might want to create, and then working with others to pursue our dreams.

Finally, the world that lies in the future is still an open question. Who will create it? We will, or rather, communities of people will. What I experience in the future will be greatly affected by what my fellow pilgrims think, believe, and do in the present. No matter what I think my personal truth might be or how much I value my own individual path, the decisions I make will affect others around me, for better or for worse, just as theirs will affect me. We will go into the future as individuals as much as ever, but the relationships, the conversations, the planning, and the doing of pilgrims in community will affect all of us. Our interface with others will greatly determine what we experience and how we draw meaning from and give purpose to our lives—and how we contribute to the lives of others.

As pilgrims we simply do not walk alone. Others have preceded us, and others are currently walking alongside us or walking in different directions or to other places. Many are seeking God, meaning, and the fullness of life in one way or another, just as we are. Further, the Spirit often chooses to speak to us and lead us through others, making relationships with spiritually vital people very important.

Pursuing God within community, then, can offer many benefits. For greater safety and security, pursuing God within a community of sincere, knowledgeable pilgrims can be reassuring and helpful. For greater knowledge and wisdom, interacting with both learned people and those from other traditions and faiths in the broader world can be quite fruitful. For encouragement and support for the journey, finding the right kind of community offers companionship, perspective, and essential help along the way. On the other hand, those who try to go it alone or who refuse to listen to others set themselves up for futile wandering at best and disaster at worst. Spiritual arrogance, rooted in self-centeredness and an overly self-confident reliance on one's own thinking and experience, can easily lead to making significant personal mistakes and to hurting others.

Sometimes finding a church that feels like a good fit is really hard. Sometimes others don't want to resolve their conflicts with us or cannot do so peacefully. Trying to develop authentic, mutually beneficial relationships is often hard work and doing so with some people seems impossible. Most of us have memories of being hurt by someone in Christian community, and some of us still carry the scars from our wounds. Finding, cultivating, and maintaining spiritually vital relationships within community sometimes may seem like too much work with too little promise. Nevertheless, in my experience, without Christian community we simply cannot experience the fullness of life God intends for us, and we will limit our spiritual growth and miss out on important aspects of Spirit-led living.

We are inseparably linked to each other. None us is so wise or enlightened that we cannot learn from others. In fact, we need each other, and we will all benefit from learning how to live better in community with each other in every imaginable and possible way. Healthy community is an essential ingredient to spiritual vitality and transformation, and learning how to journey peacefully and constructively with one another is critical for the future of our world. It is worth the effort to keep trying to find or create Christian community, for everyone's sake.

Notes

❧

Introduction

1. Victor Turner and Edith Turner, *Image and Pilgrimage in Christian Culture: Anthropological Perspectives* (New York: Columbia University Press, 1978), 7.
2. Alan Morinis, ed., *Sacred Journeys: The Anthropology of Pilgrimage* (Westport, CT: Greenwood Press, 1992), 9.
3. Kerry Egan, *Fumbling: A Pilgrimage Tale of Love, Grief, and Spiritual Renewal on the Camino de Santiago* (New York: Doubleday, 2004), 32–33.
4. Robert E. Webber, *The Divine Embrace: Recovering the Passionate Spiritual Life* (Grand Rapids: Baker Books, 2006), 32. On the importance of keeping spirituality and theology linked together, also see Mark A. McIntosh, *Mystical Theology: The Integrity of Spirituality and Theology* (Malden, MA: Blackwell, 1998).
5. Sandra Schneiders, "The Discipline of Christian Spirituality and Catholic Theology," in *Exploring Christian Spirituality: Essays in Honor of Sandra M. Schneiders, IHM*, Bruce H. Lescher and Elizabeth Liebert, eds. (New York: Paulist Press, 2006), 200. As an academic discipline, spirituality, Schneider suggests, is the study of such lived experiences separate from systematic theology (study of God and belief about God).

CHAPTER 1   Taking the Next Step

1. See, for example, Turner and Turner, *Image and Pilgrimage in Christian Culture* and Morinis, *Sacred Journeys*.

2. Resources on spiritual disciplines include: Richard J. Foster, *Celebration of Discipline: The Path to Spiritual Growth*, 25th anniv. ed. (San Francisco: HarperSanFrancisco, 1998); Tony Jones, *The Sacred Way: Spiritual Practices for Everyday Life* (Grand Rapids: Zondervan, 2005); Dallas Willard, *The Spirit of the Disciplines: Understanding How God Changes Lives* (San Francisco: HarperSanFrancisco, 1988); Timothy C. Geoffrion, *The Spirit-Led Leader: Nine Leadership Practices and Soul Principles* (Herndon, VA: The Alban Institute, 2005), ch. 3.
3. See Luke 2:46–49; 4:42–43; 5:15–16; 22:39–42.
4. See M. Craig Barnes, *Searching for Home: Spirituality for Restless Souls* (Grand Rapids: Brazos Press, 2003); Timothy C. Geoffrion, *The Rhetorical Purpose and the Political and Military Character of Philippians: A Call to Stand Firm* (Lewiston, NY: Mellen Biblical Press, 1993).
5. Brother Lawrence describes such God-sensitive daily living in *The Practice of the Presence of God*. I discuss Brother Lawrence and offer many practical suggestions for practicing the presence of God in *The Spirit-Led Leader*, ch. 2.

CHAPTER 3   **Facing Reality**

1. See, for example, Luke 18:29–30; Philippians 3:20; Hebrews 11:39–40; 12:22–24. The importance of understanding one's identity in terms of one's relationship to God is a given throughout the Bible. In the New Testament, Jesus frequently preached about the kingdom of God as a defining reality in the mindset of those who worship and serve God. Jesus also promised his disciples that in exchange for giving up all to follow him, they would receive back far more in this life and the next, thus helping them to understand themselves primarily as his followers who will be rewarded by God for their faith and faithfulness. The apostles taught that Christians are saints made holy by faith in Christ and the Holy Spirit, citizens of a heavenly Jerusalem, and members of Christ's body, the church. Paul especially stressed that believers should see themselves as *in Christ*, living *for Christ*, filled with the Holy Spirit of God and Christ. (For an

example of how Paul emphasizes Christian identity as a part of his rhetorical strategy to help believers stand firm in their faith and live worthily of the gospel, see my book, *The Rhetorical Purpose and the Political and Military Character of Philippians.*)

2. I created the title "Spiritual Life Coach" for myself as a way to capture the somewhat unusual blending of three different professional practices—spiritual direction, life coaching, and personal consulting. For a fuller description of spiritual life coaching, see www.timgeoffrion.com.

3. On the value of developing empathic skills and nonviolent communication skills, which include linking our feelings to underlying needs and listening well to ourselves, see Deborah van Deusen Hunsinger, *Pray without Ceasing: Revitalizing Pastoral Care* (Grand Rapids: Eerdmans, 2006), 55–62, 79–98.

4. Ibid., 73–74. Hunsinger cites research by psychologist Albert Mehrabian from his article "Communication without Words," *Psychology Today* 2, no. 9, 52–55.

5. The importance of learning to listen well cannot be overemphasized, especially in light of our world's generally poor ability to resolve conflicts peaceably. Listening well is also important for leadership and in management. Deborah Hunsinger's book is an excellent resource for clergy and anyone involved in caring relationships. I address the subject and offer some practical suggestions for managers and organizational leaders in "Listening Well," chapter 7 in *The Spirit-Led Leader.*

CHAPTER 4 Seeking Inner Change

1. For example, see Mark 7:21–22; Romans 1:28–32; 1 Corinthians 6:9–11; and Galatians 5:16–23.

2. Robert S. McGee, *The Search for Significance: Seeing Your True Worth through God's Eyes* (Houston: Rapha Publishing, 1994).

3. Jesus taught repentance from sins and faith in God for forgiveness, within the context of ancient Judaism. After his death and resurrection, and the outpouring of the Holy Spirit, Jesus's followers expanded Jesus's message to include faith in him, as the Son of God, for salvation and life in the Spirit as a means to

repentance. Over time, various theological traditions, most notably Catholics and Protestants, have differed on how and to what extent believers are purified and transformed. Much work has been done in recent years to reconcile Protestant and Catholic views of justification (how someone is made right before God) and to affirm the many common beliefs held among theologians today. For one scholarly resource on the latest efforts to find common ground between Catholic and Protestant views, see David E. Aune, ed. *Rereading Paul Together: Protestant and Catholic Perspectives on Justification* (Grand Rapids: Baker Book House, 2006).

4. *Star Tribune*, sec. E, December 31, 2007, 2.

5. For additional resources, see Tilden H. Edwards, *Living in the Presence: Spiritual Exercises to Open Our Lives to the Awareness of God* (San Francisco: HarperSanFrancisco, 1995); Richard J. Foster, *Celebration of Discipline*; Geoffrion, *Spirit-Led Leader*, chapters 2 and 3 especially; Gerald G. May, *The Awakened Heart: Opening Yourself to the Love You Need* (San Francisco: HarperSanFrancisco, 1991); Jones, *The Sacred Way*; Dallas Willard, *Renovation of the Heart: Putting on the Character of Christ* (Colorado Springs, CO: NavPress, 2002).

6. Sometimes, when we are in the grip of addiction, our ability to refrain from sin or avoid certain ways of thinking seems beyond any help we know. If you feel that way, you are not alone. All people suffer from some intransigent habit or tendency that is out of sync with God's will for their life. Do not give up. At such times, in addition to seeking professional help and spiritual counsel, you may especially need to look to the grace of God for forgiveness as well as for power to release the hold the addictions are exerting. For good insight into the nature and prevalence of addiction in everyone's life and to the role of grace in the face of such addiction, see Gerald G. May, *Addiction and Grace: Love and Spirituality in the Healing of Addictions* (New York: HarperCollins, 1988).

INTERLUDE   In Pursuit of God

1. I am indebted to my theologian friend Etienne Veto for his portrayal of how Christians will one day be united with God. Of course, he is not responsible for any way I have failed to clearly pass on this understanding of the Christian hope.

CHAPTER 5   Knowing God

1. *Gnosis* means "knowledge" in Greek. Gnosticism is a catch-all term that refers to the teaching of religious groups, especially prominent in the second century AD, that salvation came by receiving special or secret knowledge from God. As far as scholars can tell from a relatively small amount of extant literature, gnostics were typically dualistic and thought in terms of light and darkness, good and evil, righteous and unrighteous, and spirit and flesh, with little or nothing between the poles. Some taught that the world was created by a lesser god and that Christ came from a good God and was a spirit who appeared to be a man so as to redeem human spirits. The vast majority of Christian leaders and churches eventually rejected gnosticism because its adherents failed to acknowledge that Jesus was fully human, elevated their secret beliefs over apostolic teaching, promoted an alternative means of salvation to the rule of faith (initiation into the secret mysteries instead of faith in Jesus Christ as taught by the apostles), and generally did not recognize the goodness of creation and the value of human existence in their dualistic worldview.
2. Peter Rollins, *How (Not) to Speak of God* (Orleans, MA: Paraclete Press, 2006), 53.
3. For a thorough academic treatment of many of the issues related to the role of experience in theological thinking, see Mark A. McIntosh, *Mystical Theology: The Integrity of Spirituality and Theology* (Malden, MA: Blackwell Publishers, 1998).

CHAPTER 6 Following Jesus

1. See Geoffrion, *The Spirit-Led Leader* for more autobiographical information related to how I learned to trust in God and experience the love and grace of God (chapters 8 and 9).

2. Wayne A. Meeks, *Christ Is the Question* (Louisville: Westminster John Knox, 2006).

3. Now, to read the Gospel accounts more as testimonies is not to say they are not historical. In fact, they are exactly historical, because that is what ancient historiography was all about: telling a story through the eyes of the writer and his or her sources. That is what all historical writing does, and pre-Enlightenment writers seemed to be freer than most historians today to assemble the facts, stories, and opinions of others in ways that best fit their overall understanding of the story they are telling. The modern historian values attempting to be as objective as possible, and the postmodern historian insists on declaring one's biases and subjective point of view. As far as anyone can tell, ancient historians chose and shaped stories in ways that fit their rhetorical objectives, some of which they make explicit and some we are left to guess.

4. *Monogené*, in the original Greek text, literally means "only begotten" or unique in a class.

5. To know Jesus as the Son of God is not to recognize his maleness but to honor his identity with God and unique relationship with God the Father. As human parents and their biological children have a special physical relationship to one another because of a shared DNA, so God the Father and Jesus the Son share a unique connection—divine DNA of some unfathomable quality—that theologians for centuries have wrestled to understand. In the defining work of the Councils of Nicaea (AD 325), Constantinople (AD 381), and Chalcedon (AD 451), church theologians refined concepts that are basically incomprehensible to most people: Jesus Christ was of one substance with the Father, he was both fully God and fully human, and the Trinity represents one God in three persons.

6. See Matt. 10:37–39; Mark 8:34–35; Luke 14:26–27; 17:33; John 12:25.

CHAPTER 7 Spirit-Led Living

1. See appendix A, "The Holy Spirit and Believers" for an overview of biblical teaching on the many ways the Holy Spirit interfaces with those who worship God and follow Christ.
2. See Romans 8:13–14; Galatians 5:16–23; Titus 2:11–14; 2 Peter 1:3–4.
3. Martin Luther described this phenomenon as "*simul justus et peccator*" (simultaneously righteous and a sinner).
4. For some practical suggestions and illustrations on how to be a Spirit-led church, see N. Graham Standish, *Becoming a Blessed Church: Forming a Church of Spiritual Purpose, Presence, and Power* (Herndon, VA: Alban Institute, 2005).
5. Gary A. Shockley, in *The Meandering Way: Leading by Following the Spirit* (Herndon, VA: Alban Institute, 2007) offers many helpful reflections and illustrations for pastors in particular on how to be less driven and more Spirit-led in life and ministry. He also uses the image of sailing, including tacking back and forth, as a metaphor for letting the Spirit lead us to get where God wants us to go, in God's timing, and in God's way.

CHAPTER 8 Crossing Bridges

1. Dallas Willard, *Renovation of the Heart: Putting on the Character of Christ* (Colorado Springs, CO: NavPress, 2002).
2. Dallas Willard and Jan Johnson, *Renovation of the Heart in Daily Practice: Experiments in Spiritual Transformation* (Colorado Springs, CO: NavPress, 2006), 60.
3. To be sure I am not misunderstood, I want to add that I am not passing judgment on every decision to separate from one's spouse or to get divorced. I am not talking about individuals who feel compelled to get out of a marriage because they are being abused or who are suffering in life-threatening ways.

Further, during midlife, it is not uncommon to finally face that you and your spouse have grown in different directions or that your needs cannot be met well in relationship with each other. Much soul searching is done by the conscientious person who struggles with ending an unhappy marriage. It is God's place to judge, not mine.

My concern grows out of the all-too-human tendency to act in self-serving ways and then try to justify ourselves at the expense of others. My ten years of work with troubled youth and families at TreeHouse has sensitized me to the pain of the abandoned and neglected children and spouses (usually wives) left behind because one of the parents fell in love with someone else or some dream they had.

If you are considering separating from your spouse, instead of too quickly concluding that your marriage is hopelessly damaged, be sure you have not entangled yourself with someone or something else. Staying stuck in life-destroying patterns is not good; it is often possible to renegotiate one's marriage if both partners are willing to learn new patterns of relating together, grow together in new ways, and get the professional and pastoral help they need.

POSTLUDE Staying the Course

1. "I Dreamed a Dream." From the Musicale: *Les Miserables*, by Alain Boublil & Claude-Michel Schonberg. Music by: Claude-Michel Schonberg. Lyrics by: Alain Boublil, Jean-Marc Natel & Herbert Kretzmer. (c) Alain Boublil Music Ltd. (ASCAP). Used by Permission. All Rights Reserved.
2. In fact, I learned after returning home that according to at least one study, people who live closer to the ground out in the country can preserve their spiritual life better than people in the fast-paced, technologically enhanced life in urban and suburban areas. See Richard A. Swenson, *Margin: Restoring Emotional, Physical, Financial, and Time Reserves to Overloaded Lives* (Colorado Springs, CO: NavPress, 2004) 47.

APPENDIX A The Holy Spirit and Believers

1. For a monumental work on all of Paul's references to the Spirit, see Gordon D. Fee, *God's Empowering Presence: The Holy Spirit in the Letters of Paul* (Peabody, MA: Hendrickson, 1994).

2. See Matthew 3:11; Mark 1:8; Luke 3:16; John 1:33.

3. See John 3:16; 6:44–47; 8:42; 13:34–35; 15:12; See also, 1 John 3:16–23; 4:7–16.

4. The Greek word *anothen*, found in John 3:3, can mean either "again" or "from above." In either case, the teaching is that a special kind of Spirit-initiated birth is required in order to receive eternal life. Either we are "born again," that is, in addition to our physical birth we must experience a spiritual birth, or we are "born from above," meaning that the key to receiving eternal life is a spiritual birth effected by God's Spirit (not the result of human effort).

5. Examples include Philippians 1:9–11; Ephesians 1:17–23; 3:14–19; Colossians 1:9.

Selected Bibliography

Spirituality and Spiritual Transformation

Countless books are available on spiritual growth and discipleship. Some are Bible studies, some academic and theological, others are psychological, and many are practical, written for the average believer who wants to develop a better relationship with God. Here I offer a number of resources I have found inspiring, insightful, or thought-provoking that focus on the Christian's experience with God, and, in many cases, offer practical suggestions for spiritual growth and transformation.

Barton, Ruth Haley. *Sacred Rhythms: Arranging Our Lives for Spiritual Transformation*. Downers Grove, IL: IVP Books, 2006. A very readable, insightful, and practical book on how to grow deeper spiritually and experience more spiritual vitality. Barton writes out of personal experience with becoming overstressed in ministry due to neglecting her physical, emotional, and spiritual needs. She offers guidance for listening to our inner longings better and creating disciplines to open ourselves better to God's transforming love and transformative work in our lives.

Blackaby, Henry T., and Claude V. King. *Experiencing God: How to Live the Full Adventure of Knowing and Doing the Will of God*. Nashville: Broadman and Holman, 1994. Blackaby draws on years of pastoral experience in his best-selling resource for individuals and congregations. He gives practical guidelines for an experiential relationship with God. He urges readers to look for places where God is actively working and to join God there.

Bloesch, Donald G. *Spirituality Old and New: Recovering Authentic Spiritual Life*. Downers Grove, IL: IVP Academic, 2007. A solid, readable theological treatise on spirituality from an evangelical perspective, which the author routinely calls a "biblical" reading. He covers "Mystical Reli-gion," "Biblical Religion," and "A New Spiritual Vision." He provides an extensive treatment of "Classical Mysticism," "Biblical Personalism," "The New Spirituality (New Age)," "Worldviews in Collision," and a concluding chapter, "For Christ and His Kingdom."

Foster, Richard J. *Celebration of Discipline: The Path to Spiritual Growth*, 25th anniv. ed. San Francisco: HarperSanFrancisco, 1998. This book is the modern classic on spiritual disciplines. Foster provides an excellent orientation to these practices for the newcomer to faith as well as for those who are eager to grow spiritually.

———. *Prayer: Finding the Heart's True Home*. San Francisco: Harper-SanFrancisco, 1992. This book is another foundational book for under-standing the many different kinds of prayer that Christians utilize as they seek transformation, greater intimacy with God, and fruitful min-istry. A classic.

Fowler, James W. *Becoming Adult, Becoming Christian: Adult Development and Christian Faith*. San Francisco: Jossey-Bass, 2000. This reprint of Fowler's influential work from the late 1970s, published in 1980, offers thought-provoking insights into the various stages that Christians are likely to go through as they mature spiritually. His final (controversial) stage, which very few believers reach according to his assessment, embraces more openness and mystery in relation to how God works in the world and focuses more on love than specific doctrinal beliefs. While the first several stages follow one another in a linear and logical progres-sion, the final stage posited leaps to a different order and way of relat-ing to and understanding God.

Geoffrion, Jill Kimberly Hartwell. *Christian Prayer and Labyrinths: Path-ways to Faith, Hope and Love*. Cleveland: Pilgrim Press, 2004. One of seven published books by this author, who offers many practical tools for appreciating and using the labyrinth as a spiritual resource. This volume provides an explicitly Christian perspective on walking the labyrinth and maximizing the opportunities it affords those who seek God on its path.

———. *Pondering the Labyrinth: Questions to Pray on the Path*. Cleveland: Pilgrim Press, 2003. This book was written in response to expressed needs for resources that could be used by those seeking personal and spiritual growth through labyrinth walking and prayer. The hundreds of meaningful questions can serve the spiritual pilgrim well on or off the labyrinth. Divided into four sections, "About Labyrinths," "Questions to Ponder as You Experience the Labyrinth," "Questions to Ponder Away from the Labyrinth," and "Questions to Ponder for Special Reasons," this book is highly accessible and especially useful for those who would like to learn creative ways to seek God with their bodies as well as their minds and hearts.

Hagberg, Janet O., and Robert A. Guelich. *The Critical Journey: Stages in the Life of Faith*. Salem, WI: Sheffield Publishing, 2nd ed., 2005. Bob Guelich (now deceased) and Janet Hagberg offer an excellent resource that grows out of deep spiritual and psychological insight into personal growth and relating to God. In a humble, yet profound way, they offer thoughtful, insightful, and practical teaching on various stages in the Christian faith journey and on spirituality, which they define as "the way in which we live out our response to God." The latest edition includes additional material both for individuals and pastors and leaders.

Jones, Tony. *The Sacred Way: Spiritual Practices for Everyday Life*. Grand Rapids: Zondervan, 2005. *The Sacred Way* provides an excellent introduction to spiritual practices in contemporary language. In a down-to-earth style, Jones shares his own journey and offers many practical suggestions along with thoughtful commentary on ancient practices that are still relevant to the person who feels drawn by God to develop a deeper spiritual life.

Lawrence. *The Practice of the Presence of God*. This little book, printed by various publishers of hardcover and paperback editions, is a classic guide to living with a continual sense of awareness of God throughout one's day in all circumstances. Brother Lawrence, a member of the Carmelite order (Order of Our Lady of Mount Carmel) in seventeenth-century Paris, connected with God while washing dishes, working in the garden, or doing other commonplace chores, and thereby learned how to adore God and to notice God's activity in his life amid the mundane. The book offers many of his insights and practices.

Loder, Ted. *The Haunt of Grace: Responses to the Mystery of God's Presence*. Philadelphia: Innisfree Press, 2002. This book is a collection of reworked sermons, which are responses to the haunt of grace, reflecting the author's own struggle "to live more fully, freely, creatively, and joyfully in relationship to the haunt of grace." (19). Loder writes: "Surely mystery is an essential ingredient, if not the essential of our common life and this earth in which we are all rooted" (15). "Our experience of mystery is what Augustine called the restlessness of our hearts until they find their rest in God" (16). "We are haunted by grace. We are invited, urged, perhaps compelled, to respond to that haunt" (18).

May, Gerald G. *Addiction and Grace: Love and Spirituality in the Healing of Addictions*. New York: HarperCollins, 1988. A former psychiatrist and spiritual guide, May provides piercing insight into the physiological and emotional quality of addictions of all kinds, from the well-known addictions to alcohol to what some might consider minor compulsions, such as addictions to watching movies or eating desserts. Hope for addicts—which include everyone, in his opinion—comes from God's grace to help release us from the hold addictions have on us.

———. *The Awakened Heart: Opening Yourself to the Love You Need.* San Francisco: HarperSanFrancisco, 1991. In *The Awakened Heart,* May guides readers to look to God to meet our needs for love. This book offers an extended discussion of Brother Lawrence's practices.

McGee, Robert S. *The Search for Significance: Seeing Your True Worth through God's Eyes.* Houston: Rapha Publishing, 1994. McGee offers penetrating insight into human fears and shame and our need to feel significant. His book is both a theoretical and a practical tool to help readers overcome their fears and to trust in God's love, redemption, and sanctification to be secure and to feel significant.

McIntosh, Mark A. *Mystical Theology: The Integrity of Spirituality and Theology.* Malden, MA: Blackwell Publishers, 1998. McIntosh has written a thorough academic treatment of many of the issues related to the role of experience in theological thinking.

Ortberg, John. *God Is Closer Than You Think: If God Is Always with Us, Why Is He So Hard to Find?* Grand Rapids: Zondervan, 2005. This book is filled with hundreds of nuggets of spiritual wisdom accompanied by immensely practical guidance. Ortberg is funny, transparent, a gifted communicator, psychologically astute, and above all, very helpful to ordinary Christians who want to know God more personally. His premise is that the glue that holds Scripture together is God's promise to be with us (Immanuel). Through a steady stream of engaging and moving stories from real life, his book tells and shows readers how to better recognize God's presence in us and all around us, and how to embrace a life of letting God work through us to benefit others.

Scorgie, Glen G. *A Little Guide to Christian Spirituality: Three Dimensions of Life with God.* Grand Rapids: Zondervan, 2007. Scorgie's book is a readable, engaging, and clear introduction to Christian spirituality from an evangelical perspective. As the publisher notes, this resource "offers a model of Christian spirituality with three dimensions: the first relational (Christ with us), the second transformational (Christ in us), and the third vocational (Christ through us). It is designed to help students think more clearly about Christian spirituality, understand its basic dynamics, and utilize classic and contemporary resources with discernment." Glen draws on his sabbatical pilgrimage experiences to Iona Abbey in Scotland and elsewhere to add depth and feeling to the many principles he discusses. For those who want to go deeper, a valuable (but not overwhelming) bibliography is included.

Shults, F. L., and S. J. Sandage. *Transforming Spirituality: Integrating Theology and Psychology*. Grand Rapids: Baker Academic, 2006. Brilliant exposé on spiritual transformation blending psychological, theological, and spiritual formation perspectives. Written from an academic point of view, *Transforming Spirituality* is not an easy read but offers the perspectives of both a philosopher-theologian and a practicing psychologist with many insights worth mining for the motivated reader.

Smith, Martin L. *The Word Is Very Near You: A Guide to Praying with Scripture*. Cambridge, MA: Cowley Publications, 1989. An Episcopal priest and author, Smith helps readers understand that God takes the initiative in communicating with us. We can respond out of a sense of continuing the conversation God began. Smith offers practical tools and suggestions for praying with Scripture.

Swenson, Richard. A. *Margin: Restoring Emotional, Physical, Financial, and Time Reserves to Overloaded Lives*. Colorado Springs, CO: NavPress, 2004. Dr. Swenson argues that "progress" has produced overloaded lives in an unprecedented way, causing much unnecessary pain and suffering. Those who want to find greater peace, joy, and fulfillment in life must create greater margin in multiple dimensions of their life. At the core of his worldview is his conviction that commitment to following Christ means valuing simplicity and contentment and rejecting the allure of status, wealth, and power. When we have more margin—"the space between our load and our limits" (p. 69)—we have room to breathe, to enjoy life, and to be better able to engage in the demands and opportunities of life without stressing out. Though the book is repetitious, Swenson offers good advice with many practical suggestions for creating a healthier life.

Webber, Robert E. *The Divine Embrace: Recovering the Passionate Spiritual Life*. Grand Rapids: Baker Books, 2006. This book offers a historical perspective on "how spirituality became separated from the divine embrace," followed by a discussion of how spirituality can be returned to the divine embrace. Webber helpfully discusses spirituality in the context of story: God's story, our story, and our story of life with God. He focuses on God's story of expressing love through Christ's death on the cross, our story of coming within reach of his saving embrace, and what it means to rediscover our mystical union with God. Webber acknowledges the experiential dimension of spirituality while insisting that the experience is always rooted in the story from which it came.

Willard, Dallas. *The Spirit of the Disciplines: Understanding How God Changes Lives.* San Francisco: HarperSanFrancisco, 1988. A professor of philosophy at the University of Southern California and a nationally known speaker on spiritual growth, Willard presents a powerful and challenging book calling Christians to take responsibility for their own spiritual maturity. Action is required for those who want to develop character and to live fruitful lives.

————, and Jan Johnson. *Renovation of the Heart in Daily Practice: Experiments in Spiritual Transformation.* Colorado Springs, CO: NavPress, 2006. Willard and Johnson offer a clear presentation of Willard's beliefs that transformation best occurs when we have a vision for the change desired (V), set our intention on pursuing that vision (I), and then take advantage of the means of transformation (M). Willard's VIM paradigm is a helpful way to think about and pursue spiritual growth. The bulk of the book offers thoughtful, challenging devotionals on various aspects of growing spiritually and transformation.

Pilgrimage-Related Resources

Of the numerous books that focus on the pilgrimage theme, many are memoirs related to specific treks, while others use the concept loosely and suggestively, without actually exploring the notion of spiritual pilgrimage as a way of life. Here I offer just a few resources that I have found helpful or worth reading for those whose interest in pilgrimage goes beyond a specific journey to a sacred site, who are interested in either understanding better why pilgrims make their journeys, or how pilgrimage can serve as a metaphor for one's spiritual life as a whole.

Bodo, Murray. *The Place We Call Home: Spiritual Pilgrimage as a Path to God.* Brewster, MA: Paraclete Press, 2004. Of all the books on pilgrimage that I have read or seen, Bodo's book comes the closest to the basic concept of *One Step at a Time.* Bodo, a Catholic priest, teacher, and author of twenty-one books, has written a gentle book on pilgrimage. His memoirs form the basis for the book, especially his trip to Assisi, Italy. The book has depth but is not penetrating. Thoughtful, and thought-provoking, but not intellectual or scholarly. A good read for those looking for wisdom and spiritual truth from someone who has devoted his life to God and spiritual growth.

Cousineau, Phil. *The Art of Pilgrimage: The Seeker's Guide to Making Travel Sacred.* Berkeley, CA: Conari Press, 1998. Cousineau has written a brilliant book, a bit dated now, demonstrating his broad knowledge of various religious traditions and offering good insight into what is needed to become a more spiritually sensitive person from an eclectic point of view. Cousineau succeeds at offering an authentic personal experience, thoughtful and knowledgeable reflection, and helpful questions for reflection. He portrays pilgrimage as metaphor for the daily life.

Morinis, Alan, ed. *Sacred Journeys: The Anthropology of Pilgrimage.* Westport, CT: Greenwood Press, 1992. Alan Morinis, anthropologist, filmmaker, and writer, offers two chapters on theoretical issues followed by ten chapters of case studies from all over the world, spanning diverse cultures and religions. The book is a collection of anthropological studies of pilgrimage from a time when very little work had been done in this area. Morinis explains that anthropologists have found that the bulk of pilgrims are not necessarily concerned with transition in their lives (as Victor and Edith Turner argued) but are seeking a particular type of community experience and want "to establish direct contact with [their] deity."

Rupp, Joyce. *Walk in a Relaxed Manner: Life Lessons from the Camino.* Maryknoll, NY: Orbis Books, 2005. Catholic nun Joyce Rupp wrote a book on her thirty-seven-day pilgrimage along the Camino de Santiago, drawing out spiritual lessons she learned along the way. The account is personal and authentic.

Turner, Victor, and Edith Turner. *Image and Pilgrimage in Christian Culture: Anthropological Perspectives.* New York: Columbia University Press, 1978. Victor Turner, former professor at the University of Chicago, and his wife, Edith, were groundbreaking in their work on pilgrimage. One of their key contributions is to help readers understand pilgrimage as a liminal experience, as the authors offer research and insight into how individuals and groups function within the rare context of significant transition, especially when marked by pilgrimage.

Especially for Pastors and Other Leaders and Congregational Ministers

Spirit-led living is not only for individuals but also for congregations and ministers engaged in community building, ministry, and mission. While vital spirituality may be deeply personal for individuals, it is also foundational to healthy congregations working together to serve Christ effectively. Here are a handful of good resources written for pastors, leaders, and congregations to promote greater spiritual dynamism in ministry and to help them learn how to foster greater spirituality among the members of churches, church staff, or coworkers.

Ackerman, John. *Listening to God: Spiritual Formation in Congregations.* Herndon, VA: Alban Institute, 2001. This book is particularly helpful for pastors and other spiritual leaders who want to help congregations learn how to listen to God in the context of community. Ackerman offers helpful insights into various preferences of worship styles to increase the leader's ability to work with all members of the congregation.

Hunsinger, Deborah van Deusen. *Pray without Ceasing: Revitalizing Pastoral Care.* Grand Rapids: Eerdmans, 2006. Hunsinger, a professor of pastoral theology at Princeton Theological Seminary, has written a very readable, well-researched, and highly practical resource for pastors who value a rich spiritual dimension to pastoral care. Key concepts include: *koinonia*; listening to God, self, and others; and prayers of various kinds. One of Hunsinger's specialities is peaceful conflict resolution, and she offers an excellent presentation on empathy and nonviolent listening.

Geoffrion, Timothy C. *The Spirit-Led Leader: Nine Leadership Practices and Soul Principles.* Herndon, VA: The Alban Institute, 2005. Designed for pastors, executives, administrators, managers, coordinators, and those who see themselves as leaders and want to fulfill their God-given purpose, *The Spirit-Led Leader* addresses the critical fusion of spiritual life and leadership for those who not only want to see "results" but also care as deeply about who they are and how they lead as they do about what they produce and accomplish. One of my goals in writing this book was to present a new vision for spiritual leadership as partly an art, partly a result of careful planning, and always a working of the grace of God.

Quinn, Robert E. *Building the Bridge as You Walk on It: A Guide for Leading Change.* San Francisco: Jossey-Bass, 2004. The third book in

Quinn's trilogy on deep change and leadership, this one, like the others, is clearly written; chock full of insights, practical suggestions, and questions; with numerous illustrations. This book draws heavily on his earlier books to help individuals envision a better future for themselves and to move successfully toward that vision. Quinn emphasizes that the most effective leaders are those who are "results centered, internally directed, other-focused, and externally open." An outstanding resource for those who truly want to understand the dynamics involved in growing personally and becoming a leader who can inspire change in others. Quinn writes, "This book is about how real people find the courage to make deep change" (p. viii).

————. *Deep Change: Discovering the Leader Within*. San Francisco: Jossey-Bass, 1996. Quinn draws on business experience to illustrate the serious danger of not changing, which leads to "slow death." His argument is compelling, and his illustrations are helpful to those who want to come to grips with the need for change within themselves and in their organizations. Though this book is not written from an explicitly Christian perspective and is designed especially for business leaders, Quinn's insights are valuable for anyone seeking to grow personally or professionally.

Rice, Howard. *The Pastor as Spiritual Guide*. Nashville: Upper Room Books, 1998. Rice portrays pastoral ministry as primarily a spiritual vocation, describing several key roles the pastor plays (worship leader, teacher, social change agent, manager) as "spiritual guidance." The pastor is a spiritual director whose primary responsibility is to nurture the spiritual life of the congregation out of a deep sense of personal spirituality.

Shockley, Gary A. *The Meandering Way: Leading by Following the Spirit*. Herndon, VA: Alban Institute, 2007. Written from his personal experience as a pastor, Shockley offers thoughtful personal reflections on learning how to trust the leading of the Holy Spirit better and not be so driven as a pastor. He uses the image of sailing and stresses the importance of learning to tack back and forth as the Spirit leads in order to get where God wants us to go, in God's timing. Gary's book would be especially helpful for pastors who need to slow down, trust the Spirit better, get a life outside of ministry, become more real, and help parishioners learn the same kind of Spirit-sensitive way of living.

Standish, N. Graham. *Becoming a Blessed Church: Forming a Church of Spiritual Purpose, Presence, and Power*. Herndon, VA: Alban Institute, 2005. Standish writes out of his own long-term experience as a pastor of a Presbyterian church in Pennsylvania. This is a very practical and inspiring book on pastoral, spiritual leadership, which emphasizes discerning the Spirit's leading and working in the congregation and the leadership.

————. *Humble Leadership: Being Radically Open to God's Guidance and Grace.* Herndon, VA: The Alban Institute, 2007. Standish follows up his previous books on church leadership by focusing on the quality of the leader him- or herself. Above all, he emphasizes the need for humility and openness to God, and to expect God to lead and provide the grace needed for a congregation to fulfill its calling.

Thompson, C. Michael. *The Congruent Life: Following the Inward Path to Fulfilling Work and Inspired Leadership.* San Francisco: Jossey-Bass, 2000. Thompson runs a private consulting practice that focuses on organizational and individual leadership development; he also works with the Center for Creative Leadership. The Congruent Life is filled with helpful insights and illustrations on personal fulfillment and successful leadership based on an integrated life, characterized at the core by a vibrant spirituality.

Thrall, Bill, Bruce McNichol, and Ken McElrath. *The Ascent of a Leader: How Ordinary Relationships Develop Extraordinary Character and Influence.* San Francisco: Jossey-Bass, 1999. *The Ascent of a Leader* contrasts the ladder of capacity with the ladder of character. While most leaders start out trying to increase their capacity to advance in status and responsibilities, the authors argue that developing one's character is even more important. Ultimately, the successful leader will integrate capacity and character.